LEADING THE BLIND

LEADING THE BLIND

A CENTURY OF GUIDEBOOK
TRAVEL 1815–1914

ALAN SILLITOE

MACMILLAN

First published 1995 by Macmillan

an imprint of Macmillan General Books
Cavaye Place London SW10 9PG
and Basingstoke

Associated companies throughout the world

ISBN 0-333-64225-2

9 8 7 6 5 4 3 2 1

A CIP catalogue record for this book is available from
the British Library

Phototypeset by Intype, London
Printed by Mackays of Chatham PLC, Kent.

My thanks to Jane Dunlop,
Librarian of the Royal Geographical Society

CONTENTS

CHAPTER ONE

OFFICER EATEN BY A BEAR

In 1861, Baedeker's guidebook to Switzerland informs us that an English officer fell into the bears' den at Berne and was 'torn in pieces after a desperate struggle'. Like the eternal conundrums that have puzzled poets, such as who cleft the Devil's foot, what song the Sirens sang, and what secret was concealed by the Gordian knot, I was curious to solve this one, at least as far as knowing the man's name, but a letter to the mayor's officer at Berne querying his identity brought no response.

Murray's handbook for 1874 gave more details of the officer's fate, saying that he was 'destroyed by the large male bear, having fallen in an attempt to pass along the wall separating the two dens. The struggle was long, and took place in the presence of many witnesses, and, it is said, of an armed sentry, who did not interfere.'

Later editions of the same book tell us that the victim was Swedish, a Captain Lorck, who was killed 'owing to the stupidity of his companion, who might easily have caused him to be rescued, but lost his head'. One wonders which of the bears dined off that, and whether it was at all palatable.

Being torn apart by bears was only one pitfall of travel in the Victorian Age, and others, albeit less terminal, will be mentioned later. Macmillan's guide to Switzerland, 1904, informs us that carrots and cakes to feed the bears were sold at the various stalls. Visiting the bear pit a few years ago I noticed that the safety rails were such as to make it impossible for anyone to suffer the same fate as Captain Lorck.

After the Congress of Vienna in 1815 had promised peace on the mainland of Europe for a long time to come, people from Great Britain went 'abroad' in ever-increasing numbers. The Industrial Revolution had enriched many, and enabled far more to travel than had been the case before the Napoleonic Wars. The following paragraph from the *Observer* of 18 November 1822 nicely sums up the futility of that series of conflicts:

> It is estimated that more than a million bushels of human and inhuman bones were imported last year from the continent of Europe into the port of Hull. The neighbourhood of Leipsig, Austerlitz, Waterloo and of all the places where, during the late bloody war, the principal battles were fought, have been swept alike of the bones of the hero and the horse which he rode. Thus collected from every quarter, they have been shipped to the port of Hull and thence forwarded to the Yorkshire bone grinders who have erected steam-engines and powerful machinery for the purpose of reducing them to a granulary state. In this condition they are sold to the farmers to manure their lands.

By the 1840s railways and steamships were linking places of importance, though travellers still went by coach (often their own) or as well-to-do pedestrians in regions of scenic beauty. The bicycle had become popular by the end of the century, and the motor omnibus made its appearance a little later, before the Great War in 1914 ended an era of travel which was certainly more arduous – and therefore more interesting – than it is today when people are transported in an hour over what in those times would have taken days, if not weeks.

Before the French Revolution only the rich could make their way, at least in any style, to foreign places. William Beckford – 'England's wealthiest son', as Byron called him – moved around in a glamorous equipage, followed by retainers and his own cook; while Arthur Young, the gentleman-farmer from Suffolk, went through France to investigate the state of agriculture, and thereby left a pre-Revolutionary picture of that country so unique that his book was often required reading in French schools through much of the nineteenth century.

Shelley and his entourage, in 1814 and 1816, travelled on foot and by donkey, from Paris to the Alps, at the cost of sixty pounds. On leaving Switzerland they just managed to get home on the twenty-eight pounds remaining.

Later travellers might have a more viable budget, but their educational levels varied, from the accomplished Classical scholar to the newly rich manufacturer whose wife and growing children persuaded him that it was 'the thing' to go abroad. The galleries, castles and Gothic cathedrals of Europe – but especially the cities of Florence, Venice and Rome – were soon overflowing with English tourists.

No writer was more biting against what he considered the tide of vulgarity crowding through Europe than Thackeray: 'Times are altered at Ostend now; of the Britons who go thither, very few look like lords, or act like members of our hereditary aristocracy. They seem for the most part shabby in attire, dingy of linen, lovers of billiards and brandy, and cigars and greasy ordinaries.'

The educated and snobbish considered themselves 'travellers' rather than 'tourists', reluctant to associate with the uncultured mob who were thought to give their country a bad name. The German author of a guide to Nuremburg, writing about the castle, observed that 'in the summer time the cheerful voices of German philistines or inquisitive Britons soon drove me from this haunt'.

Practical ways of ameliorating the unlettered condition of tourists were undertaken by two guidebook publishers, John Murray of London, who produced a *Hand-book for Holland, Belgium, and North Germany* in 1836, and Karl Baedeker of Coblenz, whose guide to the same countries came out in 1839. Their works were of most use to the educated, who must have been their main readers. In Murray's *Southern Italy*, 1853, all quotations from Classical authors are given in the original, as if it would be an insult to translate them for readers. French was certainly necessary to receive full benefit from Augustus J. C. Hare's illustrated cultural guides for Italy and France which appeared later in the century.

Such books instructed potential travellers as to how they should behave on leaving home ground, and described in economical prose the countries whose names they bore, so that even today one learns a great deal of the conditions at that time. Topographical exactitude and honest assessment were the criteria, but there were also lists of hotels, with comments and prices, and precise catalogues of each great picture gallery. Notable buildings were pointed out and described, the gems of European civilization marked with an asterisk in case anyone should walk by them unawares.

Baedeker was to comment that his firm was the first to use asterisks, 'single or double, as marks of commendation for hotels and restaurants, for views and sites of outstanding natural beauty, and for works of architecture and art', the object being to 'familiarise his readers with the merits, in general esteem, of the things they encountered on their travels; "starred in Baedeker" became a synonym for high quality'.

Guidebooks, then, were the educated dogs which led the blind, giving the latest information on travelling conditions, but also instructing those who needed to have the blanks in their knowledge filled in, much of which, it might be said, is still of interest for the traveller today. The English editions of Baedeker's guidebooks were in a sense more democratic, in catering for the tourist of modest means. Quotations were kept as few and as short as possible, and his meticulousness may have appealed more to the engineer than the pedant.

The early Murray handbooks were written for the rich and cultured traveller who could afford a private carriage and to employ a courier. His readers were assumed to be on a higher social level, though the law is sometimes laid down heavily on how travellers should behave, indicating that the so-called upper classes may not have been above a bit of rough stuff when dealing with recalcitrant foreigners.

In *France*, 1848, we are told that Englishmen 'have a reputation for pugnacity in France: let them therefore be especially cautious not to make use of their fists, however grave the provocation, otherwise they will rue it. No French magistrate or judge will listen to any plea of provocation; fine and imprisonment are the offender's inevitable portion.'

Mary Wollstonecraft Shelley, in her *Journal of a Six Weeks Tour*, gives this stricture some point when she relates an event at the beginning of her journey with Shelley down the Rhine in 1816:

> Our companions in this voyage were of the meanest class, smoked
> prodigiously, and were exceedingly disgusting. After having
> landed for refreshment in the middle of the day, we found that
> our former seats were occupied; we took others, when the original
> possessors angrily, and almost with violence, insisted upon our
> leaving them. Their brutal rudeness to us, who did not under-
> stand their language, provoked Shelley to knock one of the fore-
> most down: he did not return the blow, but continued his
> vociferations until the boatmen interfered, and provided us with
> other seats.

The handbooks of John Murray and Karl Baedeker became the
two chief rivals out of many guidebook series, but Baedeker produced the cheaper item which sold therefore in greater numbers.
Less durable, and printed on thinner paper, the maps and plans
were mostly coloured and easy to read, while the black and white
maps in the early Murray's books, sometimes without scale, were
more difficult to follow.

The Baedeker series is still going, though the quality has
deteriorated since the introduction of glossy photographs; the only
remaining Murray is a handbook to India. In France Adolphe
Joanne began his series of travel guides in 1841, which in 1916
were renamed *Les Guides Bleus*, published in English only after the
Great War. Although the *Blue Guides* of today, with the *Guides
Bleus* in France, are perhaps the best both for detail and cartography,
the prize for the best maps and plans of all time must be shared
between Murray's last edition of *Switzerland*, and Baedeker's *United
States*, 1909.

In the nineteenth century such books guided travellers to all
parts of Europe, and sometimes to places beyond. With a Baedeker
one could travel as far as Peking, or across Canada and the United
States, while Murray even published handbooks to Japan and New
Zealand.

Trawling through the various titles and editions enables one to
confect a fair picture of what it was like to travel in the century up
to the Great War of 1914, of the pleasures, dangers, traps and rare

experiences which the tourist was warned against but no doubt often encountered.

The flood of tourists had a civilizing influence on some parts of the Mainland, in that the money spent was an economic blessing. The disadvantages have often been pointed out, but English gold helped to finance modern infrastructures, giving employment on all levels, and sustaining those inn owners who were to become a solid part of the middle class. As Murray writes in *France*, 1848: 'By official returns it appears that there are at present in France 66,000 English residents. Supposing the average expenditure of each to be 5 francs a day, the sum total will amount to about 4,820,000 pounds per annum.'

From *Switzerland*, 1892, we learn that: 'The great annual influx of strangers is of the same importance as some additional branch of industry or commerce would be. It has been estimated that in 1880 there were over a thousand inns in Switzerland especially built for the use of travellers, the capital value of the buildings and their contents and sites being put at nearly 13 million pounds sterling.'

The death of an officer in the bear pit at Berne was not the only accident which befell a tourist during that century up to 1914, when the days were good if you had the money to travel. Before going on to chronicle others I will refer to *The Tourist's India* by Eustace Reynolds Ball (1907 edition). This tells of an incident which had a happier outcome than the one at Berne.

The great sight of Karachi is the sacred Crocodile Preserve at Magar Pir, some seven miles off. There are hot springs here which feed a shallow tank containing nearly a hundred crocodiles . . .

The story, usually thought to be fictitious, of the Englishman who for a bet crossed the tank by jumping successively from the backs of these crocodiles is, it seems, based on fact. The hero of this foolhardy feat was a certain Lieutenant Beresford, a friend of R. F. Burton. When Burton and his companion were visiting the crocodiles' tank they noticed that these reptiles and certain islets of reeds happened to make an almost continuous bridge across the tank. This prompted the daring subaltern to hazard the feat of crossing by hopping from one crocodile to another. To the amazement of the spectators he succeeded in this apparently mad attempt. Sir Richard Burton had already successfully performed an equally daring feat. He managed to muzzle a crocodile by means of a lasso, and then jumped on the reptile's back and enjoyed a somewhat zigzag ride.

Reading these guidebooks has for many years been a pleasurable pastime for me, and I shall lead the reader through their combined maze, picking out whatever illuminates the larger picture of travel in a bygone age.

CHAPTER TWO

HURDLES

Before going abroad in the first half of the nineteenth century, a passport was needed, the price for which was four shillings and sixpence. By 1913 it had gone down to two shillings. Regarding the indignity of having to carry such a document John Murray wrote, in 1848: 'Of all the penalties at the expense of which the pleasure of travelling abroad is purchased, the most disagreeable and most repugnant to English feelings is that of submitting to the strict regulations of the continental police, and especially to the annoyance of bearing a passport. As this, however, is a matter of necessity, from which there is no exemption, it is better to submit with a good grace.'

A visa was also called for, at the cost of five francs, a process which had to be gone through before every journey. 'Beyond this the new regulations present no impediment to well-intending and respectable travellers.'

What people should take with them, and how they were to dress when they got to wherever they were going, was the subject of much advice from Murray. 'The warning cannot be too often repeated, or too emphatically enforced upon the traveller, that, if he value money, temper, comfort, and time, he will take with him as little luggage as possible. In cases, however, where the travelling party is large it is a great mistake to distribute it in many small packages. Three large portmanteaus are infinitely better than six small ones: they are more easily found on arrival, more quickly opened at the custom-house, cost the same when you are charged by weight, and of course half when you are charged by package.'

Walking was more in vogue than it is today, and you were advised to: 'Provide yourself with a pair of *shooting-boots* with cloth or leather tops in England, where alone they can be procured good, with a pair of thin boots for dress. This arrangement will prevent the necessity of loading yourself with a large stock of boots, boot-trees, and boot-cases.' He goes on to say that for the walker the buttoned boots should be double-soled and provided with hobnails: 'The experienced pedestrian never commences a journey with new shoes, but with a pair that have already been conformed to the shape of the feet.'

With regard to wearing-apparel, the best rule was 'to choose that which is not conspicuous or unusual – a light loose morning coat for travelling, which will keep off dust and rain: even the English shooting-jacket has of late become familiar to foreigners.' While a better and cheaper knapsack could be acquired abroad: 'Portmanteaus are better in England than anywhere else.'

The ablutions of Englishmen were of prime importance: '*Soap* is indispensable, being a rare article in Continental inns.' Another necessity was: 'A portable *india-rubber bath*, with a bellows to distend it, packing into the compass of about a foot square, an immense comfort in summer in a hot and dusty climate.'

A flask for brandy or kirschwasser would be useful on mountain excursions, but 'it should be remembered that spirits ought to be resorted to less as a restorative than as a protection against cold and wet, and to mix with water, which ought never to be drunk cold or unmixed during a walk. The best restorative is tea . . .'

Carey, an optician with a shop on the Strand, was said to make excellent pocket telescopes, 'about four inches long, combining, with a small size, considerable power and an extensive range . . . Spectacles are almost indispensable in railway travelling, for those who ride in 3rd class carriages, to protect the eyes from dust and cinders. Those ladies who take an interest in mountain scenery, or excursions from the high road, will find great advantage in a saddle constructed by Mr. Whippy, in North Audley Street. The crutch is separable, for the convenience of packing.'

The first obstacle in the path of the British traveller was of course the sea, whether it was twenty miles wide as at the Channel, several hundred across the North Sea (German Ocean, in those days) or a week's voyage to Spain and Portugal. Paddle-wheeled steamers were soon crossing to all major ports of the Continent, their fore-decks packed with carriages. Boats left from St Katharine's Wharf on the Thames, but there were two rapid-return crossings every day from Folkestone. English steamboats from Dover took about two hours to Calais, the fare for a pedestrian being ten shillings, and the cost of transporting a carriage two guineas. On this route Murray says that the French steamers were 'very bad', though without giving the reason.

If you needed to wait a day or two at Folkestone, for a calmer sea perhaps, you could get bed and breakfast at the South-Eastern Hotel for six shillings. A cup of tea cost sixpence, a slice of sponge cake one penny, and a pork pie a shilling. For service, the advertise-ment says, 'one shilling per day will be charged to each Visitor, who, if staying only a portion of a day will have to pay accord-ingly'.

Few guidebooks mention the torments of seasickness, a topic which rarely appeared in their pages till the advent of air travel in the 1920s. The subject was not, however, neglected in Baedeker's *Travellers Manual of Conversation*, 1856, which tells one how to express in four languages the following degrees of sickness: 'The wind increases. See that great wave which is coming to break against our vessel. I fear we shall have a storm; the sky is very dark towards the west.'

'The rolling of the vessel makes me sick.'

'Steward, will you assist this lady to go on deck; she is very unwell.'

'Smell some eau de Cologne, it will do you good.'

'I am very much inclined to vomit.'

'Drink some Gin; it will strengthen your stomach, and you will feel relieved.'

'I must lie down in my hammock.'

Certain guidebooks helped to pay their way with an advertisement section, though it was never the case with Baedeker, who was thus able to claim impartiality for any deleterious comments. An advertisement against the dreaded *mal de mer* appeared, later in the century, in Ward Lock's *Guide to Sherwood Forest*, though why *there* is impossible to imagine. The effect of *Roach's Seasick Draughts* was bolstered by a testimonial from *a lady*: 'And here I have something to say which I expect all voyagers to accept with grateful joy. A distinguished physician advised me to get for a young friend who was going out to Gibraltar, some of ROACH'S celebrated draughts for the prevention of seasickness. The remedy had never been known to fail in its effects. The young lady who took them last year found them perfectly efficacious both on the journey out and home . . . Sold in boxes, containing Six, for 4/6; or 12 Draughts, 8/6.'

An extensive consideration of seasickness was found, as it should have been, in the invalid's guide *Winter and Spring on the Shores of the Mediterranean*, 1875, by James Henry Bennet, MD, who claimed to have discovered the perfect means of avoiding the malady:

The stomach should be absolutely empty before going on board, but to avoid exhaustion a good meal should be taken three, four, or five hours before, according to the nature of the digestion. Then, one or two hours before embarking, some very strong coffee, tea, or spirits and water, should be taken, without milk or other food. This is to tonify the nervous system . . .

Once on board, repose should be enjoined, the recumbent position is best, and nothing whatever, solid or fluid, should be taken for twelve hours or more, even then very little. As there is nothing left in the stomach, or given it to digest, it remains quiescent under difficulty. The reason that medicines given in sickness do no good is that they are not absorbed. Once even nausea commences the stomach refuses to absorb liquids or to digest solids, and the more there is in it the worse it behaves. The best stimulant in my experience is very strong black coffee. Scores and scores of my friends and patients have escaped seasickness in the short passages by observing these rules, and have diminished suffering in long ones.

Brown's *Madeira, Canary Islands, and Azores* agrees with the above advice, adding that: 'When attacked by vomiting the greatest comfort is to be found in lying down. A belt drawn tightly round the stomach is at times a relief. As a remedy a solution containing bicarbonate of soda, chloroform, or bromide of potash and sal volatile is of great assistance. Efforts should be made to keep the digestive organs at work. For this purpose a few apples and dry biscuits are in every way most convenient. It is rarely that sickness gives much trouble the second day.'

Our traveller could put his sorrows in their place should all these seasickness remedies fail, by taking in Murray's comments on the exigencies of the French police and their passport system, which emphasized that as soon as he stepped ashore at Calais every man's hand would be against him:

In France, more than in any other country in Europe at the present time, the passport is liable to be demanded at all times and places, and should *always be carried about the person*. The gendarmes are authorised to call for it not only in frontier and fortified towns, but in remote villages: they may stop you on the highway, or waylay you as you descend from the diligence – may force themselves into the salle à manger or enter your bedroom, to demand a sight of this precious document. It is needless to expatiate on this restraint, so inconsistent with the freedom which an Englishman enjoys at home, or to show that the police are a pest to the harmless and well conducted, without being a terror to evil-doers; it is the custom of the country, and the stranger must conform, or he has no business to set his foot in it. It must be allowed that the police perform their duty with civility, so as to render it as little vexatious as possible.

Woe to the traveller who loses his passport, or leaves it behind. Those who do so 'are liable to be marched off to the judge de paix, or préfet, often a distance of 10, 15, or 20 miles, on foot, unless they choose to pay for a carriage for their escort as well as themselves; and if no satisfactory explanation can be given, may at last be deposited in prison.'

In the epilogue to *An Inland Voyage* Robert Louis Stevenson relates in his fey yet charming manner that he was arrested by a gendarme during a pedestrian tour of France soon after the Franco-Prussian War of 1870–71. The vital paper had been left behind in his valise, and neither charm nor argument prevented him being incarcerated, albeit for less than an hour, in the damp cellar of a police station. He was uncertain as to whether or not he would be detained for trial, but was released on the arrival of his more appropriately dressed companion, who vouched for him as a bona fide traveller. Even so, neither of them was allowed to continue their walk, being put on the next train for Paris.

The nineteenth century became comparatively peaceful and tolerant towards its end, but an intense spy mania nevertheless surrounded a country's defence installations. Guidebooks frequently contained the following warning, as in Baedeker's *Northern France*, 1909: 'Sketching, photographing, or making notes near fortified places sometimes exposes innocent travellers to disagreeable suspicions or worse, and should therefore be avoided.'

In the same author's *Russia*, 1914, we are told that 'even in less important places the guardians of the law are apt to be over-vigilant. In order to escape molestation the photographers should join the Russian Photographic Society.' In no guidebook to Britain was the traveller given similar warnings regarding arsenals and naval bases.

Such rules have of course remained in force during much of the present century. In 1967 my Finnish publisher, to whom I showed the detailed military maps I intended using to motor my way around the USSR, warned me not to take them or I would be sure to get into trouble. While driving in the Ukraine my Russian friend was plainly worried when I stopped to photograph the landscape, though neither bridges nor fortresses were visible, and he was even more harassed when I levelled my camera at the streets of Czernowitz.

Travellers have always been fair game for the secret police. In

1954 I was arrested in Barcelona and detained for a day, though not in a cell. I never knew for what reason, and after lengthy questioning and a close examination of my passport I was released.

One hopes that our Victorian traveller did not suffer too much from seasickness, having taken his luck on the weather. The boats were much smaller than they are today, and wrecks were not uncommon in the Channel. During a violent storm in January 1857 the steamer *Violet* foundered off the Goodwins. She had left Ostend the previous night, and hit the sands at two in the morning, going down with all passengers and crew.

The most agreeable crossings to the Continent must have been those enjoyed by J. P. Pearson, recounted in his three-volume magnum opus *Railways and Scenery*. In 1901 he took the ship from Grimsby to Hamburg, having bought a year's season ticket for the amazingly low price, even then, of sixty shillings. 'The state rooms were spacious, and almost invariably each passenger (so few used this route) could have one of them all to himself. The open fire in the dining saloon was most cheery, and the writer recalls some pleasant evenings sitting around it on his trips across the North Sea.'

CHAPTER THREE

GETTING THERE

The next barrier met with by the British traveller, after the two-hour crossing, were foreigners, who made sure that having got him into their country they were not going to make it easy for him to get out, for he would discover that his passport in France was (Murray) 'not valid for travelling through the country, nor for quitting it, until it has received the signature of the Minister of the Interior. It is therefore taken away from the traveller at the sea-port where he lands, and is forwarded by the police to Paris, while a temporary passport is given him to carry him on to Paris, and 2 francs must be paid for it. Until the traveller reaches Paris this will carry him through all parts of France, but not out of the country. He cannot depart until he has exchanged it for his original passport.'

Supposing then that the traveller has more or less recovered from the crossing, he or she now has something more to worry about, for when the steamboat reaches port (Murray again) 'the shore is usually beset by a crowd of clamorous agents for the different hotels, each vociferating the name and praises of that for which he is employed, stunning the distracted stranger with their cries, and nearly scratching his face with their proffered cards. The only mode of rescuing himself from these tormentors, who often beset him a dozen at a time, is to make up his mind *beforehand* to what hotel he will go, and to name it at once. The agent or Commissionaire of the house then steps forward, and the rest fall back, while he takes the new arrival under his protection, extricates him from the throng, and conducts him to his quarters.'

Even this procedure was far from simple, because passengers were not allowed to take their baggage into town with them, it being conveyed at once 'from the vessel to the Custom-house by the Custom-house porters, who are answerable for the safety of everything. The owner, instead of appearing himself to claim it, had better send his servant, or the Commissionaire of the inn, instructing him with the keys, in order that he may open and clear each package. This is his usual duty, and the landlord of the inn, who employs him, is answerable for his honesty. Personal attendance at a Custom-house is by no means calculated to put the traveller in a good humour. Indeed, it is a severe trial to his patience, first to wait till his turn comes, amidst the elbowing of porters, and next to look on while his well-packed trunk is tossed over with a cruel, hard-hearted sort of civility which leaves nothing to complain of, and everything to lament.' (Murray.)

Baedeker's *Paris* 1874, says: 'In order to prevent the risk of unpleasant detention at the custom-house travellers are strongly recommended to avoid carrying with them any articles that are not absolutely necessary. Cigars and tobacco are chiefly sought for by the custom-house officers. Six cigars and about an ounce of tobacco only are free of duty. Books and newspapers occasionally give rise to suspicion and may in certain cases be confiscated.'

'Indeed,' Murray suggests, 'the search into baggage is often more severe in the presence of the traveller, which seems sometimes to give rise to a suggestion of smuggling. He that would keep his temper, and does not grudge a fee of two francs to the Commissionaire, will intrust to him his keys, and, dismissing the care of his baggage from his thoughts, amuse himself for an hour or so, when he will probably find his effects conveyed to his chamber, very often not opened at all, generally only slightly examined.'

Getting into Abroad threatened at times to become an obstacle race, though Murray endeavours to prevent the British traveller from turning it into an assault course. 'Those who would travel with comfort should be particularly on their guard against rendering themselves liable to detection or penalty at the foreign Custom-houses. They should avoid taking anything which is contraband, either for themselves or for their friends; for it too often happens that travellers on the continent are meanly solicited to take those things for their friends who are abroad which they dare not send by the public conveyance, thus rendering their travelling friends liable to penalty and punishment.'

If after such Kafka-like turmoil our gentleman-traveller wishes to recuperate for a few days in the Calais area, before proceeding to Paris, there are several hotels to choose from. First on the list is the Hotel Dessin, said to be very good, one of whose rooms was slept in by the author of *A Sentimental Journey*, still marked as 'Sterne's Room'. Also singled out is that which was occupied by Sir Walter Scott.

Murray describes the sights of the town and gives something of its history, then goes on to tell us, should the traveller wish to make a romantic pilgrimage, that 'Lady Hamilton (Nelson's Emma) died here in great misery. Her remains, refused a resting place in consecrated ground, were interred in a timber-yard, about 20 yards beyond the Port de Calais.'

Should the traveller be tempted to take a day's trip down the coast to Boulogne he will find a quarter of the population to be English. The town is within eight hours of London, Murray says, and has become 'one of the chief British colonies abroad; and, by a singular reciprocity, on the very spot whence Napoleon proposed the invasion of our shores, his intended victims have quietly taken possession and settled themselves down. The town is enriched by English money; warmed, lighted, and smoked by English coal; English signs and advertisements decorate every other shop door, inn, tavern, and lodging house; and almost every third person you meet is either a countryman or speaking our language; while the outskirts of the town are enlivened by villas and country houses, somewhat in the style and taste of those on the opposite side of the Channel. There are at least 120 boarding schools for youth of both sexes, many of them under English managers.'

Thackeray in *Vanity Fair* gives a further view of English travellers on the Continent, those among them who have 'swindled in all the capitals of Europe. The respect in those happy days of 1817–18 was very great for the wealth and honour of Britons. They had not then learned, as I am told, to haggle for bargains with the pertinacity which now distinguishes them. The great cities of

Europe had not been as yet open to the enterprise of our rascals.
And whereas there is now hardly a town of France or Italy in
which you shall not see some noble countryman of our own, with
that happy swagger and insolence of demeanour which we carry
everywhere, swindling inn-landlords, passing fictitious cheques
upon credulous bankers, robbing coachmakers of their carriages,
goldsmiths of their trinkets, easy travellers of their money at cards
– even libraries of their books: thirty years ago you needed but to
be a Milor Anglais, travelling in a private carriage, and credit was
at your hand wherever you chose to seek it, and gentlemen, instead
of cheating, were cheated.'

If our traveller at Calais was already regretting his departure
from home the pier jutting out from the shore gave an occasional
view of the white cliffs of England. This must have been a tantaliz-
ing sight to those who were also exiles, 'fugitives from creditors, or
compelled from other causes,' hints Murray, 'to leave their homes: a
numerous class both here and at Boulogne. There are many of
our countrymen besides, who reside merely for the purpose of
economising; so that the place is half Anglicised, and our language
generally spoken.'

Murray also mentions the local fishermen and their wives, who
dress in picturesque costume and occupy their own quarter of the
town, where the streets, 'are draped with nets hung out from
the fronts of the houses to dry, and in dress and manners they are
distinct from the rest of the inhabitants, speaking a peculiar patois,
and rarely intermarrying with the other townsfolk. They are an
industrious and very hardworking race, especially the women, and
very religious: the perils and vicissitudes of their hard life reminding
them more nearly than other classes of their dependence on
Providence.'

According to Baedeker, the men's wives are called *matelottes*,
and 'exercise unlimited sway on shore, whilst the sea is the undis-
puted domain of their husbands'.

During a pause in his solitary walk along the seafront, or while
sitting in the dining room of his hotel over a long half-English
meal, our traveller may ponder on the remarks in his handbook
concerning accommodation in the rest of France. He will not be
reassured, for Murray tells him that: 'On the whole, the inns of

France are very inferior to those of Germany and Switzerland, in the want of general comfort, and above all of cleanliness – their greatest drawback. There is an exception to this, however, in the bed and table linen. Even the filthy cabaret, whose kitchen and salon are scarcely endurable to look at, commonly affords napkins and table-cloths clean, though coarse and rough, and beds with unsullied sheets and white draperies, together with well-stuffed mattresses and pillows, which put German cribs and feather-beds to shame.'

Presumably referring to the toilet facilities, he goes on: 'Many of the most *important essentials*, on the other hand, are utterly disregarded, and evince a state of grossness and barbarism hardly to be expected in a civilised country; the provisions for personal ablution are very defective: the washing of floors, whether of timber or tile, seems unknown. In the better hotels, indeed, the floors are polished as tables are in England, with brushes attached to the feet instead of the hands; but in most cases they are black with the accumulated filth of years, a little water being sprinkled on them from time to time to lay the dust and increase the dark crust of dirt.'

Murray divides French hotels into two classes: 'Those which make some pretension to study English tastes and habits (and a few of them have some claim to be considered comfortable), and being frequented by Englishmen, are very exorbitant in their charges.' Then: 'Those in remote situations, not yet corrupted to exorbitance by the English and their couriers; where the traveller who can conform with the customs of the country is treated fairly, and charged no higher than a Frenchman.'

The traveller is advised to bargain for a room on arrival at an inn, though he is told to be careful because doing so can 'sometimes lead the landlord to suppose that you are going to beat him down, and he may therefore name a higher price than he is willing to take, and thus you may cause the exorbitance which you intend to prevent.'

French hotels are nevertheless compared favourably to those in Germany, since they will 'furnish at almost any hour of the day, at 10 minutes or ¼ hour's notice, a well-dressed dinner of 8 or 10 dishes, at a cost not greatly exceeding that of the table-d'hôte. In remote places and small inns, never order dinner at a higher price than 3 francs: the people have only the same food to present, even if they charged 10 francs. A capital dinner is usually furnished at 4 fr. a-head; but the traveller who goes post in his own carriage will probably be charged 6, unless he specifies the price beforehand.'

It was usual to dine at a common table in French inns, but Murray says they are '*rarely* resorted to by the most respectable townspeople, or by ladies, as in Germany. The majority of the company almost invariably consists of commercial travellers but of a stamp very inferior to those of the same class in England, who swarm in all the inns, and are consequently the most important personages. Without denying that there are exceptions among these gentry, it is impossible to have sojourned in France for any time without the conviction that a more selfish, depraved, and vulgar, if not brutal, set does not exist, and gentlemen will take good care not to encourage their approaches, and to keep a distance from them. They commonly sit down to table with their hats on, and scramble for the dishes, so that the stranger who is not on the alert is likely to fare very ill; and if females be present, not only do not pay them that attention which is customary in all civilised countries at a dinner-table, and used at one time to distinguish the French, but, as Mrs. Trollope remarks, constantly "use language which no Englishman would dream of uttering in their presence," evincing an utter want of all sense of propriety and decency. English ladies, therefore, will be cautious of presenting themselves at a French table-d'hôte, except in first-rate hotels, where English guests form a considerable part of the company, and at well-frequented watering-places.'

In confirmation of the above, Delacroix remarks in his notebook (1855) that the effect of a good meal in the provinces 'was not entirely spoiled by the company of some commercial travellers, whose chatter is always the same mixture of nonsense and ineptness'.

Various guidebooks convince our traveller that he may need several periods of repose, as well as a few large brandies, before setting out on his journey to the interior. The cafés in which he may have to bide his time when he gets there received a somewhat better press than the hotels:

'We have no equivalent in England for the Cafés in France, and the number and splendour of some of these establishments, everywhere seemingly out of proportion to the population and to other shops, not only in Paris, but in every provincial town, may well excite surprise. They are adapted to all classes of society, from the magnificent *salon*, resplendent with looking-glass, and glittering with gliding, the decorations of which have perhaps cost 4000 or 5000 pounds, down to the low and confined *estaminets*, resorted to by carters, porters, and common labourers, which abound in the back streets of every town, and in every village, however small and remote. The latter sort occupy the place of the beer-shops of England, furnish beer and brandy, as well as coffee, and, though not so injurious to health and morals as the gin-palaces of London, are even more destructive of time: indeed, the dissipation of precious hours by almost all classes in France produces as bad an effect on the habits of the people.' (Murray.)

Such pompous moralizing did not admit that even the gentleman-traveller might at times be guilty of dissipating the precious hours. Certainly, the French seemed more able to enjoy life than their English counterparts, for in the evening the cafés 'are most crowded, and even in the most respectable (except the first-rate Parisian cafés) the company is very mixed. Clerks, tradesmen, commercial travellers, soldiers – officers as well as privates, and men in blouzes, crowded about a multitude of little marble tables, wrangle over provincial or national politics, or over games of cards or dominoes, while others perspiring in their shirt-sleeves surround the billiard-table. The rattling of balls, the cries of waiters hurrying to and fro, the gingling of dominoes, and tinkling bell of the mistress who presides at the bar, alone prevail over the harsh din of many voices, while the splendour of mirrored walls and velvet seats is eclipsed behind a cloud of unfragrant tobacco-smoke.' What a picture of pleasure island for the sin-preoccupied English!

However many days our traveller stayed in Calais or Boulogne, he had sooner or later to pay his hotel bill, before setting out for the fleshpots of Paris. Twenty-five francs to the English sovereign allowed him to live well and cheaply, his room costing about two shillings a night, something like five pounds at today's rates. Dinner and breakfast would add on another ten, amounting to forty-five pounds for three days of demi-pension. Baedeker advises that 'the bill should be obtained every two or three days, in order that errors, whether accidental or designed, may be detected. When the traveller intends to start in the morning, he had better pay, or at least examine, his bill over night, as overcharges are apt to escape detection in the hurry and confusion of departure.'

In 1848 the quickest way of getting to Paris from the coast was to take the diligence as far as Arras or Abbeville, then go by recently opened railway. 'France has allowed herself to be outstripped by her neighbours, not only by England, but also by Belgium, Prussia, and Austria, in these means of extending national resources and civilisation, which the country more especially stands in need of.' (Murray.)

Murray describes the diligence as being a 'huge, heavy, lofty, lumbering machine, something between an English stage and a broad-wheeled waggon.'

It is composed of three parts or bodies joined together: 1. the front division, called *Coupé*, shaped like a chariot, holding 3 persons, quite distinct from the rest of the passengers, so that ladies may resort to it without inconvenience, and, by securing all 3 places to themselves, travel nearly as comfortably as in a private carriage. The fare is more expensive than in the other parts of the vehicle.

2. Next to it comes the inside, holding 6 persons, and oppressively warm in summer.

3. Behind this is attached the *Rotonde*, 'the receptacle of dust, dirt, and bad company,' the least desirable part of the diligence.

The *Banquette*, an outside seat on the roof of the coupé, tolerably well protected from rain and cold by a hood or head, and leather apron, but somewhat difficult of access until you are accustomed to climb up into it. It affords a comfortable and roomy seat by the side of the conductor, with the advantages of fresh air and the best view of the country from its great elevation, and greater freedom from the dust than those enjoy who sit below. It is true you may sometimes meet rough and low-bred companions, for the French do not like to travel outside; and few persons of the better class resort to it, except English, and they for the most part prefer it to all others. It is not suited to females, owing to the difficulty of clambering up to it.

What no guidebook mentions – nor the phrase manuals of the age either – is the problem of *land* sickness when travelling by a badly sprung coach on sometimes indifferent roads. Almost as common as seasickness, all we get in the way of chit-chat from phrase books dealing with road travel are: 'Can I take my dogs with me by coach?'

'Are there any robbers on the road?'

'Keep away from the ditch: it is a bog full of mud. You must put on the drag.'

'If you drive well, and behave yourself civilly, I shall give you something for drink-money.'

The coaches in France were ruled over by a conductor who was 'paid by the administration, and expects nothing from the passengers, unless he obliges them by some extra service. He is generally an intelligent person, often an old soldier, and the traveller may pick up some information from him.'

Though the methods of transport were far slower in the 1840s, they resembled the holiday procedures in France today, in that during the month of August 'the diligences on all the great roads are thronged with school-boys and collegians, with their parents and masters, in consequence of the breaking up of the establishments of education in Paris, all hurrying home at once into the provinces'.

On the way to Abbeville or Arras our traveller will learn from Murray's *Hand-Book of Travel Talk* how to get himself and his impedimenta safely into the train. The diligence, said to be more roomy than an English stagecoach, and therefore less tiring, went at the rate of about six miles an hour, and even less when the roads were bad, so there was sufficient time to practise the few phrases necessary: 'Pray, Sir, where is the railway station? Where can one get tickets? Where is the luggage-office? I hear the whistle of a train which is arriving.'

If our traveller, after a fight for his seat, becomes bored with looking out of the window – at better scenery as the train went south – perhaps he will go back to his handbook and read the section on 'The English Abroad': 'It may not be amiss to consider the causes which render the English so unpopular on the Continent; as to the fact of their being so, it is to be feared there can be no doubt. In the first place, it arises from the number of ill-conditioned persons who, not being in condition to face the world at home, scatter themselves over foreign lands, and bring no little discredit upon their country. But in addition to these, there are many respectable and wealthy persons, who, through inattention, unguardedness, wanton expenditure in some cases, niggardly parsimony in others, but, above all, from an unwillingness to accommodate themselves to the feelings of the people they are among, contribute not a little to bring their own nation into disrepute. The Englishman abroad too often forgets that he is the representative of his country, and that his countrymen will be judged by his own conduct; that by affability, moderation, and being easily pleased, he will conciliate; whereas by caprice, extravagant squandering, or ill-timed niggardliness, he affects the reception of the next comer.'

Eugene Delacroix, in 1855, recorded in his notebook that, in the train from Dieppe to Rouen, there were three Englishmen in the first-class carriage whom 'you would suppose comfortably off. They were very badly dressed, especially one who was really dirty, his clothes were even torn. I do not understand this complete contrast with their former habits; I noticed the same thing on my trip to Baden and Strasbourg. A day or two later, when I was making my examination of the pictures, I met Lord Elcho, and even his clothes were not particularly clean. The English have changed entirely and we French, on the other hand, have adopted many of their former habits.'

'There are many points, however,' continued Murray, 'in which our character is misunderstood by foreigners. The morose sullenness attributed by them to Englishmen is, in perhaps nine cases out of ten, nothing more than involuntary silence, arising from his ignorance of foreign languages, or at least from his want of sufficient fluency to make himself rapidly understood, which prevents his enjoying society. If an Englishman were fully aware how much it increased the pleasure and profit of travelling to have made some progress in foreign languages before he sets foot on the Continent, no one would think of quitting home until he had devoted at least some months to hard labour with grammars and dictionaries.'

Our traveller being young and rich will be allowed to feel at ease on the Continent, however, and throwing aside such pompous strictures with a smile of superior amusement, joyfully commit himself to the diversions of Paris, the undoubted capital city of the civilized world.

CHAPTER FOUR

PARIS

Before anything else can be done in the capital our impatient traveller must either take or send his provisional passport to police headquarters, 'where the original will be given in exchange for it. It is better to send a valet de place or commissionaire for it than to go for it: the commissionaire being known to the officials is more likely to be attended to than a stranger, speaking French perhaps scarcely intelligible. The commissionaire may, it is true, play false, and declare that the passport is not arrived, in the hope of detaining the traveller at his hotel; and the best way to prevent this is to promise him an extra douceur in the event of his securing the passport at once. The stranger who undertakes to do this for himself will find it a very disagreeable and tiresome business, the passport offices being open only at fixed hours, being situated in distant parts of the town, and being beset by crowds of applicants.'

Having seen to these formalities our traveller is now free to enjoy the town, and we will assume he has already found accommodation, because Murray's guide tells him that there are nearly four thousand hotels in Paris, as well as six thousand cafés and numerous restaurants. Concerning the latter: 'The smallness of the quantity of solid food supplied is a difficulty for the English. A card is handed the diner on entering, containing a priced list of all the dishes supplied, and the waitress (for the service is performed by modestly-dressed females) marks those ordered, and expects a few sous to be left on the table for her.' Murray goes on to say that: 'Ladies may dine at Restaurants mentioned in this handbook without the slightest impropriety or feeling of annoyance.'

In a possibly idealized version of street life we are told that on fine summer evenings, 'coffee, ices, etc., are supplied out of doors, and the streets facing the principal cafés, the Boulevards, Champs Elysées, etc., are covered with little tables and chairs, occupied by groups of well-dressed ladies and gentlemen sipping coffee and ice, or smoking cigars'. Our traveller must have fitted with alacrity into such a scene, though his Baedeker advised tourists to 'scrupulously avoid these cafés where the chairs placed outside in summer are in unpleasant proximity with the gutters'.

Paris, to paraphrase Baedeker the greatest treasure-house of art and industry in the world, possessed 'English hotels, English professional men, English "valets de place", and English shops; but the visitor who is dependent upon these is necessarily deprived of many opportunities of becoming acquainted with the most interesting characteristics of Paris.'

On installing himself at his hotel the traveller will of course note the following: '*Articles of Value* should never be kept in the drawers or cupboards at hotels. The traveller's own trunk is probably safer; but it is better to entrust them to the landlord, from whom a receipt should be required, or to send them to a bankers.'

For those who would wander freely, a paragraph was provided concerning public safety: 'In the E. quarter are numerous manufactories and the dwellings of those who work in them. Here was the hotbed of insurrection and the terror of Paris in troubled times.' Baedeker remarks that the annual consumption of wine in Paris was thirty-nine million gallons, or thirty gallons a head for the whole population. He also tells us that the Parisian police 'are so efficient and well-organised, that street-robberies are less frequent than in most other large towns. Beware, however, of pickpockets, who are as adroit as the police are vigilant, and are particularly apt to victimise strangers.'

Our traveller on his perambulations may think to pick up a trifle or two at an auction, but Baedeker has another word in his ear: 'Strangers are cautioned against making purchases in person, as trickery is too frequently practised, but a respectable agent may be employed to bid for any article they may desire to purchase.'

Should the traveller wish to go to the theatre, warning is given against ticket touts, 'who frequently loiter in the vicinity and endeavour to impose on the public . . . The attendants of the cloak-rooms are often troublesome in their efforts to earn a "pourboire". One of their usual attentions is to bring footstools, for the use of ladies; and they have a still more objectionable practice of bringing the cloaks and shawls to the box before the conclusion of the performance in order to secure their gratuity in good time.'

The theatre is said to present a highly characteristic part of Parisian life, but, in some, 'ladies are not admitted to the orchestra stalls'. Murray tells us that most of the forty theatres in Paris are devoted to light comedy with music, but 'the subjects and treatment of many of the pieces render them unfit for the ears of English ladies'.

As for the *cafés chantants*, spectators sit in the open air, and 'listen to singing and music by performers outrageously overdressed . . . The company is not the most select, and the performance tends to be immoral. Respectable people keep aloof.'

While the farces at the Théâtre du Palais Royal are said to be of a character 'not always exceptionable', the concerts of the Conservatoire de Musique 'enjoy a European celebrity. The highest order of classical music, by Haydn, Beethoven, Mendelssohn, etc., as well as by the most celebrated French and Italian composers, is performed with exquisite taste and precision.'

Our traveller might well look in at one of the many balls given in the summer because, though the society 'is by no means select, they deserve to be visited by the stranger on account of the gay, brilliant, and novel spectacle they present. The rules of decorum are tolerably well observed, but it need hardly be said that ladies cannot go to them with propriety. Dancing takes place every evening, but the place is frequented by different people on different evenings when many handsome, richly dressed women of the "demi-monde" and exquisites of the boulevards assemble here, while on the other evenings, when the admission is 3 francs, and women enter without payment, the society is still less respectable.'

Bals Masqués du Grand-Opéra took place every Saturday evening, and presented 'a scene of boistrous merriment and excitement, and if visited by ladies they should be witnessed from the boxes only. The female frequenters of these balls wear masks or dominoes, the men are generally in evening costume.'

Should our gentleman-traveller wish to call at the Stock Exchange, the Bourse, he may walk along boulevards which were once paved, but 'as the stones had frequently been employed in the construction of barricades, they were replaced in 1850 by a macadamised asphalt roadway'. The Municipal Authorities of Barcelona, it was once said, solved that problem by numbering the cobblestones so that they could be put back in the correct order after each *pronunciamiento*. In Paris: 'The trees with which the boulevards are flanked are a source of constant trouble to the municipal authorities, being frequently killed by the gas lamps'.

The Bourse is open for business from midday, we are told, but visitors are admitted to the galleries from nine o'clock onwards. Numerous private carriages drive up, and 'the money-seeking throng hurries into the building. The deafening noise, the shouting, the excited gestures of the spectators, and the eager cupidity depicted in their features, produce a most unpleasant impression on the mind of the neutral spectator.'

Baedeker's *Paris*, 1874, appeared only three years after the upheavals of the Commune, but as soon as order had been restored the tourists flocked back. England had always been much like a box at the theatre, from which heads wagged censoriously at disturbances on the Continent.

From the Bourse our traveller might make his way to the Place de l'Hôtel de Ville, where public executions occurred up to 1830. 'Hither,' Murray said, 'Catherine de Medici and her son came in 1574 to see the torture and death of Montgomeri, for having accidentally slain in a tournament Henry II her husband. In 1676 the Marchioness de Brinvilliers, the notorious poisoner, was burnt here. Madame de Sevigné, a spectator, describes the scene in one of her letters. Cartouche the robber was broken alive here in 1721: and Damiens, so late as 1737, was put to death under the most protracted tortures (torn asunder by 4 horses), for attempting to assassinate Louis XV. In 1766 Lally Tollendal, the brave antagonist of the English in India, was hurried to execution with a gag on his mouth.'

Accounts of horrors abound in all guidebooks of the period,

and indeed the various French upheavals were in a traveller's living memory, as the Second World War is with us today. At the Place de la Concorde the '*Guillotine* was erected, Jan. 21, 1793, for the execution of Louis XVI. The scaffold was raised a few yards to the w. of the pedestal. The king commenced an address to the people, but was not allowed to finish it; on a signal from Santerre, who commanded the soldiers, the king was seized from behind, bound to the bascule, or setting-plank, and thrust under the axe. No sooner had the head fallen than the crowd rushed in to dip hands, pikes, or handkerchiefs in the blood.'

And then on 16 October Marie-Antoinette, 'the once beautiful queen, the most maligned of her sex, but innocent of all moral guilt; she preserved her calm dignity to the last . . . The blood thus shed like water remained in pools around the spot for the dogs to lick up, and on one occasion the oxen employed to drag a classic car in one of the theatrical processions of the Convention stood still in horror at the tainted spot.'

Baedeker reminds us that from 1793 to 1795 'upwards of 2800 persons perished here by the guillotine'. He also recounts that the last stand of the Communards, in 1871, took place – conveniently – in the Père Lachaise cemetery, where several hundred insurgents took up their position and 'planted cannon near the tomb of the Duc de Morny and the conspicuous Beaujour monument, using the latter as their guard-house. A few days later the batteries of Montmartre opened their fire upon the cemetery, destroying seven or eight monuments and injuring others. On the 27th the defenders of the cemetery, as well as those insurgents who on being driven back from the barricades of the Château d'Eau and the Place de la Bastille had sought refuge here, were compelled to abandon it, many however, being captured and shot. Near the wall of Charonne, which bears numerous marks of bullets, 147 National Guards, who had been taken prisoner at the barricades, were shot a few days later.'

From the cemetery it is not far distant to the famous morgue which, Murray tells us, 'is a place where bodies of the murdered, drowned, or of suicides, are exposed until they are recognised. On entering, a glazed partition will be seen, behind which are exposed the bodies of men and women found dead or drowned, and unowned. They are stretched naked, with the exception of a piece of leather over the loins, upon black marble slabs; the clothes found hang on pegs above them, and a stream of water is trickling over the bodies. Each corpse is exposed for 3 days, and there are usually 3 or 4 at a time, often hideously bloated and distorted, the majority being taken from the river. About 200 are carried to the Morgue every year on average, of whom about one-sixth are women and one-sixth new-born infants. The greatest number are found in June and July, the fewest in December and January. Gambling at the Bourse is the most fruitful cause of suicide. 15 fr. is paid for every corpse brought in. The larger proportion are never claimed by their friends, and are buried at the public expense. A perpetual stream of men, women, and children pour in and out of this horrible exhibition, to gaze at the hideous objects before them, usually with great indifference.' Baedeker adds: 'The painful scene attracts many spectators daily, chiefly persons of the lower orders.'

Baedeker also devotes a section to the Catacombs, which used to be quarries, and date from Roman times, extending under a great part of Paris, with sixty entrances in different suburbs. Several streets in the southern part of the city, situated above these quarries, having begun to show symptoms of sinking, 'steps were taken by the government in 1784 to avert the danger by constructing piers and buttresses where the upper surface was insufficiently supported. About the same time the Council of State ordered the removal of the bodies from the Cemetery of the Innocents, and others, which were closed at the period, to these subterranean quarries. In 1786 the catacombs were accordingly converted into a vast charnel-house. During the Revolution and the Reign of Terror, immense numbers of bodies and bones brought from various quarters were thrown into these cavities, in confused masses; but in 1810 a regular system was organised for the more seemly disposition of these remains, and the preservation of their resting-place. New pillars have since been erected to support the roof, excavations made to admit more air, and channels dug to carry off the water. The galleries and different compartments are completely lined with human bones, arranged with great care, and intermingled with rows of skulls.'

More interesting than the Catacombs was the network of sewers. Just as the Victorians thought it important to pay attention to the stomach, and what frequent and copious sustenance was put into it, so they were interested in how the detritus was carried away in the common cloaca, such fascination perhaps reinforced by their recognition that the only possible equality on earth afforded to human beings was in the disposal of what their biological systems ejected. The Paris sewers were, said Baedeker, 'so admirably constructed and well ventilated that parties, including even ladies, have frequently been formed to explore them. This system of drainage has been so beneficial to the public health that the annual death rate has been been reduced to 22–25 per thousand. If these statistics be correct, Paris is the healthiest capital on the continent, as indeed one would expect from the fact that, with the exception perhaps of Hamburg, it is the only continental city provided with a complete system of underground drainage.'

According to Baedeker a stay of a fortnight or three weeks was enough to give the traveller a superficial idea of 'the innumerable attractions which the city offers, but a residence of several months would be requisite to enable him satisfactorily to explore its vast treasures of art and industry'.

We will assume, however, that he is ready to leave, and continue his several months' tour of the Continent and the Middle East. In the sitting room of the hotel he will unfold the cloth-bound and dissected map of Central Europe which opens elegantly from the form of a book, engraved by B. R. Davies, and published by Edward Stanford of 6 Charing Cross in 1873. The British always journeyed with good maps, and the beautifully coloured and engraved specimen no doubt carried by our gentleman-traveller showed 'all the Railways in use with the Stations. Also the principal roads, rivers and Mountain Ranges', in a coverage extending from the Atlantic to Russian Poland, and from the Mersey to Bosnia (then part of the Turkish Empire). The scale of twenty-four miles to an inch makes its size somewhat awkward for unfolding in a crowded diligence or railway carriage, but most convenient for planning purposes; with a one-franc bottle of wine to hand, our traveller's finger moves languidly towards Switzerland.

In 1874 a first-class railway ticket from Paris to Basel cost sixty-three francs, the distance of 328 miles being covered in twelve hours. If our Victorian traveller intended stopping along the way he will have noted the following in Murray's handbook:

'It has been the custom of the English, who traverse France on their way to Italy or Switzerland, to complain of the monotonous features of the country, and to ridicule the epithet "*la Belle France*", which the French are wont to apply to it. By a "beautiful" country, a Frenchman generally understands one richly fertile and fully cultivated; and in this point of view the epithet is justly applied to France. It is also most fortunate in its climate. Many of its vineyards, the most valuable spots in the country, occupy tracts of poor, barren, and waste land, in appearance, which in our climate would be absolutely unprofitable . . . In France, the features of nature are broad and expanded, and you must often traverse 50 or 100 miles to encounter these pleasing changes which, in Britain, succeed one another almost every 10 miles.'

The writer goes on to say that, in compensation for this supposed dullness of terrain: '. . . glorious monuments of architectural skill and lavish devotion are far more stupendous in their proportion than the cathedrals of England, but have this peculiarity, that scarcely one of them is finished: thus Beauvais has no nave, Amiens has no towers, Bourges no spire.'

It was a time, we are reminded, when French provincial towns were being improved for the social convenience of their inhabitants, many completely remodelled, with straight streets and handsome shops replacing narrow and crooked lanes: 'There are many institutions and establishments in French towns,' said Murray, 'deserving high commendation and imitation in England: such are the Abattoirs, or slaughterhouses, always in the outskirts; the public Cemeteries, always situated outside the walls: even the Public Walks to be found in every French town, though not suited altogether to English ideas of recreation, yet show an attention to health and enjoyment of the people which would be worthy of imitation on our side of the Channel.'

CHAPTER FIVE

SWITZERLAND

The first problem our traveller must consider on entering Switzerland is the complication of money. In his Murray of 1838 he will perhaps already have noted that: 'There is hardly a country in Europe which has so complicated a currency as Switzerland; almost every canton has a Coinage of its own, and those coins that are current in one canton will not pass in the next. Let the traveller, therefore, be cautious how he overloads himself with more small change than he is sure of requiring.'

One English sovereign could be exchanged for 17 Swiss francs, 4 batzen and 6 rappen. If any French cash remains in his pocket he will get 7 batzen and 8 rapps for each franc. In the German-speaking provinces a Swiss guilden will net 60 kreutzers, and a ducat 30. The Zurich florin is divided into 16 (good) batzen and 40 rapps, and again into 40 schillings of 4 rapps each. At Geneva a French 5-franc piece will fetch 3 livres, 1 sol and 9 deniers. In the Grisons canton a florin contains 15 (light) batzen and 60 kreutzers, or 70 blutgers, which is the equivalent of 1 French franc 76 centimes, or 16 English pence. In the southern or Ticino part of the country the lira contains 20 solidi, each of 4 quatrini. Perhaps the Norfolk jacket of those days had more pockets than it does today. By 1850, however, the Swiss currency was brought into conformity with that of France.

Having sorted out the above problem, if he ever did, our traveller will take out his map of the country at the first good inn he comes to, though the remarks in his Murray concerning the complexity and variation in measuring distance will not be reassuring, for they are 'reckoned not by miles, but by *stunden* (hours' walking) or leagues. The measures of length given in the following routes have been taken from the most perfect tables that could be procured; but the Editor is aware that there must be many errors, and that an *approach to accuracy* is all that can be expected from them. The length of the stunde has been calculated at 5278 metres, or 2708 toises or 1800 Bernese feet; 21,137 of such stunden go to a degree of the Equator. To make their measurement agree with the actual pace of walking, it is necessary to advance 271 Paris feet in a minute . . . Since the correction of weights and measures in 1833–34, $\frac{3}{10}$ of a metre, or 3 decimetres, or 132,988 Paris lines has been constituted the legal Swiss foot, and 16,000 Swiss feet 1 stunde.'

Folding his map with a sigh, if not in a fit of absolute vexation, our traveller will notice that on the Italian side of the Alps things are even worse. Regarding distances in Piedmont, 'it is nowhere more strangely felt than in this route to the Val d'Aosta from Turin. With maps, post-books, descriptions of the valley, and the latest authority of the government before us, neither distances nor measures can be reconciled. Whether the miles are geographical, 60 to a degree, or of Piedmont, 40 to a degree, is not mentioned; and no measure from the scales of three of the best maps will agree with either of the quantities described in the three best works, which ought to be of authority since they are sanctioned by the government; so that the distances named can only be approximations.'

Before taking to the road it will be learned that travelling by diligence in Switzerland has greatly improved in the last twenty years but, even so: 'On some routes, particularly in going from one canton into another, passengers are sometimes transferred into another coach, and run the chance of waiting several hours for it, being set down in a remote spot to pass the interval as they may, and this not unfrequently in the middle of the night.'

Those who wish to hire a carriage and driver will observe that: 'Before making an engagement, it is prudent to consult the landlord of the inn or some other respectable inhabitant – (N.B. not the waiter) – to recommend a person of approved character to be employed. As there are many very roguish voituriers, ready to take advantage of the traveller on all occasions, such a recommendation will be a guarantee, to a certain extent, for good behaviour. The landlord should be referred to apart, not in the presence of the coachman, nor, indeed, with his cognizance. It is a bad plan to intrust a waiter or inferior person with the negotiation; he will most probably sell the traveller to the voiturier, and make a job for his own advantage.'

The rate of travelling was about forty miles a day, at a speed of five miles an hour, and Murray suggests that the traveller hire one set of horses for the whole tour, since it would not be easy to change them at every town he came to. He would then be free from the 'manoeuvres of petty inn-keepers, who will often pretend that none are to be had, and will throw every impediment in the way of his departure'.

Perhaps our traveller, for reasons of economy, decides to go where he will by charabanc, the national carriage of Switzerland, which Murray describes as having the body of a gig, or being like a bench which is 'placed sideways upon four wheels, at a very little distance from the ground. It is surrounded by leather curtains made to draw, whence it has been compared to a four-post bedstead on wheels. There is a larger kind of char, in which the benches are suspended by thongs, not springs, across a kind of long waggon, and are arranged one behind the other. The char-à-bang is a very strong and light vehicle, capable of carrying two persons, or three at a pinch, and will go on roads where no other species of carriage could venture. It is convenient, from being so low that one can jump in, or alight without stopping the horse, while it is going on; but it is a very jolting conveyance.' Many lines of railway were opened in Switzerland during the ensuing decades, though the diligence continued in use until motor buses took its place after the turn of the century.

In 1838 the country was already well provided with hotels, though Murray has much to say about them. The approach to a high-class city establishment in summer 'exhibits rather a character-istic spectacle. The street before it is usually filled with several rows of vehicles of all sorts, from the dirty and rickety calèche of the

German voiturier, to the neat chariot of the English peer, and the less elegant, but equally imposing, equipage of the Russian prince. Before the doorway is invariably grouped a crowd of loitering servants and couriers, of all nations and languages, and two or three knots of postilions and coachmen on the look-out for employment. During the height of the season, should the traveller arrive late in the evening, the chances are against his being admitted, unless he had sent or written beforehand to secure rooms.'

An already familiar system of graft is now outlined: 'Couriers, voituriers, guides, and boatmen, are apt sometimes to sell their employers to the innkeepers for a gratuity, so that travellers should not always implicitly follow the recommendations of such persons . . . The innkeepers hitherto have been very much at the mercy of this class of persons, who invariably fare sumptuously, and certainly not at their own expense. It not unfrequently happens that the attendance which ought to be bestowed on the master is lavished upon his menials. Whenever a new inn is started, it is almost invariably by the lavish distribution of high gratuities to coachmen, couriers, and the like, and by pampering them with the best fare, that the landlord endeavours to fill his house, to the prejudice both of the comfort and the purse of their masters.'

However: 'It may be laid down as a general rule, that the wants, tastes, and habits of the English are more carefully and successfully studied at the Swiss inns than even in those of Germany. Thus, at most of the large inns, there is a late table-d'hôte dinner at 4 or 5 o'clock, expressly for the English; and the luxury of tea may always be had in perfection.'

We are told that there were generally two sets of charges, one for the Swiss, or Germans, and another for the English, 'on the principle, that the latter have both longer purses, and also more numerous wants, and are more difficult to serve. It is often remarked by the English that the Germans pay very little to the servants at inns; but they should bear in mind how much less trouble the Germans give, and how slight the attendance which they require generally speaking.'

Baedeker's *Switzerland*, 1873, expands on this theme, and he clearly has the English in mind when stating that some guests are more demanding than others, and 'give orders totally at variance with the customs of the country, and express great dissatisfaction if their wishes are not immediately complied with; others travel with a superabundance of luggage, which is often apt to embitter their enjoyment; and there is also a numerous class whose ignorance of foreign languages causes them frequent embarrassment and discomfort.'

Murray, occasionally endeavouring to be fair, tells his readers that: 'Swiss inns have the reputation of being expensive, and the innkeepers of being extortionate. A recent journey through the greater part of the country had scarcely afforded an instance of either; but, where such cases have occurred, notice will be taken of them', a very real threat indeed.

Later in the century the traveller was reminded that the hotel-keeper, in some parts of the country, was often the only wealthy inhabitant, and might also be a local magistrate. 'Consequently, it is sometimes difficult to obtain redress against them for an injury or act of insolence, owing either to the interest they possess with the courts, or to their being themselves the justices. As a rule, however, they are respectable men, and difficulties seldom arise.'

Perhaps it was a complaint to Murray which caused him, a few years later, to insert the following: 'The drainage in some of the larger houses had been badly reported of within the last few years. Any cases where such complaints continue, will be noted in future editions' – another entry which, if hotelkeepers read the book (maybe a copy which some traveller had accidentally left behind), would remind them that their living could be in jeopardy if they failed to call in the plumber. Murray goes on to say, however, that cleanliness was to be met with everywhere, until one reached the Italian side of the Alps, and went into Savoy and Piedmont.

Swiss hotelkeepers were even more highly thought of by Murray when he saw them as willing caterers to the Bible-backed English travellers of the Victorian Age. Several hotelkeepers went so far as to 'build *English chapels* as an inducement to our travellers to pass the Sunday with them; in many mountain inns an English clergy-man is offered free lodging with the same object, and the guests of other nations are ejected from the public sitting-room while English service is performed'.

By the beginning of the Great War there were fifty-two English churches in the country, as well as 124 hotels where, in the season, services were held.

Joining the zig-zag peregrinations of our traveller around Switzerland and Piedmont, we can look at the merits (and sometimes demerits) of a few hotels mentioned in Murray's first edition. If our traveller is an Alpine enthusiast he will find that the hostelry on the summit of the Faulhorn (8140 feet) is '. . . totally abandoned to the wind and rain in October, but affords 3 very tolerable apartments, and one or two lofts; still it is but sorry sleeping accommodation, the désagréments of which are hardly compensated to ladies by the *uncertain* beauty of the early view of the glaciers: for gentlemen the quarters are good enough.' Baedeker tells us, about the same inn thirty-five years later, that: 'A single traveller is often required to share his room with another.'

The posthouse of the Mont Cenis, on the other hand, is a tolerable place to put up, 'where travellers may regale on the excellent trout of the lake, and sometimes on ptarmigan, for which they will, however, pay handsomely'.

The isolated six-thousand-foot peak of the Rigi drew many travellers, but Murray describes the scene and possible disappointments in such a way as to make the potential pilgrim wonder whether the ascent would be worthwhile. During summer nights, the hotel near the top was 'crammed to overflowing every evening; numbers are turned away from the doors, and it is difficult to procure beds, food, or even attention. The house presents a scene of the utmost confusion, servant maids hurrying in one direction, couriers and guides in another, while gentlemen with poles and knapsacks block up the passages. Most of the languages of Europe, muttered usually in terms of abuse or complaint, and the all-pervading fumes of tobacco enter largely as ingredients into this Babel of sounds and smells, and add to the discomfort of the fatigued traveller. In the evening the guests are collected at a table-d'hôte supper; after which most persons are glad to repair to rest. It takes some time, however, before the hubbub of voices and the trampling of feet subside; and, not unfrequently, a few roystering German students prolong their potations and noise far into the night.'

Let Baedeker continue the account, which in this case easily matches the style of Murray: 'Half an hour before sunrise, the Alpine horn sounds the reveille. All is again noise, bustle, and confusion. As the sun will wait for no man, eager expectants often indulge in impromptu toilettes of the most startling description. A red Indian in his blanket would on these occasions be most appropriately dressed, and would doubtless find many imitators but for the penalty imposed on visitors borrowing so tempting a covering from the hotel. The sleepy eye soon brightens, the limb stiffened by the exertions of the preceeding day is lithe again in that exciting moment; the huge hotel is for the nonce without a tenant; and if the eager crowd are not, like the disciples of Zoroaster, ready with one accord to prostrate themselves before the great source of light and life, there are probably few whose thoughts do not turn in silent adoration towards that mighty hand which created "the great light which rules the day." '

Murray ends with a ray-by-ray description, in the best romantic tradition, of the stunning sunrise which the guests would see, if they were lucky.

In a more remote part of the country our traveller's way leads him along the 'savage' valley of the Romanche to the 'miserable village of La Grave where there is a wretched inn. The author was once detained there in a storm, and the filth and misery of such a *gîte* cannot be imagined. It is rare to find bread there. Eggs, however, may be had, and good wine.' The same accommodation was still, 'wretched, bad, and dear' more than thirty years later.

On one of the main routes between northern and southern Europe lay the Great St Bernard Hospice, a massive stone building at the highest point of the pass, 'where it is exposed to tremendous storms from the north-east and south-west. The chief building is capable of accommodating 70 or 80 travellers with beds: 300 may be sheltered; and between 500 and 600 have received assistance in one day. The Drawing Room, appropriated to the reception of strangers, especially ladies,' is where 'the brethren do the honours to their visitors. The room . . . is hung with many drawings and prints, presents sent by travellers in acknowledgement of the kind attentions which they had received from the brethren. A piano was among the presents thus sent, by a lady.'

A somewhat sour note is sounded by Murray's comments on

the chapel services, which were attended on Sundays, in favourable weather, by peasants from the neighbouring valleys: 'The tawdry ornaments of Catholic ceremony and worship in the chapel weakens the impressive character of the establishment and its devotees, for whom the most unfeigned respect must exist; but as their religious peculiarities are never obtruded upon strangers, and as their most valuable duties are performed in obedience to the dictates of their religion, no man has a right to make them a ground of offence.'

Sojourners were expected to put a donation into a box in the chapel, of not less than they would have paid had they stayed at a hotel. As Murray reminds them: 'The resources of the brethren are small, and in aid of them, collections are regularly made in the Swiss cantons; but this has been sometimes abused by imposters, who have collected as the agents of the hospice.'

It was while crossing the Alps in 1873, thirty-five years later, that the young Joseph Conrad, who put up at a boarding house, heard English for the first time, spoken by English engineers building the St Gotthard tunnel. On the same trip he recalled an 'unforgettable Englishman wearing a knickerbocker suit, with short socks and laced boots, whose calves, which were exposed to the public gaze and to the tonic air of high altitudes, dazzled the beholder by the splendour of their marble-like condition and their rich tone of young ivory'.

Some of the remote inns were so bad that one wonders why travellers ventured into such regions, but a guidebook left no viable route undescribed. At Brussone the inn was said to be the most detestable in Piedmont. 'Filth and its accompanying goitre, disgust in every direction, and the Cheval Blanc with its dirty hostess cannot be forgotten.' Two inns there are named in a later edition without comment, the Cheval Blanc not being specifically mentioned.

The inn at Macugnaga, 'which may be endured by an Alpine traveller, and which may subdue an alpine appetite, offers all its bad accommodations with so much civility, as almost to reconcile the traveller to disgust, starvation, and want of rest. Myriads of fleas, and nondescript food do not promise well for rest and refreshment; but the little host who keeps the inn – of whom Aesop was the prototype – boasts of his having studied the *cuisine* at Lyons;

he seems to have fitted himself for the service of Harpagon. Still the inn may be endured, for the sake of the palace of nature in which it is placed.' By 1874 this judgement had changed to 'fair quarters with good cuisine'.

Winding our way up the valley of the Germanasca, the house of Mr Tron is passed, 'a singularly handsome structure in such a situation. He is a man remarkable for his hospitality; but this virtue does not extend to his wife and family, and the stranger who expects to receive it will fare ill in his absence.'

In the neighbourhood of Muotta the 'ancient and primitive' convent of St Joseph will provide accommodation for the night: 'The sisters are poor, and their mode of living homely; they make their own clothes and their own hay; the superior is called Frau Mutter. They receive visits from strangers without the intervention of a grating, and will even give lodging to a respectable traveller. Whoever avails himself of this must remember that the convent is too poor to afford gratuitous hospitality.'

A more interesting experience could be had at the baths of Leuk, where: 'The accommodation is as good as can be expected, considering that the houses (except the Hôtel Maison Blanche) are made of wood, not very well built, shut up and abandoned from October to May. From the dreariness of the situation, the coldness of the climate, and the defects of the lodging, few English would desire to prolong their stay here, after satisfying their curiosity by a sight of the place. The baths and adjacent buildings have been three times swept away by avalanches . . .'

The notion of risk may stimulate the jaded traveller, but the concupiscent voyeur would surely be tempted to linger at Leuk due to the following: 'Four hours of subaqueous penance are, by the doctor's decree, succeeded by one hour in bed; and many a fair nymph in extreme negligé, with stockingless feet, and uncoifed hair, may be encountered crossing the open space between the bath and the hotels. From their condition one might suppose they had been driven out of doors by an alarm of fire, or some such threatening calamity.'

By 1873, according to Baedeker, the system had changed: '. . . the patients, clothed in long flannel dresses, sit up to their necks in water in a common bath, where they remain for several hours together. Each bather has a small floating table before him, from which his book, newspaper, or coffee is enjoyed. The utmost order and decorum is preserved. Travellers are invited to view this singular and somewhat uninviting spectacle.'

The early Murray's rarely failed to point the traveller's eye, supposing he should need it, in the direction of good-looking women. Those of the Grindelwald were said to enjoy the reputation of 'being prettier, or rather, less plain than those of most other Swiss valleys'. The Val Anzasca seems even better endowed: 'I rarely saw a plain woman: their beautiful faces and fine forms, their look of cheerfulness and independence, and their extreme cleanliness, continually arrested attention.'

The hotel at the Baths of Monastier is welcome because 'the filth and privations of those passed *en route* reconciles the traveller, and almost persuades him that it is tolerable. The mineral waters here are both drunk and employed in baths, and are so abundant that they are employed to turn a mill.'

Many of the strictures against hotels in the early guidebooks tend to disappear or become modified in later editions, the crusading spirit of Murray and Baedeker in favour of their readers having taken effect. Hotels were by now a speciality of Switzerland, and 'the modern establishments are models of organisation on a most extensive scale. The smaller inns are often equally well conducted, and indeed in French and German Switzerland a really bad hotel is rarely met with.'

Baedeker, however, could still remark that: 'Wine is often a source of much vexation. The ordinary table wines are sometimes so bad that the traveller is compelled to drink those of a more expensive class, which indeed is the very aim and object of the landlord. The wisest course is to select a wine which is the growth of the country.'

Vandalism of various kinds was frequently attributed to the English, as in the village church of Hindelbank, where there was a monument to Madame Langhans, who died in childbirth. 'It is by a sculptor, named Nahl, and represents her with her child in her arms, bursting through the tomb at the sound of the last trumpet. Its merit, as a work of art, has been much exaggerated. The chief figure is injured by the loss of the nose, which Glütz

Blotzheim asserts (it is to be hoped unfoundedly) was the wanton act of an Englishman.'

Perhaps the famous scratching by Byron of his name on a pillar of the Castle of Chillon could also be classed as vandalism but, when I visited the place, a frame had been put around it. Baedeker lessens the heinousness of this act by telling us that Victor Hugo and Eugène Sue also scored their names there.

The orderliness of Switzerland has become proverbial, but the criminal statistics of the district around Locarno, Murray writes, 'show a large amount of crime in proportion to the number of inhabitants'. On the other hand certain villages in Piedmont 'encourage a pride of birth and birthplace . . . their characters are distinguished for honesty and industry, and few communities have a higher moral tone. Crime is almost unknown among them, and if disputes arise the magistrate elected by themselves hears the complaint, and effects an amicable settlement. Their educational attainments are of a higher order than is usually found in such a class, especially in such a place.'

In Switzerland proper, according to Baedeker, the traveller in the Bernese Oberland 'should possess a considerable fund of patience and of the smallest coin of the realm. Vendors of strawberries, flowers, and crystals first assail him, and he has no sooner escaped their importunities than he becomes a victim to the questionable attractions of a chamois or marmot. His admiration must not be engrossed by a cascade, be it ever so beautiful, or by a glacier, be it ever so imposing and magnificent; the urchin who persists in standing on his head, or turning somersaults for the tourist's amusement, must have his share of attention. Again, if the route happens to pass an echo, a pistol shot is made to reverberate in one's ears, and payment is of course expected for the unpleasant shock. Swiss damsels next make their appearance on the scene, and the ebbing patience of the traveller is again sorely tried by the national melodies of these ruthless songsters. Then there is the Alpine horn which, although musical when heard at a distance, is excruciating when performed close to the ear. The fact is, the simplicity and morality of the aboriginal character in these once sequestered regions has been sadly corrupted by modern invasion. These abuses had become so crying, that the attention of

Government was directed to them, and commissioners were sent to inquire into the matter. Their advice is, "Give to nobody"; the remedy therefore lies principally with travellers themselves.'

Locomotion for the traveller on certain routes was far from easy. The hotelkeepers between Andermatt and Como 'generally provide good carriages with trustworthy drivers. Extortionate demands, however, are occasionally made, especially on the Italian side, a spurious printed tariff being sometimes exhibited. Though the government has curbed the importunities of guides, drivers, and landlords, the boatmen and carriage-drivers of Brunnen are still noted for the exhorbitance of their charges.'

The romance of travel, and its possible dangers, is highlighted in Murray when he comes to Novasca: '. . . this spot offers to the traveller some of the most sublime horrors encountered in the Alps. Here a grand cataract bursts out from a rift in a mountainous mass of granite, where all is denuded to absolute sterility. Below it, a thousand enormous masses of granite are bouldered by the materials brought down and thrown upon them by the fall.'

More chilling matter is to come. Murray tells us that, a mile above Novasca,

there is a terrific gorge where enormous precipices overhang the course of the Orca, which tumbles through a succession of catar-acts between these herbless precipices. The path which leads to the summit is cut out of the rocks, and a flight of steps, practi-cable for mules, is carried up through the gorge; sometimes on the actual brink of the precipice which overhangs the foaming torrent; in others, cut so deep into its side, that the rocky canopy overhangs the precipice. In some places there is not room enough for the mounted traveller, and there is danger of his head striking the rocks above him. This extraordinary path extends half a mile. In its course, crosses are observed, fixed against the rock to mark the spots of fatal accidents: but as three such accidents happened in company with an old miscreant who lived at the foot of the Scalare, suspicions were entertained of these having been murders which he had committed there. He underwent severe examin-ations; yet, though no doubt existed of his guilt, there was not evidence enough to convict him. It is believed that, at the spot where the crosses are placed, he pushed his victims over in an unguarded moment, where a child, unheeded, might have destroyed a giant.

Our traveller would sooner or later bring Geneva into his itinerary, and put up at the Hôtel des Bergues, 'a grand establishment, recently built, facing the lake – expensive'. Reading the page of history in his Murray he would learn that: 'The feuds arising between the high and low town were not few, nor void of interest; indeed, they would fill a long and amusing historical chapter: they often led to bloodshed, but the democrats below generally brought their exalted neighbours to reason by the simple expedient of cutting off the water-pipes, taking especial care to guard the hydraulic machine which furnished the supply to the upper town, and which is situated in their quarter.'

Thirty thousand people were said to visit the town every year, and one object of interest was the Natural History Museum. 'There is the skin of an elephant, which lived a long time in a menagerie in the town, but at length becoming unruly, was shot.'

Some of the inhabitants remembered the horrors of the French Revolution, associated with the Botanic Gardens. 'On this spot took place fusillades and butcheries, too horrible to be detailed, in which the blood of the most respectable citizens of the town was shed, condemned to execution by a band of wretches, most of whom were their fellow-citizens. Here, as in other places, subjected to the madness of the reign of terror, the atrocities were committed by a mere handful of assassins, while thousands looked on, disapproving, but yet not raising a voice to condemn, nor an arm to resist.'

On the nearby lake, the village of Clarens, sentimentally described by Rousseau in *La Nouvelle Héloïse*, was a poor and dirty place, says Murray, 'far less attractive than many of its neighbours, and it probably owes its celebrity to a well-sounding name, which fitted it for the pages of a romance. The spot on which the beautifully 'bosquet de Julie' is sought for is now a potato field.'

In the historical note on Geneva Baedeker tells us that Jean Jacques Rousseau, the son of a watchmaker, was born there in 1712, and lived in the town during his early youth. 'His writings, which exhibited ability of the highest order, exercised a great influence over the opinions of his age, but their tendency was highly injurious to society, and he passed a troubled and agitated life. At the instigation of Voltaire and the university of Paris, and by order of the magistrates of Geneva, his *"Emile"* and *"Contrat Social"* were burnt in 1763 by the hangman.'

Well might Dostoevsky, in a letter to his sister, complain that 'Geneva is a dull, gloomy, Protestant, stupid town with a frightful climate, but very well suited for work.'

If our traveller came towards Mont Blanc from the Valley of Aosta he would find that it was 'more perhaps than any other in Piedmont afflicted in a horrid degree with cretinism and goitre. Nowhere are they more prevalent than in this beautiful valley. The peasantry appear squalid and filthy a race of beings generally stunted and diseased. Of the whole population in the neighbourhood of Aosta, one in fifty is a cretin; and above half are more or less goitred. Some of these are horrid objects. Tumours as large as their heads are appended to their throats, varying in number, size, and colour. The dirt, deformity, and imbecility of the inhabitants presented a scene so wretched, that it harrowed our feelings. Not a well-dressed or decent-looking person is to be met with; all bear the marks of poverty, disease, and wretchedness; and this too amidst scenes for which nature has done so much. Something weighs upon the people like a curse. Many conjectures have been offered upon the cause of goitres and cretinism. Labour, food, water, air, have all been offered in explanation; but none of these account for it satisfactorily. The opinion of our guide was, that it was chiefly owing to the villainously dirty habits of the people most afflicted with it. He said that among the mountaineers this was the general opinion; and though it sometimes descended in families, and often was observed in infancy, yet it might be traced to the filthy habits of preceding generations.' Similar views were expressed in later editions but, by the end of the century, guidebooks had ceased referring to the disease, which suggested that it had more or less died out.

To reach Chamonix and Mont Blanc from Geneva Baedeker recommends taking the diligence as far as St Gervais, then walking the rest of the way in six or seven hours over a five-thousand-foot col – no great feat for a pedestrian, then or now. The highway is, however, 'beset by all sorts of vagabonds, who plant themselves in the way openly as beggars, or covertly as dealers in mineral specimens, guides to things which do not require their aid, dealers in echoes, by firing small cannon where its reverberation may be heard two or three times. Such idle nuisances should be discountenanced.'

All guidebooks gave advice on walking, suggesting that inexperienced Alpine travellers should accustom themselves, for some time before they set out, to look down from heights and over precipices, 'so that, when they really enter upon a dangerous path, the eye may be familiarized with the depths of the abyss, and the aspect of danger, and the head relieved from vertigo which the sudden sight of a precipice is otherwise apt to produce'.

No one should attempt to cross a glacier without a guide, who must always be allowed to take the lead. Only double-soled boots should be worn, Murray says, 'with iron heels and hob-nails; the weight of a shoe of this kind is counter balanced by the effectual protection afforded to the feet against sharp rocks and loose stones, which cause contusions.'

Blistered feet should be rubbed with spirits before going to bed, 'mixed with tallow dropped from a candle into the palm of the hand; on the following morning no blister will exist. The spirits seem to possess the healing power, the tallow serving only to keep the skin soft and pliant. To prevent the feet blistering, it is a good plan to soap the inside of the stocking before setting out.'

Baedeker says that, in spite of possible discomforts: 'The pedestrian is of all travellers the most capable, both physically and morally, of enjoying a tour in Switzerland. The first golden rule is to start on his way betimes in the morning. If strength permits, and a suitable halting-place is to be met with, a two hours' walk may be accomplished before breakfast. At noon a moderate luncheon is preferable to the regular table-d'hôte dinner. Repose should be taken during the hottest hours, and the journey then continued till 5 or 6 p.m., when a substantial meal may be partaken of.'

He has much to say on the drawback of having too much luggage, which renders the travellers a prey to porters at every stop. 'Who has not experienced the exultation which attends the shouldering of the knapsack or wielding of the carpet-bag, on quitting a steamboat or railway station? Who in his turn has not felt the misery of that moment when, surrounded by his "impedimenta", the luckless tourist is almost distracted by the rival claims of porters, touters, and commissionaires? A light game-bag amply suffices to contain all that is necessary for a fortnight's excursion. A change of flannel shirts and worsted stockings, a few pocket-handkerchiefs, a pair of slippers, and the necessary "objets de toilette" may be carried with hardly a perceptible increase of fatigue. A piece of green crêpe or coloured spectacles to protect the eyes from the glare of the snow, and a leather drinking-cup will also be found useful . . .'

The foremost 'Rule' for the enthusiast is that he should curb his ardour at the beginning of the tour, and rarely exceed ten hours a day. In the tone of the fatherly schoolmaster Baedeker tells him: 'Animal spirits are too often in excess of powers of endurance; overtaxing the strength on a single occasion sometimes incapacitates altogether for several days. When a mountain has to be breasted, the prudent pedestrian will pursue the "even tenor of his way" with regular and steady steps; the novice alone indulges in "spurts". If the traveller will have a third golden maxim for his guidance it may be, "When fatigue begins, enjoyment ceases." '

We are forewarned about the chilling reality of actual experience. 'The first night in a *Chalet* dispels many illusions. Whatever poetry there may be theoretically in a bed of hay, the usual concomitants of the cold night-air piercing abundant apertures, the ringing of the cow-bells, the sonorous grunting of the swine, and the undiscarded garments, hardly contribute to that refreshing slumber of which the wearied traveller stands in need.'

Baedeker's edition of 1911 frowns heavily on: 'The senseless habit of breaking empty bottles and scattering the fragments (which) has led to inconvenience and even danger near some of the more frequented of these club huts. Bottles when done with should be deposited in some suitable spot where they will be out of the way.'

As for experiencing the rarefied effects of air in the mountains, Francis Galton in *The Art of Travel* suggests a cruel and bizarre method of gauging it: 'On the high plateaux newcomers must expect to suffer. The symptoms are described by many South American travellers; the attack of them is there, among other names, called the *puna*. The disorder is sometimes fatal to stout plethoric people; oddly enough, cats are unable to endure it. Numerous trials have been made with these unhappy feline barometers, and the creatures have been found to die in frightful convulsions.'

The first view of Mont Blanc from the northwest is obtained at Sallenches, where the traveller enters the bustling courtyard of the hotel of that name and, during the season, 'never fails to meet numerous travellers going to or from Chamonix; the latter imparting their impressions of the wonders of Mont Blanc, and their adventurous scrambles in the presence of the "monarch" to the listening expectants of such enjoyment; – all is excitement.'

A few miles beyond Sallenches is St Gervais, 'a little fairy spot, in a beautiful valley, where excellent accommodation may be had *en pension*; hot mineral baths for the sick, and delightful walks around this little paradise for the convalescent... One of the pleasures of this place is its solitude, amidst scenes so beautiful and wild, that it would be difficult to find it, without a guide.'

This difficulty might have been a positive advantage on 11 July 1892 for, to quote from Edward Whymper's guidebook to the area, 'the whole of the central (and oldest) portion of these buildings, and the farther ends of the two wings, were erased by the sudden bursting of a sub-glacial reservoir... The flood first coursed down the valley, and at its mouth half obliterated the village of Bionnay. It then joined the Bon Nant Torrent, and did little further mischief until it was compressed between the walls of the Gorge of Crepin; from the lower extremity of which it issued with tremendous violence, and in a few minutes battered the Baths to ruin, and swept away and drowned the greater part of the visitors. Those who were in the building on the left escaped; but, with few exceptions, all who were in the central and in the farthest blocks perished. How many were lost is unknown. It is supposed that at the Baths alone the number exceeded one hundred and twenty.'

Whymper's guide, one of the most thorough, tells us in the introduction, under practical matters: 'Soap. – There is a great

opening for soap in Alpine regions, and at the present time it pays
to carry a cake.' As for those who travel light, meaning pedestrians,
'. . . inkeepers look with suspicion upon travellers with little or no
baggage, and are apt to thrust them into the very worst rooms'.

Chamonix, while not in Switzerland, is dealt with in Murray
because of its nearness to Mont Blanc. Out of several good inns
he recommends the Hôtel de Londres et d'Angleterre, since this is
'the oldest establishment, and has never forfeited the reputation of
being one of the best held and appointed inns to be found in the
Alps; where Victor Tairrez and his excellent wife are so practised
in their acquaintance with, and their provision for, the wants of
travellers, especially English, that more *confort* will be found there
than in almost any other inn out of England'.

As opposed to this solid praise Murray takes hotel guests to
task, sternly reminding them that: 'At Chamonix and elsewhere,
the travellers' books at the inns are great sources of amusement;
often containing, in remarks of preceding travellers, useful information. A most disgraceful practice has too often prevailed, of
removing leaves for the sake of autographs; it is difficult to imagine
any act more unworthy, for this selfish gratification they destroy
what would be pleasure to hundreds.'

Whymper, a great Alpinist himself, discusses with the reader
the advisability or otherwise of employing guides, concluding that:
'Everyone must decide for himself. Some persons are competent to
carry out all the excursions that are mentioned. A larger number,
however, are not equal to this.'

Baedeker says that the services of a guide are unnecessary in
good weather on well-trodden routes, and that: 'The traveller may
engage the first urchin he meets to carry his bag or knapsack for a
trifling gratuity.' Guides were said to be indispensable, however,
for expeditions among, 'the higher mountains, especially on those
which involve the passage of glaciers. Only novices undervalue their
services and forget that snowstorms or mist may at any moment
change security to danger. As a class, the Swiss guides will be
found to be intelligent and respectable men, well versed in their
duties, and acquainted with the people and resources of the country.'

He tells us in his preface that: 'The achievements of the English
and Swiss Alpine Clubs have dimmed the memory of the pioneers

of these icy regions, whilst latterly the fair sex have vied in deeds of daring with those by whom the dangers of adventure are more appropriately encountered.'

A chapter in Whymper's guidebook is devoted to accidents in the Mont Blanc area, one of which, in 1909, 'did not present any great novelty. In September a tourist named Eugène Ribaud, who was said to be an architect of Lyons, leant against a balustrade in the Gorge of Trient, which gave way, and he fell to the bottom of a cliff, where his corpse was found.'

Sixty-two climbers and guides were killed from 1820 to 1909, and details are given of each accident. One that did not end fatally is a good example of stiff-upper-lip reporting:

On the 11th of July, 1861, a large party of tourists was assembled on the top of the Col de Miage, with the object of discovering whether an ascent of Mont Blanc could be made from this direction. Whilst the rest were stopping for breakfast, one of the party, Mr. Birkbeck, went aside, and the others did not at first remark his absence. When it was noticed, his track was followed, and it was found that he had fallen down precipitous slopes of snow and ice, and was descried nearly half a mile away, at the foot of the slope, at the head of the French Glacier de Miage. His friends went to his assistance as quickly as possible, but nearly 2½ hs. elapsed before they could reach him.

Between the place where Mr. Birkbeck commenced to slide or fall and the place where he stopped there was a difference of level of about 1700 feet! The slope was gentle where he first lost his footing, and he tried to stop himself with his fingers and nails, but the snow was too hard. Sometimes he descended feet first, sometimes head first, then he went sideways, and once or twice he had the sensation of shooting through the air. He came to a stop at the edge of a large crevasse. When reached, it was found that he was almost half-skinned by abrasion and friction. By his passage over the snow, the skin was removed from the outside of the legs and thighs, the knees, the whole of the lower part of the back and part of the ribs, together with some from the nose and forehead. He had not lost much blood, but he presented a most ghastly spectacle of bloody raw flesh. He was transported to St. Gervais, and remained there in a critical condition for some weeks, but ultimately recovered better than might have been expected.

The worst accident took place near the summit, in 1870, when eleven persons perished. Three Americans who led the expedition did not have any mountain experience, but set out with three guides and five porters. 'The next day several persons in the Valley of Chamonix endeavoured to watch their progress through telescopes. The weather aloft was bad. The wind is said to have been frightful. Even from below the snow was seen whirling about, and it was noticed from time to time that they had to throw themselves down to escape being carried away by the wind.

'*No one returned*, and fourteen Chamonards started, to try to learn something, but snow was falling heavily and drove them back.' Among those eventually discovered was Mr Bean, 'sitting down, with his head leaning on one hand and the elbow on a knapsack still containing some meat and bread and cheese'. In his notebook was a letter to his wife: 'My dear Hessie, – We have been on Mont Blanc for two days in a terrible snowstorm. We have lost our way and are in a hole scooped out of the snow at a height of 15,000 feet. I have no hope of descending. Perhaps this book may be found and forwarded. We have no food; my feet are already frozen, and I am exhausted; I have only strength to write a few words. I die in the faith of Jesus Christ, with affectionate thoughts of my family; my remembrance to all. My effects are in part at the Hôtel Mont Blanc, and partly with me in two portmanteaux. Send them to the Hotel Schweitzerhof at Geneva; pay my bills at the hotel, and heaven will reward your kindness.'

The first woman to be killed during this period was when a Mr and Mrs Marke set out with Miss Wilkinson and two guides to climb Mont Blanc. Their porter was a youth called Oliver Gay. 'At the top of the Corridor the ladies were fatigued, and remained behind with the porter, while Mr. Marke and the guide continued the ascent. The latter were half way up the Mur de la Côte when they heard piercing shrieks, and returning with all haste found that Mrs. Marke and Oliver Gay had disappeared in a crevasse. The ladies had been unable to bear the cold, and wished to move about. The porter offered his arm to Mrs. Marke, and very shortly afterwards both broke through a snow-bridge. The bodies were not recovered.'

Another female casualty occurred on 4 August 1902: 'A French lady, while crossing the place called the *Mauvais Pas* by the side of the Mer de Glace, met a party coming in the contrary direction. She attempted to pass outside, and falling about a hundred feet, was killed on the spot.'

Then there was Mr Nettleship, tutor of Balliol College, Oxford, who left Chamonix to climb Mont Blanc on 23 August 1892. He took two guides, but 'Though the morning was fine, clouds gathered, and there were indications of bad weather, before mid-day. The party, however, continued upwards, intending to stop for the night at the Refuge Vallot. An hour after leaving the Aiguille a storm broke upon them, they became bewildered, wandered about for several hours, and at last stopped, dug a hole in the snow, and remained in it all night. According to the statement of the guides, Mr. Nettleship was in good spirits, assisted in digging the hole, and even sang during the night. They had sufficient food and wine, but no extra clothing.

'The storm continued the whole of the night. On the morning of the 25th it was still snowing hard, and all tracks were obliterated. The guides advised Mr. Nettleship to remain where he was, on the chance of a change in the weather, but Mr. Nettleship urged that it was idle to remain there and die like cowards, and that they must make an effort to get away. He therefore started, the guides following him. They proceeded some little distance when Mr. Nettleship stumbled and became unsteady. The guides offered him wine and brandy, which he refused. He then cried out and fell forward, uttering some words in English, after which he took each guide by the hand, bade them goodbye, closed his eyes and expired.'

The most curious death occurred during a thunderstorm: 'Simond, who was leading, was killed instantly by a flash of lightning, which also severed the rope leading from him to Monsieur Fontaine, and caused the corpse of the unfortunate man to fall a great distance on to the glacier below. It is stated that Simond was the only member of the party carrying an ice-axe.'

*

If our gentleman-traveller made an attempt to climb Mont Blanc, we must assume that he survived, whether or not he reached the summit, for we have many more tribulations, and occasional pleasures, to keep him going. After a few weeks among ice and snow he would crave the man-made artefacts and artistic productions – not to mention the mellower climate – of Italy. But if in those early days before the railway he chose to go into that country via the coast from Nice, he could do so in a couple of days by hiring a light calèche. 'Few travellers, however, will be willing to pass over its interesting scenes in so hurried a manner. It is a country to be dwelt upon: the artist may enrich his sketch-book at every step, and the architect or antiquary will find ample field for the most interesting researches. Persons travelling in a heavy carriage, which requires four horses, should be cautioned that in some places the road is steep and narrow, and runs along the verges of precipices, whose bases, 200 or 300 feet below, are washed by the Mediterranean: parapets are not always provided in such spots; and, unless the horses are very quiet, and accustomed to the road, there is some danger.'

After Albenga we are told that: 'The streets of many of the old towns through which the road is carried are so narrow, that the walls of the houses on both sides are grooved by the marks of the axletree.'

CHAPTER SIX

GERMANY AND THE RHINE

Many travellers took the German route over the Alps so as to enjoy a stay at the various spas, either refreshing and rejuvenating themselves after whatever exertion they had undergone in England, or in preparation for encountering the heat and heavy cultural rounds of the tourist in Italy.

Murray's handbook of 1858 tells us that four steamers a week left London for Ostend in the summer, the passage lasting twelve hours, of which seven were spent descending the Thames. If our travelling gentleman thought of taking his own servant, the advice was discouraging. 'It is notorious that English servants taken for the first time to the Continent, and ignorant of every language but their own, are worse than useless – they are an encumbrance.' The traveller who required a servant was recommended to hire a foreign one or, better still, 'save himself much expense by dispensing with a servant altogether'.

The best course, though an expensive luxury, was to hire a courier: 'He relieves his master from much fatigue of body and perplexity of mind, in unravelling the difficulties of long bills and foreign moneys, sparing his temper the trials it is likely to endure from disputes with innkeepers and the like. He must make arrangements for his employer's reception at inns where he intends to pass the night; must secure comfortable rooms, clean and well-aired beds, and order meals to be prepared, fires to be lighted, taking care that his master is called in proper time, and that the horses are ordered at the right hour. He should superintend the packing and unpacking of the luggage, should know the number of parcels, etc., and be on his guard against leaving anything behind. It falls to the courier to pay innkeepers, postmasters, and postboys, and he ought to take care that his master is not overcharged. Besides this, he performs all the services of waiting and attendance, cleaning and brushing clothes, etc.'

There are disadvantages in this seemingly perfect proceeding, because a courier, as the guidebooks have already suggested, will often 'sell' by pre-arrangement the rich family he is working for to innkeepers along the road, so that what he extorts from the innkeeper 'inevitably comes out of his employer's pocket'. Perhaps the traveller could be consoled by the fact that railways were spreading through the Continent, in combination with steam navigation on the rivers. This is seen by Murphy as an argument against taking a carriage from England. 'With such expeditions and comfortable modes of travelling at command, it is far better for those who study economy at all to hire vehicles from place to place when required.'

The many confidence men on the Continent gave rise to Murray's classic 'Caution to Innkeepers and Others': 'A person or persons have of late been extorting money from innkeepers, tradespeople, artists, and others ... under pretext of procuring recommendations and favourable notices of them and their establishments in the Handbooks for Travellers. The Editor, therefore, thinks proper to warn all whom it may concern, that recommendations in the Handbooks are not to be obtained by purchase, and that the persons alluded to are not only unauthorised by him, but are totally unknown to him. All those, therefore, who put confidence in such promises may rest assured that they will be defrauded of their money without attaining their object.'

He goes on to say that the character of hotels, good and bad, inserted in the handbook, 'are given either from personal knowledge or upon unexceptionable authority of travellers whose names and residences are known to the Editor. Where the objections stated in this book no longer exist, and where a positive improvement has taken place, the Editor is always ready to listen to respectable and well-authenticated testimony, and to remove in future editions the condemnatory epithets or passages. Thus he hopes to stimulate to exertion and amendment, to protect travellers from neglect and imposition, and to do justice to deserving innkeepers.'

With such assurances our traveller will set out, the indispensable Murray buttoned into his pocket, though when he reaches Ostend he is not likely to linger after reading the following: '. . . a few hours there exhaust a traveller's patience; while the visit to the douane, and the extortions of innkeepers and commissionaires, are not likely to improve his temper.' Apart from which, travellers should be on their guard against drinking water, 'which is filtered rain-water. Seltzer water is drunk in preference.' Even so, 'Ostend is a favourite watering-place, and is much resorted to in summer; even the King and Queen of the Belgians repair hither, and occupy 2 or 3 ordinary-looking houses in the Rue Longue. There are 80 *Bathing Machines* on the beach, and the sands are very extensive and smooth, and crowded with bathers of both sexes, decorously clad in bath dresses, by order of the police.'

The handbook also deals with Holland where 'the roads run on the tops of the dykes; and, as there are no parapets or railings, there is at least the appearance of danger, and accidents sometimes happen'. Dutch hotels were said to be nearly as expensive as those of England, and inferior to those of most other countries. They were, however, generally clean, but 'owing to the humidity of the climate the beds are often damp, and should be warmed with the warming-pan, a much employed article in Dutch households'.

The subject of cleanliness clearly fascinated the writer of the handbook, though he considered the matter to be 'carried to excess in Holland; but the passion for purifying really runs to such a height among Dutch housewives that the assertion is by no means groundless: everything has an air of freshness, and the stranger in vain looks for a particle of dust. It is on the last day of the week that an extraordinary cleaning takes place. Every house door presents a scene of most energetic activity – the brushing and mopping, the scrubbing and scraping, are not confined to steps and doorways – the pavement, wall, windows, however guiltless they may be of impurity, are all equally subjected to the same course of ablution. Those spots which are out of the reach of the hand or broom do not escape a well-aimed stream from the pipe of a small engine-pump, which is always reserved for such service. The unsuspecting stranger who walks the streets is subjected to the danger of perpetual wettings. He looks up to ascertain whence the shower descends, and he perceives a diligent servant girl, stretched out of a window two-thirds of her length, and, with eyes intently turned upwards, discharging bowls full of water upon some refractory stain, imperceptible to all but herself.'

The traveller is reminded that life was formerly most fraught in Holland – and possibly still is. The town of Dort, for example, stands on an island formed by an inundation in 1421, 'when the tide in the estuary of the Rhine, excited by a violent tempest, burst through a dyke, overwhelming a populous and productive district, which it at once converted into a waste of waters called the Biesbosch . . . 72 villages and 100,000 human beings were swallowed up by the waves. 35 of the villages were irretrievably lost, so that no vestige, even of the ruins, could afterwards be discovered.'

A more immediate danger awaited those who thought to wander freely around the houses of gentlemen: 'Many of the grounds of the country seats are open; but some have notices – only in Dutch – of man-traps and spring-guns.'

On reaching Germany the Customs examination was said to be 'strict without being vexatious. The Prussian douanier (often an old soldier invalided) is above taking a bribe, or rather, government regulates matters so as to prevent his taking one. The person offering a bribe is even liable to punishment by law. Strangers are treated with invariable civility, provided they conduct themselves becomingly.'

The money problems was again infinitely difficult, this time due to the proliferation of different states and principalities, leading Murray to warn us that the values marked on German coins 'are sometimes not the value at which the coin passes'. He then goes on to juggle Friedrichs d'or, dollars, silver groschen, thalers, kreutzers and gulden with pounds, shillings and pence, which must have left our traveller's head spinning, so that it would come as something of a relief to learn that: 'Travellers in Prussia are protected by a regulation of the police from the impositions of innkeepers, who are compelled to hang up in every apartment, or at least in the public room, a *tariff*, or list of charges for lodging, food, fuel, servants, valets-de-place, etc. This is inspected periodically by a proper officer, who regulates the price of each article, and ascertains that none of the charges are exorbitant.'

All the same, our traveller must have read the following with something like exasperation: 'All innkeepers are compelled to submit to the inspection of the police the daily arrivals and departures of their guests; and not merely the name, surname, and country, but frequently the age, condition, whether married or single, profession, religion, motives for travelling, and other particulars, are required. A book called Strangers' Book, ruled into columns, and methodically classed, is presented to the traveller for him to fill up.'

Another point made is that German hotelkeepers were of a 'higher class' than their equivalents in England, and that they usually sat at the common table, 'entering familiarly into conversation with their guests'. Travellers must have responded in various ways to this blatant intrusion into their privacy, from one of welcome at gaining some picture of local conditions, to that of wishing the hotelkeeper would eat in his own kitchen where he belonged. No doubt the silent Englishman's protection against having to answer probing questions was helped by his lack of knowing what the upstart was talking about.

Let us assume that our gentleman-traveller is not too much discouraged by this and makes for Cologne where, consulting his Murray, he would put up at the Hollandischer Hof. Delacroix stayed there in 1850, and 'felt depressed by the strange jargon and the sight of foreign uniforms. The Rhine wine at dinner made me feel more reconciled to my situation, but unhappily I had the worst bed in the world, even though this is supposed to be one of the best hotels.'

From Cologne it would take our traveller fourteen and a half hours to reach Berlin by railway, 'allowing time for refreshment at Minden'. We are told that the 455,000 inhabitants of the Prussian capital included 15,000 Roman Catholics, 15,000 Jews, 5300 descendants of the French Protestants driven out of France by the religious intolerance of Louis XIV, and 15,000 soldiers of the garrison. Murray says: 'The city is situated in the midst of a dreary plain of sand, destitute of either beauty or fertility. The great number of soldiers gives to Berlin almost the air of a camp.' He evinces surprise that it had grown into the capital of a great empire. 'Owing to the want of stone in the neighbourhood, the larger part even of the public buildings are of brick and plaster. The flatness of the ground and the sandy soil produce inconveniences which the stranger will not be long in detecting. There is so little declivity in the surface, that the water in the drains, instead of running off, stops and stagnates in the streets. In the Friedrichsstrasse, which is two miles long, there is not a foot of descent from one end to the other. In the summer season the heat of the sun reflected by the sand becomes intolerable, and the noxious odours in the streets are very unwholesome as well as unpleasant.' A complaint was also made about the pavements, which were so narrow that 'two persons can scarcely walk abreast, and many are infamously paved with sharp stones, upon which it is excruciating pain to tread'.

A mere fortnight was needed to see Berlin, after which the traveller would find it tedious without the company of friends. 'The society of the upper classes is on the whole not very accessible to strangers, nor is hospitality exercised to the same extent among them as in England, chiefly because their fortunes are limited.'

Murray admitted, however, that Berlin was one of the finest cities in Europe, but then comments on the number of statues erected in the streets, most being of military men. 'A Corinthian pillar surmounted by an eagle, absurdly called National Krieger Denkmal, has been set up in the Invalids' Garden, as a monument to the 475 soldiers whose names are inscribed on the marble tablets around its base, who fell in defending the city and their sovereign from the brutal revolutionary rioters of 1848 and 1849.'

Our traveller, if an officer in the army, may be interested in the Grand Review of the garrison, which takes place in the neighbourhood of Berlin during the autumn: '20,000 troops are sometimes collected, and the manoeuvres last several days. To see the reviews to advantage a uniform is desirable, though not absolutely necessary. A good horse warranted to stand fire may be hired for a louis a day; with these you may ride on the ground and join the staff, which sometimes amounts to 500 officers of all nations. The field manoeuvres usually last several days, the regiments bivouacking at night. Ladies in carriages are enabled to see the whole by the good arrangement of the gendarmerie.'

So a fortnight of boredom will see our traveller on the train to Dresden, and accommodated in the new Hotel Victoria, or if by now looking after his pocket, at Eichler's Boarding House, 'in the English quarter'. Dresden was known as 'the German Florence', and Murray grudgingly agrees, telling us: 'Few European capitals contain a greater number of objects calculated to gratify the curiosity of an intelligent traveller. The opera is good, and music is much cultivated; the climate is generally mild and agreeable, food and lodgings are not dear. It has been much resorted to since 1830 by the English for education and economy; and for those who are not alarmed by the recent revolutionary events in Germany, is eligible as a residence.'

Perhaps life was a little too regimented for the locals, because if any wanted to cross to the other side of the Elbe on foot they had always to 'take the path on the right hand, "a rule of the road" which is enforced by the police, and prevents collision and confusion'.

Murray recommends a visit to nearby Saxon Switzerland, and especially to the fortress of Königstein, to which one is admitted on showing a passport and paying a small fee. 'This fortress once served as a state prison: it was scaled for the first time in 1848 by a chimney-sweep, at mid-day; he reached the top half dead with fatigue.'

Between Dresden and Chemnitz lies the coal district of Saxony, where a somewhat sinister picture is given of local life. The miners, of a rather primitive class, 'are enrolled in a sort of semi-military corps, of which the common workmen are the privates, and the superintendents and managers the officers. They are called out several times a year for inspection or parade, and in addition assemble in a body at certain stated times to attend miners' prayers in the church, at the funeral of a superior officer, during the visit of a royal personage, and on days of rejoicing for the discovery of a rich vein. On these occasions they appear in uniform, their leather aprons fastened on behind, leather pockets in the place of cartouche-boxes, and a large knife stuck in the girdle. The common miners march with their pickaxes shouldered, the carpenters with their axes, and the smiths with their hammers borne in the same fashion. These processions have a martial appearance, are headed by a band playing a miners' march, and accompanied by flying colours. The officers have similar uniforms, distinguished according to their rank.'

The inhabitants of the textile manufacturing town of Chemnitz receive good marks for knowing their place, with a certain sense of regret from Murray that such conditions could not exist at home: 'The stocking-weavers for the most part are not congregated into manufactories, but live in cottages of their own, the fee-simple of which they have purchased by their own earnings. They cultivate in their own gardens the potatoes and other vegetables which form their usual food, and support from the same source the animals which provide them with the small quantity of meat they consume: they live commonly with great frugality on potatoes and coffee. When the demand for manufacture is slack, they employ themselves in the fields and garden; when it is active, they devote themselves to their frames and looms. The state provides them with gratuitous instruction, which has the happiest effect both on their industry and frugality.'

If our traveller is still snorting fire and smoke from the Berlin tattoo he will call at the *Schlachtfeld* (battlefield) of Lützen, and learn – if he didn't already know – that at the first set-to in 1632, Gustavus Adolphus was killed, his body taken to nearby Weissenfels and embalmed 'in a room of the Town-house, in the presence of Bernard of Saxe-Weimar. It is recorded that his heart weighed 1 lb. 2 oz.; that the body bore the marks of 8 wounds, i.e. 5 gunshots, 2 cuts, 1 stab. A part of the wall, which was stained with his blood, is still preserved from external contact. The heart was instantly conveyed to Stockholm; but the bowels are interred in the Kloster Kirche . . .'

Before setting off down the Rhine the traveller will no doubt have read his Byron but, if not, Murray (the poet's publisher) spread 137 lines in half a dozen parts of the text, such quotations describing certain sections of the river in a more poetic way than Murray can aspire to, though a little advice from *Don Juan* might have cut the wordage down a bit: 'Plain truth, dear Murray, needs few flowers of speech.'

In 1827, when the first company of Rhine steamboats commenced operations, 18,000 passengers travelled between Cologne and Mainz, the number increasing to a million by the mid-1850s. Murray somewhat spoils the enthusiasm of the deck traveller by reminding him that 'the views in many places, looking *down* upon the Rhine from its lofty banks, far surpass those from the river itself; and the small valleys, which pour their tributary streams on the right hand and left have beauties to unfold of which the steam-driven tourist has no conception, which are entirely lost to him'.

At Coblenz Murray can't resist a dig at his arch rival in the guidebook trade: 'Baedeker, a very intelligent bookseller in the Rhein Strasse . . . keeps a good assortment of English, French, and German books, guide-books, prints, maps, etc. He has also published German Handbooks for Travellers, enriched by his own observations, and is personally acquainted with all parts of his own country.' It is related, though not in Murray, that when the original Karl Baedeker died in 1859, a solitary Englishman followed the cortège to the cemetery carrying one of the little red guidebooks as a token of his esteem.

Further upriver, at Oberwesel, we come across an infamous blood-libel story against the Jews, though Murray of course is not taken in: 'In some period of the dark ages a boy named Werner is said to have been most impiously crucified and put to death by the Jews in this place. A similar story is told in many other parts of the world; even in England, at Gloucester and Lincoln (*vide* Chaucer). It is probable that the whole was a fabrication, to serve as a pretext for persecuting the Jews and extorting money from them', which is perhaps as balanced an account as you could get in the nineteenth century. The Church of St Werner, erected to commemorate his canonization, gets an asterisk in Baedeker, the story being put down to tradition, as it is also in Thomas Cook's *Traveller's Handbook: The Rhine and the Black Forest* (1912). In Ernest Benn's *Blue Guide*, 1933, it is said to have been a legend, but the calumny is rightly omitted altogether from the *Guide Bleu*, 1939.

Should our traveller get off the boat at Worms his Murray will tell him that the synagogue 'is said to be more than 800 years old, and certainly displays in its structure the style of the 11th century . . . The Jews have been established in this spot from a very early period, and enjoyed privileges denied them in most other parts of Germany.' This is more or less true, though they were forced out by the Guilds in 1615, upon which the synagogue was destroyed and the cemetery laid waste; a year later an Imperial Decree ordered them to be readmitted. They also suffered three massacres during the times of the Crusades in the eleventh and twelfth centuries.

Frankfurt, we are told, is the cradle of the Rothschild family, and Murray goes on to say, 'The Jews, who form no inconsiderable portion of the community here, have till very lately been treated with great illiberality by the Free Town. The gates of the quarter to which they were exclusively confined were closed upon them at an early hour every night, after which ingress and egress were alike denied. This arbitrary municipal regulation was enforced, until Marshal Jourdan, in bombarding the town (1796), knocked down the gate of the Jews' quarter, along with many houses near it, and they have not been replaced since. Another law, not repealed until 1834, restricted the number of marriages among the Hebrews in the town to 13 yearly. The Synagogue, an old and curious Gothic building, is situated in the Judengasse. The Jews are no longer compelled to live in this street, but may hire or purchase houses in other quarters.'

An excursion to Saarlouis would reveal the curious fact that its 7000 inhabitants 'are partly descended from English prisoners placed here by Louis XIV'. The town was a frontier fortress of Prussia, 'with a long stone bridge over the Saar, which flows half round the town, and sometimes during the winter lays part of it under water', a circumstance which may have made the English feel very much at home.

Between Frankfurt and Cassel lies the village of Butzbach, which prompts the story from Murray that 'German vagrants, known in London as Bavarian *broom-girls*, come from this neigh-bourhood'. Several villages were said to have sent forth, for the last twenty years, 'crowds of them annually. At first they were taken

over by the broom-makers, ready to sell their brooms; but in a
short time they discovered other and less moral modes of earning
money. The speculators, perceiving this, enticed from their homes
many young girls, under pretence of hiring them as servants. Some
of these poor creatures have never been heard of by their parents;
others have returned ruined and broken in constitution; and innum-
berable actions have been brought against the planners of this
disgraceful traffic. The magistrates of these towns have at length
interfered, and any person discovered taking away a child, or any
female but a wife, is subject to heavy penalties.'

Towns along the Rhine led a precarious existence over the
centuries due to the proximity of France. Speyer, one of the oldest
cities of Germany, on the left bank of the river, had a particularly
violent history. In the Middle Ages its citizens were 'as well versed
in the use of arms as in the arts of trade. At one time they were
called upon to issue from their walls in order to chastise the lawless
rapacity of some feudal baron, who had waylaid their merchants
and pillaged their property, by having his castle burnt about his
ears and levelled with the ground.'

Such incidents were as nothing compared to its fate in the
seventeenth century, when the greatest injury was inflicted on it by
the French. After its capture by them in 1689 a proclamation was
issued to its citizens 'commanding them to quit it, with their wives
and children, within the space of 6 days, and to betake themselves
into Alsace, Lorraine, or Burgundy, but upon pain of death not to
cross the Rhine. To carry into execution this tyrannic edict, a
provost-marshal, at the head of 40 assistant executioners, marched
into the town; they bore about them the emblems of their profession, in the shape of a gallows and wheel, embroidered on their
dress. On the appointed day the miserable inhabitants were driven
out by the beat of drums, like a flock of sheep. The French soldiers
followed them, after having plundered everything in the deserted
town, which was then left to the tender mercies of executioners
and incendiaries. In obedience to the commands of the French
commander, trains of combustibles were laid in the houses and
lighted, and in a few hours the seven-and-forty streets of Speyer
were in a blaze. The conflagration lasted 3 days and 3 nights; but
the destruction of the town did not cease even with this. Miners

were incessantly employed in blowing up the houses, walls, fountains, and convents, so that the whole might be levelled with the
dust and rendered uninhabitable. The Cathedral was dismantled,
the graves of the Emperors burst open and their remains scattered.
For many years Speyer lay a desolate heap of rubbish, until at last
the impoverished inhabitants returned gradually to seek out the
sites of their ancient dwellings.'

Such a taste of 'history' should have lasted till the end of Time,
but a hundred years later the Revolutionary army under Custine
captured the town after six assaults, and repeated 'all the wanton
acts of atrocity and cruelty which their predecessors had enacted a
century before'.

If our traveller is rich (and on this journey he needs to be) he will
want to experience the various spas and bathing establishments in
the Rhineland and the Black Forest, paying particular attention to
those described in his handbook, which tells him that for the
Germans 'an excursion to a watering-place in the summer is essential to existence, and the necessity of such a visit is confined to no
one class in particular, but pervades all, from emperors and princes
down to tradesmen and citizens' wives.'

The number of bathing-places and mineral springs in Germany
alone now amounts to several hundred: and every year adds to
the list names which, though seldom heard in England, are not
without their little sets and coteries. The royal and imperial
guests repair to them not merely to get rid of the trammels and
pomp of sovereignty, though it is universally the case that they
move about with no more show than private individuals, but
they also seek such occasions for holding private congresses, for
forming secret treaties, alliances etc.; family arrangements and
matrimonial connections are also not unfrequently there con-
cocted. The minister repairs thither to refresh himself from the
toils of office, but usually brings his portfolio in his travelling
carriage, nor does he altogether even here bid adieu to intrigue
and politics. The invalid comes to recruit his strength – the
debauchee to wash himself inside and out, and string his nerves

for a fresh campaign of dissipation – the shopkeeper and the merchant come to spend their money and gaze on their betters – and the sharper and black-leg, who swarm at all the baths, to enrich themselves at the gaming-tables at the expense of their fellow guests.

Every amusement was to be found at such places, as well as 'all the artists, and artificers that contribute to the enjoyments and the follies of indulgence – actors from Vienna – gaming-table keepers and cooks from Paris – money-lenders from Frankfurt – singers from Berlin – shopkeepers, voituriers, pastry-cooks, mountebanks, dancing-masters, donkey-lenders, blacklegs, mistresses, lacqueys – all bustling and contriving in their several vocations to reap the short harvest of profit which the season affords.'

In short, if you were financially sound, it seemed a wonderful place to be, and Murray's disapproval was unlikely to deter the rakish sensibilities of our traveller, though Murray kept on trying:

The system of the day commences with a bath taken before breakfast. Afterwards follow excursions in the environs, walks in the gardens, visits to the cafés and billiard rooms, and, above all, the pleasures of the Grand Saloon, which occupy the gay world till dinner. This last-mentioned place of rendezvous is the greatest centre of attraction; and, with the exception of much more gaiety, more avowed vice, and the absence of all pretence at rational resources, acts the part of the library at an English watering-place. After depositing your hat and stick with the *gendarmes* at the door, you enter the grand saloon – invariably a splendid room. On one side of a crowd of motley but well-dressed and gay-looking persons (I regret to say of both sexes) are pressing over each other's heads, round large banks of *Rouge et Noir*. An anxious silence reigns, only interrupted by the rattling of the roulette, the jingling of Napoleons and francs, and the titters and jokes of the few whose speculations are a matter of mere frolic. Pretty interesting women were putting down their Napoleons, and seeing them swept away, or drawing them in doubles, with a *sang-froid* which proved that they were no novices in that employment.

Having brought our traveller to the salivating state where temptation is impossible to resist, Murray comes down the heaviest of fathers: 'The Licensed Gaming-Houses at the German watering-places are a disgrace and shame to the minor princes, who not only tolerate them, but derive revenue from granting the permission, to the destruction of morality and honesty among their own subjects, as well as among thousands of strangers. English travellers should be placed especially on their guard against the sharpers who haunt the continental watering-places. The chances of being *robbed* are much greater than was formerly the case in Paris, as none of the precautionary measures are taken to prevent cheating in Germany. The princes who tolerate such a system must be content to bear the reproach of avarice and cupidity.'

The primary purpose of the spas was, or ought to have been, the curing of the sick; those who go there solely for that reason should 'consult their own physicians before leaving home. It is also prudent and customary to ask the advice of the physician resident at the baths as well before commencing a course of waters.'

Regarding the practical application of the treatment, Murray recommends that the water be drunk on an empty stomach, and a short walk taken between each draught, 'but violent exercise is to be avoided. The bath also should never be taken after eating, and during bathing a strict attention to diet is advisable. Tea, pastry, acids, vegetables, fruit, and cheese should be avoided, and but little should be eaten at each meal. Wine, if light, may be sparingly used . . .'

The first point of either sin or pleasure (or both) at which our traveller might call could be Ems, 'which seems essentially a ladies' watering-place: it is much frequented by the fair sex, and its waters are considered particularly efficacious in the complaints of females. It is on the whole a quiet place, and little or no raking goes on here . . .'

Schlangenbad, in a delightful though at that time a somewhat remote situation, was so named because of 'the great number of snakes and vipers, as well as the harmless kind, which not only abound in the neighbourhood, but even haunt the springs themselves, for the sake of the warmth yielded by the water, or for the frogs, the food of the viper. The old man who manages the baths will exhibit some of them.'

Such reptiles are not mentioned in Thomas Cook's guidebook of a later date, but Baedeker seeks to reassure those who might fear them, saying that the place 'takes its name from the harmless snake (coluber longissimus) which is occasionally found here but is really native to S. Europe'.

Even so, our traveller might linger a day or two because Murray says that the baths are one of the most 'harmless and delicious luxuries of the sort I have ever enjoyed; and I really quite looked forward to the morning for the pleasure with which I paid my addresses to this delightful element. The effect it produces on the skin is very singular: it is about as warm as milk, but infinitely softer: and after dipping the hand into it, if the thumb be rubbed against the fingers, it is said by many to resemble satin.'

None of the hotels at Homburg are rated as any good; moreover: 'The town consists of a long main street, chiefly of new houses, on one side of which are the wells and Kursaal, and on the other at the end the gloomy *Schloss*. The waters are very valuable in cases of disordered liver and stomach.'

After the usual fulmination against those who run the gaming-house, Murray concludes: 'Let those who are disposed to risk their money inquire what is the character of the managers, and be on their guard. The expense of such an enormous and splendid establishment must be paid out of the pockets of travellers. About 50,000 florins are lost here annually by the public in play.' The only manufacturing activity in Homburg was that of '*black stockings*', articles in very great request, no doubt, by the gentlemen who most numerously resort hither every summer'.

Those who behave sinfully have the opportunity of attending an English church service, which is given every Sunday. 'The number of English visitors increased so much of late that the place assumes the appearance of a settlement of our countrymen. This influx has the effect of diminishing its advantages of cheapness and retirement, as within a few years the price of everything has been raised nearly one half. After October the soil and climate are extremely damp – the grassy banks are oozing with water, which the granitic substratum will not absorb, and the hotels and lodging-houses suffer greatly from moisture.'

Water from the hot springs, which is conveyed through the

town in pipes to supply the different baths, 'loses little of its warmth in the passage; but the supply greatly exceeds the demand, so that some of the sources are used by the townspeople to scald their pigs and poultry'.

At the other Baden, near Vienna, where the scenery is compared by Murray to that of Matlock, the warm springs were said to be even more attractive than those at the German spa. 'Not a few, who though in perfect health, use the bath together, males and females mixed promiscuously, and sit, or move slowly about, for an hour or two, up to the neck in the steaming water. The ladies enter and depart by one side, and the gentlemen by another; but in the bath itself there is no separation: nay, politeness requires that a gentleman, when he sees a lady moving, or attempting to move, alone, shall offer himself as her supporter during the acquatic promenade.'

The Black Forest Baden was hyphenated to a second Baden, to remind people that it was the original bath, and to prevent any upstart watering-hole from claiming the honour. The Castle rose high above the town, but to Murray it was 'only remarkable for its situation and the curious *dungeons* beneath . . .'

. . . originally the dungeons were only accessible from above, by a perpendicular shaft or chimney running through the centre of the building, and still in existence. The visitor, in passing under it, can barely discern the daylight at the top. According to tradition, prisoners, bound fast in an arm-chair and blindfolded, were let down by a windlass into these dark and mysterious vaults and winding passages, excavated out of the solid rock on which the castle is founded. The dungeons were closed, not with doors of wood or iron, but with solid slabs of stone, turning upon pivots, and ingeniously fitted. Several of them still remain; they are nearly a foot thick, and weight from 1200 to 2000 lbs. In one chamber, loftier than the rest, called the *Rack Chamber*, the instruments of torture stood; a row of iron rings, forming part of the fearful apparatus, still remains in the wall. In a passage adjoining there is a well or pit in the floor, now boarded over, originally covered with a trap-door. The prisoner upon whom doom had been passed was led into this passage, and desired to kiss an image of the Virgin placed at the opposite end; but no sooner did his feet rest on the trap-door than it gave way beneath his weight, and precipitated him to a great depth below, upon a machine composed of wheels, armed with lancets, by which he was torn to pieces. The secret of this terrible dungeon remained unknown until, as the story goes, an attempt to rescue a little dog, which had fallen through the planking above the pit, led to the discovery, at a depth of many yards, of fragments of ponderous wheels set around with rusty knives, with portions of bones, rags, and torn garments adhering to them.

As the nineteenth century progressed guidebook prose became less prolix, and Baedeker deals with the above in a single sentence: 'The curious subterranean vaults with stone and iron doors were perhaps once used as dungeons' – a far cry from the romantic horrors detailed in Murray fifty years before, and possibly coming from the notion that one could justifiably encourage forgetfulness of such sadistic vileness on the assumption that similar practices would never surface again, the Nazi period at that time impossible to imagine.

By 1914 80,000 people a year visited Baden-Baden. Public gambling had been suppressed in 1872 (though it was allowed again under the Nazis) when it became more of a health resort. Bradshaw's *Dictionary of Bathing Places* said that the waters contained mineral properties for the cure of 'uric acid diathesis, gout, catarrhal affections of the throat and larynx, dyspepsia, chronic catarrh of the stomach and intestines, and bladder diseases', which made the waters of Baden-Baden 'stand unrivalled'. The waters were chiefly taken in the morning from 7 to 8 o'clock, while the band was playing, and: 'Special cabins were provided for the purpose of gargling.'

In spring and autumn 'grand musical festivals are held; and in winter chamber music, symphony and vocal concerts'. The town orchestra had fifty-two members. The theatre, 'a handsome and beautifully decorated building,' says Thomas Cook's guidebook, 'was opened in 1862 and inaugurated by Hector Berlioz.' The Hamburg Amerika Shipping Line *Guide Through Europe*, 1914, tells us that the theatre 'has a memorial tablet to Berlioz, the composer whose setting of Faust has become so famous'.

Another feature just prior to the First World War was that 'air trips may be taken in Zeppelin's air-ships in the Municipal Flying Ground'.

CHAPTER SEVEN

NORTHERN ITALY

D. H. Lawrence walked to Italy, and Goethe travelled by coach, as did Beckford and Heine, and countless others, some of note, most of course not. In the latter part of the nineteenth century tourists went by train, and aircraft today make it even more effortless.

Problems only began on reaching the frontier, though the traveller no doubt hoped that later compensations would erase all memories of difficulty. Old grumble-guts Murray, in *Northern Italy*, 1883 tells us what to be prepared for: 'Passports are no longer indispensable, but all travellers are advised to secure with them this important *certificate of nationality*.' Baedeker, in 1897, says, 'The countenance and help of the British and American consuls can, of course, be extended to those persons only who can prove their nationality.' Murray remarks that at the Custom-house luggage is opened and sometimes carefully searched. 'Even in the case of persons giving an assurance that their luggage contains no prohibited article, the concealment of which will, if discovered, entail trouble and annoyance, the examination will probably be persisted in. This severity of search has been increased under the present Italian Government, and it is especially enforced upon travellers arriving by the St. Gothard Railway.' That is to say, British, the majority of whom used that route. One also had to note: 'The Italian custom-house officers would consider it an insult to be offered money.'

Murray's *Switzerland*, 1891, consoles the traveller with the fact that he will have little difficulty in facing the Italian customs; though he then goes on to say that, at Chiasso, 'the head officials have made themselves notorious in the execution of their duty and discourtesy towards travellers'.

After the early Murray handbooks, in which it was assumed that travellers could afford to be extravagant, later editions positively extol niggardliness. Concerning railway travel in Italy: 'The clerks at the stations sometimes refuse to give change; it is therefore desirable to be *always prepared with the exact amount of the fare*', which is seconded by Baedeker, who adds: ' "Mistakes" are far from uncommon on the part of the ticket-clerks or the officials who weigh luggage.' He also says: 'During the last few years an extraordinary number of robberies of passengers' luggage have been perpetrated in Italy without detection, and articles of great value should not be entrusted to the safe-keeping of any trunk or portmanteau, however strong and secure it may seem.' Anyone tempted to carry arms in defence of life and belongings while in the country was told by Bradshaw: 'Revolvers are liable to be confiscated.'

A humantiarian view is taken by Baedeker, as shown by the following: 'The enormous weight of the trunks used by some travellers not unfrequently causes serious and even lifelong injury to the hotel and railway porters who have to handle them.' But the suggested remedy would also benefit thieves, who would not suffer a hernia in their attempts to carry them away: 'Travellers are therefore urged to place their heavy articles in the smaller packages and thus minimize the evil as far as possible.'

Accommodation at hotels in the large provincial cities was generally good, Murray says, and nearly equal to those elsewhere, 'but at intermediate stations and off the main routes they are often very dirty, and infested with vermin to an extent of which those who travel only in winter can have no idea . . . When off the lines of railway or main road, those who wish tea and coffee in the evening should carry milk with them from the place where they slept the previous night, as it is often not to be had at the inns on the road. The tea at the smaller inns is generally so bad that travellers will do well to carry their own supply, together with a small metal teapot.'

English travellers, here as elsewhere, were apt to be charged higher prices, and 'it *will save trouble and annoyance to fix beforehand the prices to be paid for everything.* The second floor is preferable to the first, and the traveller will do well to remember that on account of the defective drainage in most towns of Italy, it is always better to incur the fatigue of ascending a number of stairs than to sleep on or near the ground floor. In the smaller towns it would be absurd to expect the comforts and conveniences of great cities: travellers never gain anything by exacting or requiring more than the people can supply; and if they have sufficient philosophy to keep their temper, they will generally find that they are treated with civility.'

Dr James Henry Bennet, in his health-seekers' guidebook to benign climates, *Winter and Spring on the Shores of the Mediterranean*, 1875, gives a rather idealized version of travelling by carriage, asking us to remember that 'the driver for the time is your servant, and must do your bidding, and everything should be arranged in conformity with previous habits and laws of hygiene, provided the written agreement be not infringed. Thus the journey becomes a pleasure, and a source of health instead of a trial of strength, as often occurs.'

His plan called for the traveller to get up at six or seven, 'to take a cup of tea or coffee, and to start at seven or eight, the carriage being closed at the top as a protection against the sun, open at the sides, and prepared for the day's campaign by a comfortable arrangement of umbrellas, books, maps, and provisions. The latter usually consisted of a basket of bread, meat, biscuits, wine, and fruit, provided before starting, with Liebig's extract of meat, a little of which makes bad soup good, and a bottle of Dunn's extract of coffee which transforms any kind of milk, cow's, sheep's, goat's, or camel's, into good coffee. At nine or ten we stopped for breakfast, which can be obtained anywhere, if the traveller is contended with milk, bread, butter, eggs, and honey. Then the journey is resumed, and at twelve or one the principal stoppage of the day takes place for the dinner of the driver and his horses.'

After the traveller has eaten a solid lunch, 'the mid-day rest becomes a period of liberty, during which he can survey all around, analyse the habits and customs of the peasantry, study the architecture of their houses, farms, out-buildings, their agricultural operations, and the local botany. Finally, if agreeable, and weather permits, he can take a good hygienic walk in advance of three, four, or more miles. When tired he has only to sit down by the roadside in some picturesque nook until the carriage overtakes him. If the driver, as is usually the case, rests for a couple of hours, and four or five miles have been got over, it is nearly three before the carriage is again resumed. To me these midday strolls in advance were the pleasantest part of the day's journey. After that, progress is steadily made until six, when the final stoppage takes place. Then comes dinner, a walk, or a chat with your companions or some new acquaintances, a cup of tea, and an early retirement for the night.'

A favourable view of Italy and the Italians is found in the eight-volume series of guidebooks by Augustus J. C. Hare, who regrets the coming of the railways as the means of locomotion. In *The Cities of Northern Italy*, 1883, he says, in defence of horse-drawn transport: 'The slow approach to each long-heard of but unseen city, gradually leading up, as the surroundings of all cities do, to its own peculiar characteristics, gave a very different feeling towards it to that which is produced by rushing into a railway station – with an impending struggle for luggage and places in an omnibus – which, in fact, is probably no feeling at all. While, in the many hours spent in plodding over the weary surface of a featureless country, we had time for so studying the marvellous story of the place we were about to visit, that when we saw it, it was engraved for ever on the brain, with its past associations and its present beauties combined.'

He almost regrets that: 'The journey to Italy is now absolutely without difficulties, but the most desirable approach is that by the Corniche road along the Riviera. Then, after the dreary wind-stricken plains of Central France, and the stony arid hills of Provence, one enters Italy at Mentone by a portal like the gates of Paradise, and is plunged at once into the land of the citron and myrtle, of palms and aloes and cyclamen. Of course one must not expect that all Italy will be like these Riviera roads, and one is, as far as scenery goes, receiving the best first, but it is charming to feel the whole of one's ideal realised at the very outset.'

In order to avoid disappointment in Italy, Hare tells us that it is necessary not to expect too much, 'for it is in the beauty of her

details that Italy surpasses all other countries, and details take time
to find out and appreciate. Compare most of her buildings in their
entirety with similar buildings in England, much more in France
and Germany, and they will be found very inferior.'

Another thing to remember, so as to get the best out of travel
in Italy,

> is not to go forth in a spirit of antagonism to the inhabitants,
> and with the impression that life in Italy is to be a prolonged
> struggle against extortion and incivility. A traveller will be cheated
> oftener in a week's tour in England than in a year's residence in
> Italy. During eight whole winters spent at Rome, and years of
> travel in all the other parts of Italy, the author cannot recall a
> single act or word of an Italian of which he can justly complain;
> but, on the contrary, has an overflowing recollection of the disin-
> terested courtesy, and the unselfish and often most undeserved
> kindness, with which he has universally been treated. There is
> scarcely an Italian nobleman, whose house, with all it contains,
> would not be placed at the disposition of a wayfarer who found
> himself in an out-of-the-way place or where the inn was unbear-
> able; there is scarcely a shopkeeper, who would not send his boy
> to show you the way to a church, one, two, or even three streets
> distant; there is scarcely a carriage which would not be stopped
> to offer you a lift, if they saw you looked tired by the wayside;
> scarcely a woman who would not give you a chair (expecting
> nothing) if you were standing drawing near her house ...

I find Hare by far the best writer on Italy and of things Italian,
being able to back him up on his encomiums of general honesty.
On two occasions during one of my motor trips through the country
money was put back into my hand with a smile when I had
inadvertently given too much. Neither can I but agree when he
writes that 'nothing can be obtained from an Italian by compulsion.
A friendly look and cheery word will win almost anything, but
Italians will not be driven, and the browbeating manner, which is
so common with English and Americans, even the commonest
facchino regards and speaks of as mere vulgar insolence, and treats
accordingly ... Unfortunately the bad impression one set of travellers leaves, another pays the penalty for.'

Hare gives one instance of the heartless behaviour of tourists: 'The horrible ill-breeding of our countrymen never struck me more than one day at Porlezza. A clean, pleasing Italian woman had arranged a pretty little caffe near the landing place. The Venetian blinds kept out the burning sun; the deal tables were laid with snowy linen; the brick floor was scoured till not a speck of dust remained. The diligence arrived, and a crowd of English and American women rushed in while waiting for the boat, thought they would have some lemonade, then thought they would not, shook out the dust from their clothes, brushed themselves with the padrona's brushes, laid down their dirty travelling bags on all the clean table-cloths, chattered and scolded for half an hour, declaimed upon the miseries of Italian travel, ordered nothing and paid for nothing; and, when the steamer arrived, flounced out without even a syllable of thanks or recognition. No wonder that the woman said her own pigs would have behaved better.'

Hare is also sympathetic to the Italians on the matter of accommodation. 'In regard to hotel life, it cannot be too much urged, for the real comfort of travellers as well as for their credit with the natives, that the vulgar habits of bargaining, inculcated by several English handbooks, are greatly to be deprecated, and only lead to suspicion and resentment. Italians are *not* a nation of cheats, and cases of overcharge at inns are most unusual, except at great Anglicised hotels, where they have been gradually brought about through the perquisite money demanded by couriers.'

Baedeker, like Murray (and most other guidebook writers), airs a harder view, when he says that the second-class hotels, 'thoroughly Italian in their arrangements, are much cheaper, but they are rarely very clean or comfortable. The inns in the smaller towns will often be found convenient and economical by the *voyageur en garçon*, and the better houses of this class may be visited even by ladies. If no previous agreement has been made an extortionate bill is not uncommon. The landlord is generally prepared to have his first offer beaten down by the traveller, and in that expectation usually asks more at first than he will afterwards agree to accept. The recommendations of landlords as to hotels in other towns should be disregarded. They are not made with a single eye to the interests of the traveller.'

On the obsessive topic of cleanliness, Baedeker prepares those who leave the beaten track for privations. 'Iron bedsteads should if possible be selected, as they are less likely to harbour the enemies of repose. Insect powder, or camphor, somewhat repels their advances. The gnats are a source of great annoyance, and often of suffering, during the summer and autumn-months. Windows should always be closed before a light is introduced into the room. Light muslin curtains round the beds, masks for the face, and gloves are employed to ward off the attacks of these pertinacious intruders. The burning of insect powder over a spirit-lamp is also recommended.'

Should one wish to communicate with home, or any other place: 'A cautious traveller will take important letters to the post-office himself, or drop them into some of the letter boxes that are now distributed through an Italian town, since if given to an untrustworthy person to carry to the post-office they run the risk of being made away with for the sake of the stamps.'

We are told how useful it would be to climb, 'some tall steeple or tower' so as to get an idea of the layout of a city. Sight-seeing called forth more advice from Murray about behaviour in churches: 'The clergy do not like to have the churches considered as shows, nor are the congregations at all indifferent, as had been asserted, to the conduct of strangers, in walking about and talking during Divine Service. It might perhaps, too, be suggested to our Pro-testant countrymen, that they are not protesting against Roman Catholic errors by behaving indecorously in churches; and to reflect how they would like to see their own places of worship made objects of show during Divine Service.'

One of the first places the tourists made for, whether sons and daughters of manufacturers from the north of England, or offspring of county families (or anyone else for that matter), was Venice. Many no doubt had read Byron, and some Ruskin, but one assumes that nearly all had either Murray or Baedeker to browse over and take notice of. That being so, one can't help but sympathize with those whose living depended on extracting as much money as possible from tourists and travellers, by fair means or unfair, a process certainly made difficult by Murray's advice that: 'Travellers should insist on being taken to the shops etc. where they wish to go, and should be careful not to be imposed upon by, or accept the recommendations of, valets de place, gondoliers, and hotel servants, some of whom are in the pay of dishonest persons ... N.B. Many of the shopkeepers will take two-thirds or even less of the price asked. The prices in the Piazza of S. Mark greatly exceed those in parts of the city less frequented by strangers.'

The drinking water at Venice was said to contain 'a small quantity of iron and some vegetable matter, the latter derived from the peaty stratum through which it filters, and strangers should avoid drinking it without wine. Mosquito-curtains are usually provided to the beds; but if not, a request should be at once made for them.'

Lampugnini's guidebook *Venice and the Lagoon*, 1905, was presumably translated into English by someone whose native language was not English, since the quirkiness of style, especially in the placement of commas, is at times amusing.

'Venice is situated at the end of the lagoons of the Adriatic Sea; the lagoons are kinds of lakes or better still of, gulfs deeply surrounded with banks of sand and the lagoon is called *living* or *dead* according to the tide which it feels more or less, from this it, becomes divided into two parts, little by little from the same extension.'

The gondola, we are told, is one of the characteristic features of Venice, being 'a light boat long and narrow, in the centre is a little cabin which raises or lowers as you desire, the seats of the best are upholstered in leather and have seats for four persons, all the gondolas are painted black in conformity to a law of the XV century and, it is not permitted to have any colour, so it is impossible to know the mystery of a closed gondola, the gondolier remains on foot at the poop with a heavy rowlock of iron if, there are two gondoliers one is at the prow and the other at the poop, the gondola glides smoothly and rapidly on the waves, if there is only one person you feel a slight rolling at every stroke of the oar; at the corner of a canal or when nearing a bridge the gondoliers have a particular cry to warn and avoid collision.'

Murray says that all gondoliers must carry the police tariff, and show it if required. 'Complaints for misbehaviour or overcharge may be made to the Guardie Municipale, or at the office of the Municipality.'

Lampugnini's prose has a breathlessness which paces the blood in his account of the artistic treasures of the city. The Campanile of San Marco, we are told, 'existed until the 14th. of July 1902; the day of its fall, was situated at the point of entrance to the square and the Piazzetta; it was commenced in the X centy and finished in 1178, it was, in gothic style and had an height of 319 feet ... From the top of this belfry, which gave a splendid view of Venice, the lagoons and the Alps; was, by its fall a real artistic disaster to the city; the construction has been decreed, and the work begun but, will certainly never be possible to say of this new monument that, it will have the merit of the first one.'

Language verging on the operatic suggests an engraving by Piranesi, when he tells us that the prison by the Bridge of Sighs was built in the late sixteenth century so as to

fill in the pond of the Ducal Palace; the front of this edifice towards the canal is severe and gloomy, but the entrance towards the bank of the Schiavoni is more elegant; this part of the Palace was destined to be the residence of the six magistrates called *Gentlemen of the night criminals* ... The terrible *Pond* was the antique prison for political offences, it is still existing in the cellar, with the torture room and that of execution, here you go down by the corridor stated above; here are the dark cells on a level with the soil and the level of the water above, a low door is still shown to visitors; on the canal, by which the corpses were passed through and conveyed by gondola to the Orfano canal; one of these cells served for the prisoners of Carmagnola who were tortured and then afterwards decapitated, on the Piazzetta between two columns.

Should the visitor feel the urge to swim, Lampugnini is reassuring: 'An important thing to know about everything else, is that the Lido has not any *Mosquitoes. The bathing establishment* contains more than 600 rooms, placed on the sea in two long lines, from one part to the other is a *very large hall,* where select concerts are given every day. *There is a first class Caffee Restaurant,* with a *ladies saloon on the terrace* facing the sea which is the general rendezvous of the foreign elette society. Near the *Grand Baths* is erected the new *Hydro-electric-Therapeutic Establishment*, for massage cure, mud baths, vapour baths, light baths and the cures with the X Rays.'

Murray, on the other hand, is not at all happy with the segregational arrangements at the beach, finding that 'the line of demarcation between the baths of the two sexes is not sufficiently observed to make the bathing pleasant for English ladies, and the authorities ought to interfere'.

On that note we will leave Venice for Verona, where we can let a tear or two fall on the tomb of Juliet, if we can find it. Murray says that 'it certainly was shown in the last century, before Shakespeare was generally known to the Italians. That tomb, however, has long since been destroyed. The present one – on the garden of the *Orfanotrofio*, entered (small fee) from a little street running down to the Adige – is of red Verona marble, and before it was promoted to its present honour, was used as a washing-trough.'

Augustus Hare says that the tomb may be visited out of sentiment, but the one 'which was shown here in the last century was all chopped up long ago by relic hunters, and French and English ladies are wearing it in bracelets'.

The next stop in Pisa, 'that little nest of singing birds' (when Shelley and Byron sojourned there in 1821), and where, says Hare, 'The soft climate has a wonderfully soothing effect upon complaints of the chest, but it is horribly wet.' During a conducted tour of the famous Leaning Tower he tells us: 'The sensation of falling over is very curious and unpleasant. Those who ascend must be careful not really to fall over, as the railing at the top is not continuous, and very misguiding.'

A day trip by train to Leghorn would, according to Hare, be a disappointment. Should the traveller land from a steamer, 'the boatmen and porters are peculiarly fierce and extortionate . . . There is nothing whatever worth seeing, though . . . its shops are sometimes amusing. The place is full of galley-slaves who do all the dirty work of the town in red caps, brown vests, and yellow trousers. The Cathedral has a facade by *Inigo Jones*.'

Murray finds the place more interesting, and remarks on the Protestant cemetery, which was 'until the present century the only one in Italy, and contains the tomb of Smollett'. He also reminds us that in the sixteenth century Ferdinand I invited people of every nation and creed to Leghorn, 'seeking to escape the tyranny of their respective governments; Roman Catholics who withdrew from persecution in England; and New Christians, – that is, forcibly converted Moors and Jews, – as well as Jews who adhered to their religion, then driven from Spain and Portugal by the cruelty of Phillip II, animated and assisted by the Inquisition.'

Florence is an hour or so inland by rail from Pisa, and our traveller would find there many of his compatriots studiously referring to Baedeker or Murray on their walks around the town. Murray says that at least a week should be devoted to Florence, though, as elsewhere, mosquitoes were a problem. The large Hôtel de la Paix was well situated, with a lift, but 'some persons find the noise produced by the weir, just opposite, very objectionable'. If a hotel was inconvenient, or too expensive, there were pensions kept by Mrs Jennings, Miss Hill 'very comfortable' and Miss Clark – 'excellent food and very healthy situation'.

For those who got into trouble there was an English consul; also an English club, 'the Florence', an English baker, three English bankers, five English doctors, three English dentists and an English nurse. One could attend the Church of England, or a Presbyterian church; or wander around the studio of the English painter, R. Spencer Stanhope, or join an Artistic Society where 'classes are held for young ladies three or four times a week'.

An English sculptor was in residence, and whoever bought a piece from him had a choice of not less than four English forwarding agents to get it back to England. The purchaser would have to be careful, in taking the works out himself, not to travel via Chiasso where, says Murray in 1892, the customs officials 'will detain the goods, and refuse to answer any inquiries by letter as to the means by which they can be released, a course for which they are said to have the authority of their government'.

There were two booksellers in Florence, three English chemists and two English grocers, not to mention a picture dealer and a tailor, so that one could feel quite at home there. Even the uncertain weather seemed imported from the Home Country, for the rainfall was considerable, 'especially in the autumn and early winter. From the nature of the pavement and improved drainage it soon finds its way into the Arno; there is consequently no stagnant water in any part of the town.' From a sanitary point of view Florence was much improved since the cholera epidemics of 1854 and 1855, 'not only as regards drainage, but by the forbidding of intramural interments except in some very few cases'.

Matters of health are gone into in some detail, the city being 'exempt from specific diseases or epidemics. In October and the beginning of November, as in April and May, the climate of Florence is much less relaxing than that of Rome or Naples. Chronic dyspepsia generally diminishes in intensity after a residence in the Tuscan capital; in fact, all those diseases of a non-inflammatory character requiring a bracing atmosphere appear to be benefitted in Florence. Ague and fevers similar to those of Rome and Naples are unknown, save as the result of importation, the disease having been contracted elsewhere. Measles and scarlatina, like all other eruptive diseases occurring in Tuscany, as a general rule, run a remarkably mild course.' What all travellers had to beware of was the change from bright sunshine on the banks of the Arno to the 'dark sunless streets, which form so many funnels for cold air descending from the gorges of the Apennines. To this source may be traced most of the indisposition from which English and American visitors occasionally suffer.'

In the early part of the nineteenth century, before railways had been laid down, one travelled from Florence to Rome by diligence, information about the route being supplied by such books as *Rome in the Nineteenth Century* by Charlotte A. Eaton (1788–1859), which was a sort of proto-guide in two volumes first published in 1820. The author was an erudite lady whose occasional attempts to be fair with regard to travelling conditions in Italy after the Napoleonic Wars only serve to highlight her frequent blasts of complaint. The work, one of the more popular, went into four editions.

Her 150-mile journey to Rome by *vetturino* took six days, and at the start she compares Italian scenery favourably to that in the south of France, but the hard conditions of travel soon heighten the tone of her justifiable strictures: 'Wretched, indeed, is the fate of those who, like us, travel *Vetturino*! In an evil hour were we persuaded to engage the trio of mules, and the man, or *Vetturino*, by whose united efforts we are to be dragged along, day by day, at a pace not at all exceeding in velocity that of an English waggon; stopping, for the convenience of these animals, two hours at noon, in some filthy hole, no better than an English pig-stye; getting up in the morning, or rather in the middle of the night, about four hours before day-break; and when, by our labours, we have achieved a distance, often of thirty miles, we are put up for the night in whatever wretched *Osteria* our evil destiny may have conducted ourselves and our mules to.'

Nevertheless, she could not deny that 'the moon *does* look larger, and shines with far more warmth and brilliancy, in the sky of Italy, than amidst the fogs and vapours of England. The scenery through which we passed was singularly beautiful. Sometimes winding round the sides of the hills, we looked down into peaceful valleys among the mountains, in whose sheltered bosom lay scattered cottages, shaded with olive-trees, and surrounded with fields of the richest fertility.'

They arrived late at the little inn of Poggibonzi, and found it by no means uncomfortable; as interesting, in fact, as many *posadas* in Spain still were in the 1950s, especially at remote places inland: 'To be sure, it smokes so incessantly that we are compelled to sit with open windows, though the air is extremely cold; but this is no uncommon occurrence. The house is tolerably clean, and the room I am writing in is very tastefully ornamented with some elegant angels painted in fresco, the beauties of which must beguile the time while we are waiting for the repast ...'

Dinner finally comes, the waiter 'placing on the table the *mines-tra*, or soup, in a huge tureen, containing plenty of hot water, with some half-boiled macaroni in it. If you don't like this kind of soup, you may have bread boiled in water; it is all the same. There is always a plate of grated parmesan cheese, to mix with the *minestra*, of whatever sort it may be, without which even Italian palates could never tolerate such a potion. This is generally followed by a *frittura*, which consists of liver, brains, or something of that sort, fried in oil. Then comes the *rosto*, which to-day appears in the shape of half a starved turkey, attended by some other indescribable dish, smelling strong of garlic.'

Our authoress-traveller and her companions found Siena to have a somewhat antiquated appearance, though later guidebooks were to see it in a better light. 'Its streets, or rather lanes, are lined with high gloomy old-fashioned houses, looking like jails, and called, or rather miscalled, palaces, which have fallen into decay like their possessors, who are too proud to resign, and too poor to inhabit them.'

She duly visits all the sites, including the library, 'which contains a great quantity of books, though I would not answer for their value', concluding that 'Siena is a very dull place. Some English friends of ours who spent a winter there found a great want of cultivated society. There is no theatre, nor opera, nor public amusement of any kind. Life stagnates here; for its active pursuits, its interests, its honours, its pleasures, and its hopes, can have no place. No happy Briton can see and know what Siena is, without looking back with a swelling heart to his own country.'

After leaving Siena, 'night closed in upon us long before we reached our destined place of rest, the wretched *Osteria* of the still more wretched village of Buon Convento. Thither, when a wearisome pilgrimage of four mortal hours had at last conducted us, its half-starved looking denizens would not admit us into the horrible pig-stye in which they wallowed themselves, but conducted us to a lone uninhabited house on the other side of the way, in which there was not a human being. We were ushered up an old ghastly staircase, along which the wind whistled mournfully, into an open hall, the raftered roof of which was overhung with cobwebs, and the stone floor was deep in filth. Four doors entered into this forlorn-looking place, two of which led to the chill, dirty, miserable holes which were our destined places of repose; and the other two, to rooms that the people said did not belong to them, one old woman assuring us they were inhabited by nobody, while the other maintained they were occupied by very honest people. In the meantime, it was certain that the frail doors of our dormitories would yield on the slightest push; that the door of the hall itself, leading upon the stairs, had no fastening at all; that the stairs were open to the road in front, and to the fields behind, the house itself having no door whatever; and thus, that whoever chose to pay us a nocturnal visit, might do so without the smallest inconvenience or difficulty to himself.'

Worse than anything was that 'the wind blew about us, and we could get no fire. But there was no remedy for these grievances, and we resigned ourselves to fate and to bed. The two hideous old beldames who had brought us our wretched supper, had left us for the night, and no human being was near us, when we heard the sound of a heavy foot on the creaking staircase, and a man wrapped in a cloak, and armed with a sword and musket, stalked into the hall.

'If we had been heroines, what terrors might have agitated, and what adventures might not have befallen us! But as we were not heroical, we neither screamed nor fainted, we only looked at him; and notwithstanding his formidable appearance, and that he had long black moustachios and bushy eye-brows, he did us no mischief, though he might have cut our throats with all the ease in the world; indeed, he had still abundance of leisure for the exploit, for he informed us that he had the honour of lodging in the house, that he was the only person who had that honour, and that he should have the honour of sleeping in the room next to ours.'

Whoever he was, Charlotte treated him like a gentleman and, after several formal good-nights, 'our whiskered neighbour retreated into his apartment, the key of which he had in his pocket, and we contented ourselves with barricading our door with the only table and chair that our desolate chamber contained; then, in uncurtained and uncoverleted wretchedness, upon flock beds, the prey of innumerable fleas, and shaking with cold, if not with fear, we lay the live-long night; not even having wherewithall to cover us, for the potent smell of the filthy rug, which performed the double duties of blanket and quilt, obliged us to discard it, and our carriage cloaks were but an inadequate defence against the blasts that whistled through the manifold chinks of the room.' They got up at four o'clock the next morning and 'began in the dark to wend our weary way from this miserable *Osteria*'.

After several hours on the road they stopped at a solitary house called La Scala. 'It was the filthiest place I ever beheld, and the smell was so intolerable, that nothing but the excessive cold out of doors could have induced us to have remained a single moment within it. Two hours, however, did we stay, cowering over the smoke of a wet wood fire, waiting till the mules were fed – for they could get something to eat, but for us there was nothing; neither bread, coffee, eggs, milk, meat, vegetables, nor even macaroni, were to be had; so that we might have starved, or breakfasted upon salt dried fish in oil, had not our *Vetturino*, more provident than ourselves, produced a store of stale loaves and hard boiled eggs, that he had laid in at Siena.'

After La Scala they toiled up apparently interminable hills: 'The countrymen were all clothed in shaggy sheep-skins, with the wool outside, rudely stitched together to serve as a covering to their bodies, and pieces of the same were tied about their thighs, partially concealing the ragged vestments they wore beneath. Their legs and feet were bare; and this savage attire gave a strange, wild effect to the dark eyes that glared at us from beneath their bushy and matted locks. Indeed their whole appearance reminded us literally of wolves in sheep's clothing.'

It was late when they stopped for the night at a lone house by the wayside and, after the usual description of its filth and squalor, she goes on: 'The *Vetturino* had providentially brought with him our supper, or else we should have got none; and it was cooked and sent up on coarse brown earthenware. Wretched as this house was, it seemed to contain a number of inmates; and the wild, ferocious appearance of those we saw, and the hoarse voices of the men whom we did not see, which frequently met our ear in loud altercation, conspired, with the appearance of the place, and the nature of the country, to make it seem fit for the resort of banditti, and the perpetration of robbery and murder.'

The doors to their rooms having neither bolts nor locks, they again barricaded themselves in, and went to bed in fear of their lives, to be awakened in the middle of the night by the fall of one of the chairs. 'Starting up in sudden trepidation, I flew to the door, stumbling in the dark over the empty dishes of the supper, and extinguished lamps, which rolled about with a horrible clatter; and assuming a courage I did not feel, I authoritatively demanded to know who was there, as I hastily attempted to repair my outworks. I was answered by a gruff voice, demanding admittance. In my fright and confusion, it was some time before I understood that it was for the purpose of lighting the fire, and that it was four o'clock. To us it seemed that the night had only just begun, but it was clear our repose was at an end; so, wrapping myself in my dressing-gown, and guided by the light that streamed through the numerous crevices of the door, I began to demolish the pile of chairs and tables I had raised. When the door was opened, there came in a woman with long, dishevelled hair, a dim lamp burning in her withered, skinny hand, followed by a man clad in sheep-skins, and bending beneath a burden of sticks. His face was half hid with black, bushy hair, and his eyes were overhung with shaggy eyebrows; he had shoes, but his legs were bare, and by his side was fastened a huge knife or axe, much resembling one formerly in use for cutting off people's heads, but which I suspect he had applied to the less obnoxious purpose of cutting the wood he was carrying.'

If one looks carefully at the other side of her Gothic account it seems obvious that the people were anxious to make them as comfortable as was possible within their primitive means. But the party proceeds on its way, without breakfast, though: 'Tea we had with us, but nothing could be got to make it or drink it in.'

On Sunday they arrived at the town of Acqua Pendente and 'the streets were filled with men wrapped in their large cloaks, who were loitering about, or standing grouped together in corners, in that apathetic state of indolent taciturnity so expressive of complete bodily and mental inertion.

'How unlike our English associations is a village in these countries, where a narrow street of dilapidated and windowless hovels, surrounded by filth, and inhabited by squalid wretchedness, is all that answers to the name! How melancholy and miserable do they seem, and how often has my fancy returned to the smiling villages of my own country, where neat cottages, and little gardens, scattered over the green, present the happy picture of humble contentment, cheerful industry, and rural happiness!'

And so our intrepid travellers went on their way. At one inn, where they got little or nothing to eat, the author says that the famed Muscat wine was so delicious that she hoped they would 'not follow the example of an old German prelate, who, it seems, drank it at this inn till he died'.

A week of filthy beds and vile food did not tame her combative spirit. 'If we did not eat, however, we were eaten; whole hosts made us their prey during the night, while we lay shivering and defenceless. This indeed is almost invariably the case throughout Italy. The people drain your purses by day, and the fleas your blood by night. They came within sight of all their endeavours!'

She was given perhaps to a fair amount of romantic exaggeration for the sake of her readers, but one must nevertheless concede that she did indeed rough it on the road to Rome. 'Our longing eyes were intently fixed on the spot where we were told that it would first appear; when, at length, the carriage having toiled up to the top of a long hill, the *Vetturino* exclaimed, "Eccola!" The dome of St. Peter's appeared in view; and, springing out of the carriage, and up a bank by the road side, we beheld from its summit, Rome!'

CHAPTER EIGHT

ROME AND NAPLES

Railways soon ran the length and breadth of Italy, so that the journey to Rome became far more comfortable. Even by the 1850s tourists could get there from London in four and a half days, by taking the train as far as Marseilles and a boat to Civitta Vecchia – where Stendhal had been the French consul in the 1830s. With regard to the shipping lines, Murray's *South Italy and Naples*, 1853, states: 'Formerly there was considerable competition between the companies; but they have latterly amalgamated, by no means to the advantage of travellers. The fares are exorbitant, and there is no longer any inducement to accelerate the speed. The complaints are consequently numerous, and travellers are frequently exposed both to annoyance and loss by the failure of the steamers to keep their engagements. Considering the importance of the line, and the large profits which the companies derive from English travellers, the proprietors should bear in mind that a want of punctuality, incivility on the part of their officers, or exorbitant charges, will inevitably force their best customers to support the French mail line exclusively, or to fall back on the old system of travelling by land.'

These complaints are omitted from the next edition of the handbook, suggesting that they had some effect; or perhaps Murray himself had been taken to task, because a note in the preface says: 'The Publisher thinks proper to state that Mr. Blewitt, the author of the former edition of this Handbook, having been prevented superintending the present, is not responsible for the changes that have been introduced in it.'

By 1872 the railway to Rome went via Paris, Munich, Innsbruck and the Brenner Pass, a distance of 1547 miles which took three days, for the fare of twelve pounds. In 1875 there were 1600 miles of railway in Italy, and 8164 by 1889. Bradshaw, in 1897, says that Rome could be reached from London in two and a half days for ten pounds.

Such progress towards becoming a great European power was not, according to Macmillan's *Italy and Sicily*, 1905, an unmixed blessing, was even 'a little precipitate, as no social transformation had taken place which correspond to the political revolution. Owing to the variety of local conditions, one district is almost a century behind another. The Italian revolution was a triumph for the middle classes, and the labouring classes had to bear an undue share of its burdens, while they profited but little from its immediate benefits.'

Most of the hotels were full when Charlotte Eaton and her companion arrived in Rome after their arduous journey from Florence, but when they found one: 'You cannot conceive, without having travelled *Vetturino*, and lodged in the holes we have done, how delightful is the sensation of being in a habitable hotel, how acceptable the idea of a good dinner, and how transporting the prospect of sleeping in a clean bed.'

Thirty years later there were not only far more hotels, but many comfortable lodging houses. Families who intended to stay a long time 'may meet with roomy and splendid apartments in some of the great palaces; in those of the Dukes Braschi, Altieri, Ceva, and Sermoneta, there is a princely suite generally let to foreigners. However respectable the landlord may appear, a formal written agreement is desirable, and a careful verification of the inventory still more so. In the Corso it will be as well to stipulate for the exclusive possession of the windows during the Carnival, or the lodger may be surprised to find his apartments converted into show-rooms during the festivities, besides being obliged to pay for a place at his own window.'

Murray also tells us that foreigners, especially the English, 'cannot be too strongly cautioned against a set of disreputable characters who are constantly hanging about the Piazza di Spagna and the neighbouring streets, offering lodgings for hire. Such fellows ought to be avoided by respectable persons; those who place any confidence in them, as regards procuring apartments, will probably have to repent having listened to them.'

For the purpose of changing money there were three English bankers in Mr Murray's list, one of whom was also in the wine business. 'It is impossible not to feel, after any competent trial, how vastly different is the treatment an average Englishman receives from an English banker above an Italian one. No silly vanity should induce any traveller to afford certain grandiose Roman establishments the opportunity of fleecing him, for they will not even do it with civility, except to a duke or other great lord.'

There was an English Club in Rome, of which it was said: 'The rules are somewhat illiberal, as regards artists residing in Rome, who are excluded.' One could find the usual English doctors and dentists, as well as grocers and chemists, who grew more numerous as the century advanced. Hotels are also noted at which the 'Anglo-American element is predominant'.

For those who liked to hunt: 'A subscription pack of hounds is now kept, numbering several of the Roman princes among the subscribers, and affords very good sport to strangers residing at Rome during the winter; as foxes are abundant, and the country well suited for hunting', but travellers were expected to send a donation to the secretary of the hunt 'towards the maintenance of the hounds and huntsmen, at the end of the season'.

You might, of course, during your stay in the Holy City, wish to be presented to the Pope, in which case, you would receive a letter a few days before informing you of the time, generally about midday, when you were expected to wear either uniform or evening dress. 'It is the etiquette that Protestants should show the same mark of respect to his Holiness as they do to their own sovereign, by kissing his hand. Roman Catholics will consider it their duty towards the head of their Church to kiss the Pope's foot or knee. The presentation of ladies, except in the case of royal princesses or crowned heads, only takes place on Sundays, after the Pope's dinner-hour.'

In the early Murray we may read – though this is condensed in later editions – that: 'The Foundling Hospital contains upwards of 3000 children; the number annually received is 1150. In 1865, the last date for which we have returns, embracing a period of 10 years, out of 11,425 received in the hospital, 9260 died.' This, in spite of the fact that: 'Few cities in Europe are so distinguished for their institutions of public charity as Rome, and in none are the hospitals more magnificently lodged, or endowed with more princely liberality', proving that if a bastard can't live well, he or she can at least die in splendour.

One charitable institution is a hospital for Poor Protestants, which 'deserves particular mention. It can accommodate 8 or 10 patients, and is well deserving of the support of our countrymen who visit Rome, as the only one where poor British Protestants can be received without being subjected to the persecution of the friars and attendants in the other hospitals to bring about their conversion to Romanism; upon no charity in Rome can the contribution of the English Protestants be more worthily bestowed.'

In a long section on climate and health we find the curious remarks that 'the progress of malaria at Rome is dependent on the extension of the population. Whenever the population has diminished, the district in which the decrease has taken place has become unhealthy; and whenever a large number of persons has been crowded in a confined space, as in the Ghetto, the salubrity of the situation has become apparent in spite of the uncleanly habits of the inhabitants.'

It was thought in those days that the dreaded malaria was more likely to strike while you were asleep, 'hence the couriers who carry the mails at all seasons between Rome and Naples make it a rule not to sleep whilst crossing the Pontine marshes, and generally smoke as an additional security'.

Murray goes to great lengths to put the perils of disease at Rome in their place, almost as if to talk them out of existence, while Baedeker's 1897 guidebook is as usual more pragmatic – and brief, but the most sensible hints seem to be those from *Rambles in Rome*, by S. Russell Forbes: 'Perhaps the health of no city in the world is so much talked about by people who know nothing whatever of the subject, as Rome. People get ill in Rome, of course, just as in any other place; but more than half the sickness is caused through their own imprudence.' Under 'Useful Hints' the author gives us: 'Avoid bad odours. Do not ride in an open carriage at night. Take lunch in the middle of the day. This is essential. It is better to take a light breakfast and lunch, than a heavy breakfast and no lunch. If out about sunset, throw an extra wrap or coat on, to avoid the sudden change in the atmosphere. There is no danger beyond being apt to take a cold. Colds are the root of all evil at Rome. Do not sit about the ruins at night. It may be very romantic, but it is very unwise. There is no harm in walking. Close your windows at night within a few inches. If you get into a heat, do not go into the shade or into a building till you have cooled down. Do not over-fatigue yourself. Follow these hints, and you will avoid that great bugbear, Roman fever.'

In 1872 Murray tells us that travellers should be on their guard against 'an unworthy practice of innkeepers, and other interested parties at Nice, Florence, and even in Paris, and to which the newspapers have unfortunately lent themselves, in discrediting the sanitary state of Rome, thereby preventing strangers resorting to it, by representing epidemics of every kind as raging in it; indeed, the same thing has been practised in Rome itself, as regards Naples. Let the traveller shut his ears to such reports, or in case of doubt apply to some of the respectable medical men at Rome or Naples for precise information on the subject.'

For travellers who were sick, or so ailing that they died, the following difficulties were likely to arise: 'Although somewhat indirectly connected with the sanitary matters at Rome, it may not be out of place here to allude to what is frequently a subject of complaint amongst foreign visitors. – The exorbitant demands made by a few hotel keepers, and the letters of lodgings generally, in the shape of indemnities in cases of death occurring in their houses. That they are fully entitled to such in case of deaths from infectious diseases, such as typhus fever, scarlatina, or small-pox, there can be no doubt, – as for re-papering the rooms and destruction of the carpets and bedding, or making them over to some charitable establishment, as is generally the case in hotels, after purification; but the case is different in the ordinary run of fatal maladies. In Rome, as elsewhere in Southern Europe, pulmonary consumption, in its later and final stages, is considered – and with some appearance of reason – to leave behind it infectious consequences: hence it has been a general custom to believe it to be dangerous to inhabit an apartment where a person labouring under phthisis has died, without a thorough disinfecting, – the removal of papering, carpets, bedding etc.; families must, therefore, be prepared for a demand under such circumstances, whereon it will be better to come to an understanding through their banker, or physician.'

From that topic we might move on to Murray's description of the Protestant burial ground which 'all foreign travellers will regard with melancholy interest. The silence and seclusion of the spot, and the inscriptions which tell the British traveller in his native tongue of those who have found their last resting-place beneath the bright skies of the Eternal City, appeal irresistibly to the heart. The cemetery has an air of romantic beauty which forms a striking contrast with the tomb of the ancient Roman and with the massive city walls and towers which overlook it. Among those who are buried here are the poets Shelley and Keats.'

Before leaving Rome for regions further south it may not be out of place to see how guidebooks deal with the subject of begging. Charlotte Eaton, at the village of Radifalconi, on the way to the city, was disappointed at not finding gems and casts from ancient medals on sale at the inn. 'The Italians seem to neglect the most obvious means of making money honestly, but spare no trouble to get at it by begging or cheating. We were assailed by a crowd of stout, sturdy clamorous beggars, any one of whom, if they had provided themselves with these casts to sell, might have made a considerable sum by us, and probably by most travellers.'

Begging is not mentioned in the early Murray guidebooks, but in the 1908 edition to Rome we read: 'It is safe to assume that all beggars are professional idlers, and of the criminal class. The honest poor do not beg. Even the physically afflicted could, in nearly every case, earn their living by work if they chose to do so. In order to meet the fierce competition in this overcrowded profession many children are intentionally maimed for life by their parents, who are then able to live in idleness on the alms obtained by the sacrifice.'

In 1897 Baedeker advises: 'Begging, which is most prevalent at the church-doors, has recently increased in frequency in the streets of Rome . . . The foolish practice of "scattering" copper coins to be struggled for by the street-arabs is highly reprehensible, and, like most idle gratuities to children, has a demoralising effect upon the recipients.'

Perhaps begging was a further corruption of tourism, because Augustus J. C. Hare, in *Cities of Southern Italy*, relates: 'Without having suffered from it, no one can imagine the pest of beggars which make a long stay in the once enchanting Amalfi almost unendurable. Three-fifths of the able-bodied men, and every other woman and child, beg. The greater part of the population now loiter idle all day long in the streets or on the beach, ready to pounce upon strangers, till the traveller, half-maddened, is driven back to his hotel, or into the higher mountains. The only hope of future comfort is *never*, under any circumstances, to be tempted to give to a beggar; once give, and you are lost.'

The South was said to begin at Naples, and judging from the remarks in most guidebooks, people ought rather to die than see it. In 1853 Murray says: 'Travellers are liable to four custom-house visitations from the frontier to Naples, which may generally be compromised for the sum of from 6 to 12 carlini. In fact the constant appeal of "buona grazia" will soon convince the traveller, however much he may disapprove of the system, that his convenience will be consulted by a compromise.'

Before entering the Kingdom of Naples we pass through the town of Aversa, which has 'acquired considerable celebrity for its lunatic asylum, called the Maddalena, established by Murat, and capable of containing 500 persons . . . one of the earliest to throw aside restraints, and to rely on moral influences founded on the basis of occupation and amusement for the cure. It was more interesting a few years ago, before the barbarous practices of the dark ages were abolished in other countries, than it is now, when the more recent system of England has left it somewhat in the background in regard to modern improvements.'

Murray expatiates tediously at times on the hotels at Naples, but his main points are that travellers should bargain with landlords on arrival and 'refuse to pay any charge which they know, from experience elsewhere, to be exorbitant. There need be no delicacy on the subject; for it is the common custom of the country. All foreigners make it a rule to adopt this precaution, and for this reason they not only pay about a third less than English travellers, but escape the annoyances and delays of disputed bills.'

There seems to have been some justification for this advice because 'the principal hotels rank among the best and dearest in Italy' but the expense of staying in them is 'greater than any which they have experienced elsewhere from the time of leaving England. No one can deny that the great hotels of Naples are distinguished by their excellent management, and by all which can reconcile the visitor to high charges; and while they continue to deserve this praise, there will always be travellers to support them without reference to expense.' He goes on to say that the landlords 'will still further consult their own interests by adopting in every branch of their establishments, and especially in the charges for apartments, a scale of prices which will put an end to the reproach that they have the dearest inns in Italy ... In these times of railroads and steam, the general public are the best patrons; and those landlords who become known for the moderation of their charges will be abundantly repaid not only by the increased number of visitors, but by the longer period during which they will be induced to stay.'

One hotel particularly noted is the newly built Hôtel des Etrangers, 'well situated, and highly spoken of for reasonable charges and an obliging landlord, who has been a courier in English families. His wife, an Englishwoman, was formerly a lady's maid in the Duke of Newcastle's family, and has introduced many English comforts into the establishment.' The hotel, renamed the Royal des Etrangers, still existed in 1912, and had an asterisk of commendation in Baedeker.

The streets at Naples were not lit at night until 1840, when oil lamps were introduced. They were shortly afterwards superseded by gas, 'which in so crowded and intricate a city has proved one of the greatest improvements which modern civilisation has effected. Within the last few years foot-pavements have been laid down in the principal thoroughfares, but such is the inveteracy of habit that even now the people can hardly be induced to relinquish their ancient custom of walking in the middle of the streets.'

The Corso of Naples, about a mile and a half in length, was

paved with flagstones and 'from morning to night, and we almost add from night to daybreak, the Corso is thronged with people and with carriages; the people shouting at the top of their voices, and the carriages threading their way between the pagodas of the lemonade-sellers, the stalls of the vendors of iced-water, the charcoal fires of the sausage dealers, and a hundred groups of busy people, whose sole occupation appears to be to pass as much of their lives as possible in the open air. It is at all times the noisiest street in Europe, and on extraordinary occasions it presents a perfect sea of human beings, swayed here and there by each successive current, and presenting to the eye of the traveller one of the most curious spectacles it is possible to imagine.'

The impression is of an Indian or oriental city today, but sixty years later Baedeker can still say: 'The life of the people in Naples is carried on with greater freedom and more careless indifference to publicity than in any other town in Europe.'

In the narrow side streets, much cooking took place in the open air, while other dealers 'tempt the crowd with fragments from the trattorie or with trays of carefully assorted cigar-ends. The female members of the community are seen going through their toilet, and performing various unpleasing acts of attention to their children, regardless of the public gaze. In summer the children often run about quite naked.'

In the words of J. C. Hare: 'Naples has been described as a paradise inhabited by devils: but they are lively, and amusing devils – insouciant and idle: good-natured and thieving: kind-hearted and lying: always laughing, except if thwarted, when they will stab their best friend without a pang. Almost everybody in Naples cheats, but cheats in as lively and pleasant a manner as is compatible with possibilities. Nearly all the officials peculate, and perhaps not more than two-thirds of the taxes ever reach the public exchequer. If the traveller is robbed, he will never secure redress . . .

'As it is the universal custom amongst the lower orders to marry at seventeen, and Neapolitan women are proverbially prolific, the tall, narrow houses in the back streets swarm with children, and are like rabbit-warrens; whole families live huddled together, but not without cleanliness or decency, though the air sometimes resounds at once with blows and cries, singing and laughter . . .

Little, however, is needed to sustain life at Naples, and there are thousands who consider a dish of beans at midday to be sumptuous fare, while the horrible condiment called pizza (made of dough baked with garlic, rancid bacon, and strong cheese) is esteemed a feast.' And so many people consider it in modern-day London.

As in most other great towns Murray assumes the traveller to have a macabre interest in cemeteries. In Naples only the rich, he says, can afford to be buried in a church, the old cemetery of Naples being used for the dead of the public hospitals, 'and for the poorest classes who cannot afford the expense of burial in the Campo Santo Nuovo or in the churches.'

The ground forms a parallelogram of upwards of 300 feet, surrounded on three sides by a lofty wall, and bounded on the forth side by an arcade. It contains 366 deep round pits, some of which are arranged under the arcade, but the greater part are in the area. The pits are covered with large stones; their number, of course, gives one for every day of the year and one over. One of them is opened every evening, and cleared out to make room for the dead of the day. A priest resides upon the spot, and towards evening the miscellaneous funeral takes place. By this time a large pile of bodies is generally accumulated. They are brought by their relatives or by the hospital servants, stripped of every particle of clothing upon the spot, and left to be disposed of at the appointed time, unattended, in most instances, by the person to whom they were bound in life by ties of kindred or feeling. The bodies are thrown into the pit, with as much unconcern as if they were the plague patients of Florence whom Boccaccio has described; quick lime is then thrown in, and the stone covering is replaced for another year. As many as forty bodies are frequently thus disposed of in a single evening. The pits when first opened are generally so full of carbonic acid gas that a light is extinguished at its mouth; and it is said that whenever they have been examined the day after a burial, the bodies have been overrun with rats and enormous cock-roaches, which clear the bones more expeditiously than the lime.

Perhaps there would be fewer dead to inter at such charnel

houses if the hospitals were run better, Murray suggests, when mentioning the main hospital at Naples: 'The extent of its resources are unknown, as its ample revenues are administered by one of the great officers of the court, who is practically irresponsible.'

One of the most painful spectacles for nineteenth-century British travellers was the treatment of animals, especially donkeys and dogs, who seem, on the whole, to have had a worse time than human beings. 'The grossest brutality to animals used to be a Neapolitan characteristic,' J. C. Hare says, adding that the local retort to ill-usage was: 'So what? They aren't Christians.' For this attitude, Hare adds, the priest was chiefly responsible.

Macmillan's guide at the turn of the century reports: 'A local Society for the Prevention of Cruelty to Animals has done a vast amount of good, though it has met with the most violent opposition from the very persons who are chiefly interested in its operations. The continual protest on the part of English travellers against acts of wanton cruelty has probably more effect upon the Neapolitan cabman than any number of police restrictions, the justice or reasonableness of which he is wholly incapable of understanding. The Society has done immense work in removing from the streets of Naples sights and sounds which were sickening to English eyes and ears. Collecting-boxes are to be found in all the best hotels.'

In 1853 the area of the Grotto del Cane, in the environs of the city, was a place for stray dogs to avoid. 'This celebrated cave, which the books of our early childhood classed among the wonders of the world, is nothing more than a small aperture, resembling a cellar, at the base of a rocky hill. The cavern, known to Pliny, is continually exhaling from its sides and floor volumes of steam mixed with carbonic acid gas . . . Cluverius says that the grotto was once used as a place of execution for Turkish captives, who were shut up within its walls and left to die of suffocation, a merciful fate compared with the lingering tortures which the Mohametan pirates of the same period inflicted on their Christian captives. It is said that Don Pedro de Toledo tried the same experiment upon two galley slaves, with fatal results. Addison, on his visit to the cavern, made a series of very interesting experiments which anticipated all those performed by subsequent observers. He found that a viper was nine minutes in dying on the first trial, and ten minutes on the second, this increased vitality being attributable, in his opinion, to the large stock of air which it had inhaled after the first trial. He found that the dog was not longer in expiring on the first experiment than on the second. It has frequently been asserted that the dog, upon which this experiment is usually performed for the amusement of travellers, is so accustomed to "die" that he becomes indifferent to his fate. We disbelieve this statement altogether, and on the simple ground that we have never seen any dog in perfect health who has long been the subject of the exhibition. The effects of the gas, moreover, are seen quite as well, if not better, in a torch, a lighted candle, or a pistol.'

Augustus Hare says in 1911, 'Extortionate wretches generally swarm in the neighbourhood with animals which they offer to "die" for the amusement of visitors; a dog is the favourite victim.' Baedeker, a few years later, tells us: 'Dogs are no longer provided for the exhibition of this cruel experiment, but the curiosity of the traveller is sufficiently gratified by observing that a light is immediately extinguished when brought in contact with the vapour.'

The final comment on this matter will be taken from Macmillan's guidebook of 1905: 'The fumes being most powerful close to the floor, a dog or other animal is soon overcome by breathing the fumes, and a wretched dog is kept in readiness for the cruel and vulgar experiment, on the consent of the inhuman visitor' – thus putting the blame where it really lay.

After seeing the churches and picture galleries of Naples, and its street life, the traveller may now visit the asterisked environs, the first of which must surely be the ascent of Vesuvius, 'for many centuries one of the most active volcanoes in the world'. The mid-Victorian Murray gives a blow by blow description of the fifty-three eruptions up to that time, in the last of which: 'A young Polish officer was struck by a mass of large size, which caused a compound fracture of the thigh, lacerating the artery in such a manner that he bled to death on the spot. An American officer was struck on the arm by a stone, which stripped the flesh down to the elbow, producing alarming haemorrhage, which endangered his life for many days.' Perhaps for the rest of his time on earth he considered that Goethe had much to answer for, in saying that Vesuvius was 'a peak of hell, rising out of Paradise', thus tempting all tourists to climb it.

The ascent was usually made from Resina, reached by railway

or private carriage, a place 'infested by self-called guides, pretended mineral dealers, and padroni of horses and mules, who are most importunate in their offers of services, which are too frequently both dear and worthless'.

A kind of sedan chair with twelve bearers 'is required for delicate ladies and invalids. A great coat or cloak, and a warm neckerchief, to put on as soon as the ascent is made, a strong walking stick, and stout boots, may be mentioned as the *desiderata* of the excursion.' During an eruption, hundreds of people assemble to witness the sight: 'When a stream of lava is rolling slowly down the mountain, the kettle is boiled on its surface and the eggs are cooked in its crevices. Coins also are usually dropped into the lava, which is then detached from the mass and preserved as a reminiscence.

'The ascent over the loose scoriae generally occupies about an hour, varying of course with the state of the cone. At times it is necessary for the guides to assist the traveller, which they do by strapping a long leathern belt around his waist, and pulling him up the steep incline by main force.'

By 1912 there was no need for such a scramble, because Thomas Cook & Co. had constructed a rack-and-pinion railway almost to the summit, to which firm the thanks of tourists were due, Baedeker says, 'for the energy with which, in face of serious difficulties, they maintain order and discipline among the guides and others, who have been accustomed for generations to practise extortion upon travellers'.

From Vesuvius our intrepid traveller would visit Pompeii, having read the Younger Pliny's vivid account, reprinted verbatim in his Murray, of its eruption in AD 79. A copy of Bulwer-Lytton's *Last Days of Pompeii* may also have been in his knapsack, and if he wanted to stay overnight, Murray would tell him that the Hôtel Bellevue was 'a new inn, close to the railway, kept by S. Prosperi, a very civil and obliging landlord'.

The guidebook leads one from ruin to ruin, describing each house in ample detail, never failing to point out the remains of the dead: 'One cast of a young girl, part of which still exists, possessed exceeding elegance of form; the neck and breast especially were perfect models of feminine beauty.'

The House of the Vestals is: 'A double house, comprising a vestibule, an atrium with the usual apartments on each side, formerly richly paved with mosaics and decorated with luxurious pictures by no means in accordance with the name given to it.'

This sneaky form of euphemism, perhaps intended by Murray's handbook to indicate those risqué ornaments a gentleman might wish to see, was employed in the description of the House of Sallust, whose Venereum 'consists of a small court, the real prototype of the Oriental harem, surrounded by a portico, of octagonal columns, a sacrarium dedicated to Diana, two sleeping-rooms at the sides with glazed windows looking into the court . . . Every part is elaborately decorated, and the paintings are appropriately expressive of the use to which the apartments were applied. The sleeping rooms contain pictures of Mars, Venus, and Cupid, and the entire wall at the back of the court is covered with a large painting, representing the story of Diana and Actaeon, an evident allusion to the danger of prying too closely into the mysteries of this portion of the mansion.'

One is also warned of, or guided to, the Tavern: '. . . a building so called from the number of cooking vessels, tripods, pots, and pans of bronze and earthenware which were found in it. The walls are covered with licentious paintings, representing the usual routine of low tavern scenes.'

Our attention is also directed to a baker's shop, where: 'The frequent occurrence of the phallus over the entrance doors, and the obscene pictures found in several of the houses, have induced the belief that this was the quarter of the courtesans.'

In the House of the Triumphant Hercules certain statues were said to be in bad taste, 'but curious from their variety and arrangement; among them are, Love riding a dolphin, a bearded satyr, a stag, a fawn extracting a thorn from a goat's foot, a goat caressing its young one lying in the lap of a shepherdess, and others which we need not particularise'.

Such paintings and statues presented problems to guidebook writers of the Victorian Age. Baedeker, as late as 1912, says of the Lupanare, which was locked: 'The bad character of the house is sufficiently indicated by the paintings and inscriptions.' In the next edition we are informed that: 'Most of the licentious paintings have been either destroyed or removed.'

At the entrance to the House of the Vettii is 'a representation of Priapus (covered) . . . Beside the kitchen is a room (locked) containing paintings not suited for general inspection and a statuette of Priapus.' Other guidebooks ignore the issue, though a later Baedeker sums it up by saying that though the best of the paintings have been removed, many of those left 'merit inspection. The scenes present a uniformly soft, erotic character, corresponding to the peaceful and pleasure-loving taste of the age.'

Visiting Capri in 1853 called for the hire of a ten-oared boat from Sorrento, at the cost of five ducats. The twenty miles there and back enabled the traveller to return the same evening, since accommodation on the island was said to be 'indifferent'. An Englishman who had spent three days there, however, was so delighted with the island's salubrity and scenery that 'he made it his residence for thirty years'. By the next edition of Murray three inns offered 'clean and tolerably comfortable accommodations'. He also mentions that the Blue Grotto was discovered by two Englishmen swimming off the coast in 1822.

By 1912 steamers took only two hours to do the journey, though Baedeker tells us that 'on windy days the roughness of the water is apt to occasion sea-sickness'. Later in the nineteenth-century, when tourists (and artists) went there in large numbers, fourteen hotels are listed, as well as numerous lodgings.

J. C. Hare comments that the natives are 'pleasant and civil in their manners, and full of courtesies to strangers. The women are frequently beautiful, and good models may be obtained here by artists more cheaply than anywhere else. One lira a day is the usual price of a model, and yet the artist may feel he is doing no injustice, as 60c. a day would be the wages of a hard day's work in the fields.'

CHAPTER NINE

SOUTHERN ITALY AND SICILY

If our traveller wants to visit the provinces south of Naples he will learn from his Murray of 1853 that the inns in the remoter districts are 'as bad and comfortless as they were in the time of Montaigne, except that the wooden shutters which kept out the light as well as wind have mostly been replaced by glazed panels. The cookery in such places is on a par with the accommodation, and we may, from experience, congratulate every traveller in the mountain and inland districts who can make his own omelet, and instruct the padrona how to cook a dish of ham and eggs. These commodities are generally to be found in the highland villages, where even milk and butter are rarely to be met with, and they are real luxuries to an Englishman after the watery soup and cheese which constitute the chief contents of a country larder.'

Baedeker tells us that Italian customers 'have no hesitation in ordering away ill-cooked or stale viands, and they often inspect the fish or meat before it is cooked and make a bargain as to the price'. He goes on to say: 'Moderation in eating and drinking is, of course, imperative. The appetite gradually decreases under a southern sun ... The traveller should be more than usually scrupulous in rejecting fish or eggs as to whose freshness there can be the slightest suspicion.'

Sixty years after Murray, Hare wrote: 'The vastness and some-times ugliness of the districts to be traversed, the barrenness and filth of the inns, the roughness of the natives, the torment of mosquitoes, the terror of earthquakes, the insecurity of the roads, and the far more serious risk of malaria or of typhoid from the bad water, are natural causes which have hitherto kept strangers away from the south. But every year these risks are being lessened, and some of the travellers along the southern railways to Sicily may well be induced to linger on the way, though, with the exception of the rebuilt hotel at Reggio, the inns of Calabria are still such as none but hardy tourists may care to encounter.'

With regard to public safety, he goes on: '. . . there is a general transmitted feeling of insecurity in the south, and it is still the custom in Calabria for lonely country houses to be prepared for a state of siege, while no Italian gentleman ventures to go out unarmed and unattended, and, on returning to his country villa, is always met at the railway station by armed servants, with horses which fail not to have pistols in their holsters. It is not a great many years since the cracking of whips was forbidden on the road from Rome to Naples, because it served as a call to brigands, and the Neapolitan peasantry still regard brigandage as by no means dishonourable: it was rather an attraction by which a young fellow secured the favour of his love, and brigands were always to be pitied and sympathised with. A pedestrian foreigner is still apt to feel, especially in Calabria, as if every man's hand was against him, and, if he travels in desolate places, entertains (though needlessly) still as much dread of a stealthy pistol or stiletto, as of the fury of the sheep-dogs, from whom the fate of Actaeon seems constantly impending. It does do to run from these latter: the sight of a man picking up a stone is usually sufficient to keep them at bay.'

The habits of domestic life in the South are said to be very primitive. 'It is a common thing for a Calabrian woman, far advanced in pregnancy, to go up to the forest for fuel, and to be there surprised by the pains of childbirth, perhaps hastened by toil. She is nowise dismayed at the solitude around her, or the distance from home, but, as in some of the Caucasian tribes, delivers herself of her infant, which she folds up in her apron, and, after a little rest, carries back to her cottage.'

In his 1853 edition Murray informs whoever is about to do the three hundred Italian miles to Reggio that no postroad in Italy is 'so little frequented or abounds in such magnificent scenery as this high road into Calabria'. Highway robbery rarely happened, except on the byroads which 'are still so much infested with robbers that no one should attempt to explore them without the advice of the local authorities'. On entering the province of Basilicata, we are told: 'It is much to be regretted that the absence of good roads, and the danger of travelling by unfrequented paths in a country so often infested with brigands, renders a large number of interesting and picturesque towns almost inaccessible to the traveller.'

Alighting from the lumbering coach we find Atella to be 'a miserable place, half dilapidated by the earthquake of 1851, with a population of 1200 souls, scarcely less wretched than their inhabitants'. The largest town in Basilicata, Rionero, with a population of ten thousand, contains 'nothing to arrest attention, except the terrible traces which at least one half of it presents of the earthquake which spread so much terror and destruction throughout the whole district round Monte Volture on the 14th August 1851'. Hare describes the area as still 'earthquake-stricken' sixty years later.

Lagonegro, where Murray's romantic prose cranks into top gear, is 'picturesquely situated in a cold and gloomy position at the extremity of a narrow glen . . . At its southern entrance the road crosses two branches of the Trecchina by bridges thrown across the deep and narrow ravines in which they flow, and proceeds thence through a bleak and gloomy defile characterised by the picturesque wilderness for which the ravines of this province are remarkable.'

A battle fought here in 1806 between the Neapolitans and the French army of Joseph Buonaparte was 'one of the few instances in which native forces showed a gallant spirit of resistance. During the second invasion towns on this route occupied by the French were the scenes of the most terrible executions. Colletta the historian affirms that he himself saw a person *impaled* "con barbarie Ottomana," by order of a French colonel who had been a prisoner in the Levant. Many others, according to the same authority, were stoned to death, or subjected to the most terrible tortures.'

Guidebooks later in the century tend to play down accounts of such atrocities, but Hare tells us that one band of brigands in 1865 'captured seven men and fourteen women, whom they took away to a place called Maccolata. News of this enormity reaching the authorities, they sent a force to encounter the brigands. The latter, finding themselves in a difficult pass, cut off two heads of their victims and sent them to the officer in command, threatening to send the rest if the pursuit were continued. While this was going on, some of the brigands were dancing and drinking, and others were playing the guitar . . . and the authorities retired.' In 1876 another gang boiled a herdsman alive in the forest of Silla, 'and compelled his subordinates to eat him'.

For all their barbarity the bandits were said to be god-fearing and superstitious, as was revealed in the trial of one Musolino in 1902: 'If he wishes his affair on hand to go well, he sends to the curé of his village a few soldi to say a mass to the Madonna for him. If it turns out well, he will perhaps send a rich necklace to the image of the Virgin in the church. To the Madonna he owes all, and would on no account offend her by eating meat on the day sacred to her.'

One band pillaged the carrier's waggon plying between the provinces and the capital, though it was strongly escorted. On one occasion they seized a waggon loaded 'with all the paraphernalia of a newly established court of justice, and, dressing up in the judge's wig and robes, amused themselves by holding a mock court of justice on an unfortunate traveller they had captured and sentencing him to immediate execution'.

Methods of repression were on a level with the ferocity of the brigands themselves. A bandit, in the early nineteenth century, whose pleasure it was to roast his prisoners alive was, says Augustus J. C. Hare, 'taken by the French troops and roasted by them between fires, blaspheming to the last'. In the days of Murat, those 'who did not die fighting usually died under torture or at the stake, or succeeded in fleeing to Sicily. Benincasa, a leader betrayed by some of his followers, was tied, like Samson, while he slept in a wood near Cassano, and taken into Cosenza. There General Manhes ordered his hands to be struck off, and him to be taken mutilated round the town of S. Giovanni, his native place. First, they cut off his right hand and tied up the stump, so as to keep him alive. He did not utter a sound, but with terrific cynicism held out the other hand to the board. The two hands were then hung by strings upon his chest. The same day he was escorted from Cosenza to San Giovanni, in Fiore. One of the soldiers gave him some food and drink. The next evening he slept, but in the morning he refused the ministrations of the priest sent to him, and ascended the ladder to his death with *sang-froid*.'

Eventually, our coach brings us, unscathed we hope, to a place called Maida, 'a small town of 2800 souls, the name of which has been made familiar to the English traveller by the victory gained by the British army under Sir John Stuart over the French army in 1806' – and which, incidentally, gave the name to a familiar district of London, Maida Vale.

The French army occupied a strong defensive position, from which it would have been hard for the British to dislodge them. Holding the smaller British army in contempt, the French advanced to what they thought would be complete victory. Against the 7000 French the British had 4800 men, and Murray quotes the despatch of Sir John Stuart: the two enemies, 'at a distance of about 100 yards, fired reciprocally a few rounds, when, as if by mutual agreement, the firing was suspended, and in close compact order and awful silence they advanced towards each other until their bayonets began to cross. At this momentous crisis the enemy became appalled. They broke, and endeavoured to fly, but it was too late; they were overtaken with the most dreadful slaughter.' It was the last time British troops fought in Italy until the First World War.

At the furthest point of Italy's big toe we reach the Rock of Scylla. The rock, 'whose dangers have been made so familiar to every reader by the Greek and Latin poets, have long ceased to be formidable, and the timid Neapolitan or Sicilian navigator sails by it without any apprehension. But although deprived of its terrors, the classical traveller will examine with lively interest this celebrated spot, immortalized by the greatest poets of ancient and modern times.'

On the road from Naples east towards Otranto, an excursion is taken off the main track to the Lake of Amsanctus, the only place known, Murray says, besides that of the Valley of Death in Java, 'where life is endangered in the open air by the evolution of noxious gases'. He quotes a Dr Daubeny, who visited the spot in 1834: 'The quantity of mephitic vapour which proceeded from the lake was such as to oblige us (the wind being in the north) to take a circuit towards the east, in order not to meet the noxious blast; instances not unfrequently occurring of animals and even men, who have imprudently ascended the ravine, being suffocated by a sudden gust of air wafted from the lake.' Baedeker says that the vapours are only deadly to small animals. Virgil described it as 'the grinning jaws of Hell', but Hare comes closest to reality when he tells us that a friend 'was able to take his morning bath from a boat in it, and although the curious onlookers veritably believed the audacious one would never come up when he took a header, he did so, enjoyed his swim, and was heartily congratulated on it'.

Murray points out that the beauty of the women of Ariano 'is the theme of every traveller', but Hare gives the palm to Tiriolo whose 'women are particularly striking for their Amazonian figures. Their dress adds to their masculine appearance. I met several who were carrying water on their heads, and I could not but admire the magnificence of their forms. They had their gown tucked up so completely behind them that it could scarcely be observed, while a piece of red cloth, employed as a petticoat, was carelessly wrapped around them, and as it opened displayed a snow-white chemise reaching to their knees. They wore neither shoes nor stockings.'

Social conditions improve, according to Murray, when the traveller reaches the Adriatic coast. 'The road along the Marina between Barletta and Bari is one of the most pleasing on the east coast of Italy, and is famous even in this country of fine scenery; but its attractions are due more to the general air of civilization and the high cultivation of the country than to any remarkable features of natural beauty.'

Confirmation of this is evident when we come to Giovenazzo, which is 'remarkable for its admirable poor-house, capable of containing 2000 persons. At present upwards of 500 children are there maintained and instructed in useful arts. In a separate part of the establishment, children and youths condemned to imprisonment by the laws are similarly instructed with a view to reclaim them from their evil habits.'

Bari, with its tolerably good inn, 'is an active but somewhat gloomy place, and . . . has several good streets, and a convenient port formed by two moles.' Hare, sixty years later, condemns the city out of hand, as having 'all the characteristics of the meanest part of Naples – flat roofs, dilapidated, whitewashed houses, and a swarming, noisy, dirty, begging, brutalised population'.

He gives a similar bill of wretchedness to Taranto, 'with its narrow streets, high white houses, and flat roofs, and its miserable, filthy scrofulous population'. He goes on to tell us of the method of farming mussels, which has been in existence for centuries. 'Ropes are plunged into the water, and, when festooned with shells, are drawn up, and carried to the market, where the purchaser choose his mussels himself, makes his bargain, and then has them detached.'

Baedeker of the same year warns us that oysters are dangerous, 'cases of typhus have been traced to the consumption of oysters from Santa Lucia, where the water in which the shellfish are kept often leaves something to be desired in point of cleanliness'.

Regarding the prevalence of Tarantella dancing, which takes place in the neighbourhood of every town, Murray quotes a medical man as saying that the spider does not produce any injurious effects whatsoever, though he adds: 'The cure [for the supposed bite of a tarantula, or 'female' madness] is a general signal for a musical holiday throughout the village in which it occurs; feasting and dancing are always added, and the process of cure is consequently so expensive, that refractory husbands, it is said, have in late years refused to sanction it', such occasions being thought of by most writers 'as the remains of the orgies observed in the celebration of the worship of Bacchus'.

The woman so stricken continues dancing, 'as long as her breath and strength allow, occasionally selecting one of the bystanders as her partner, and sprinkling her face with cold water, a large vessel of which is always placed near at hand. While she rests at times, the guests are invited to relieve her by dancing by turns after the fashion of the country; and when, overcome by restless lassitude and faintness, she determines to give over for the day, she takes the pail or jar of water, and pours its contents entirely over her person, from her head downwards. This is the signal for her friends to undress and convey her to bed; after which the rest of the company endeavour to further her recovery by devouring a substantial repast, which is always prepared on the occasion.'

Instead of a page or so, Baedeker gives only a few sceptical lines, saying that the bite of the spider was 'formerly believed to be venomous and is still said by the natives to cause convulsions and even madness, for which music and dancing are supposed to be effectual remedies'.

After commenting on the remarkable beauty of the women of Martano, Murray brings us to Otranto, 'rendered familiar to the English visitor by the romance of Horace Walpole. The realities of it, however, will by no means be commensurate with the notions inspired by that well-known fiction.' In 1480 the Turks captured the town and butchered 12,000 of its 20,000 inhabitants, and many parts of the town and neighbourhood were said to retain marks of the bombardment sustained during its recapture.

Instead of the overland journey one can go from Naples to Otranto by sea. The vessel is a light sailing boat but 'as its arrival and departure are uncertain, passengers are sometimes obliged to wait a week or a fortnight, and the length of passage is of course doubtful, sometimes occupying many days, at others only 12 hours. The fare is 5 dollars, half of which goes to the government, and half to the captain. Passengers provide themselves with everything, and the captain expects to be invited to breakfast and dinner.'

The assumption was that those who travelled to the southern part of Italy would sooner or later continue to Sicily, the nearest port to the island being Reggio di Calabria – an unfortunate town if ever there was one. At the time of Murray, 1853, the place had a very good inn, and was agreeably situated 'in the midst of natural beauties which are not surpassed by any other part of Europe', being 'a handsome and well-built town, with spacious streets, rising from the broad and very noble Marina towards the richly cultivated slopes of the hills behind it, among which are scattered numerous beautiful villas of the wealthy residents . . . It is difficult to imagine anything more delightful than a lounge in the colonnade of the fountain in a cool summer's evening when the magnificent mountains behind Messina are thrown into relief by the setting sun . . .

With these advantages, added to its agreeable and refined society, the hospitality of its inhabitants, and the amusements of a good theatre, Reggio cannot fail to offer a pleasant sojourn.'

All this changed in 1908, when an earthquake killed five thousand of the town's 35,000 inhabitants. 'Not a building escaped without injury,' Baedeker says, 'and those that remained standing had to be pulled down. But it has already been resolved to rebuild the town on its old site . . .'

Messina, across the straits in Sicily, had an even more calamitous history, for in 1740 a plague 'carried off' 40,000 people, and in 1854 cholera claimed 16,000 victims; but an account of the earthquake in 1783, given in *Pictures From Sicily*, 1864, by W. H. Bartlett, is worth recounting:

> The cries of the dying; the shrieks of those who were half-buried under the ruins; the wild terror with which others, who were still able, attempted to make their escape; the despair of fathers, mothers, and husbands, bereft of those who were dearest to them, – these formed altogether a scene of horror such as can but seldom occur in the history of the calamities of the human race. Amid that fearful scene, instances of the most heroic courage and of the most generous affection were displayed. Mothers, regardless of their own safety, rushed into every danger to snatch their children from death. Conjugal and filial affection prompted deeds not less desperate and heroic. But no sooner did the earthquake cease than the poor wretches who had escaped began to feel the influence of very different passions. When they returned to visit the ruins, to seek out the situation of their fallen dwellings, to inquire into the fate of their families, to procure food and collect some remains of their former fortunes, such as found their circumstances the most wretched became suddenly animated with rage, which nothing but wild despair could inspire. The distinction of ranks and the order of society were disregarded, and property eagerly violated. Murder, rapine, and lawless robbery reigned among the smoking ruins . . .

In 1848, when the people of Messina rebelled against the king of Naples, the place was mercilessly bombarded, and the Neapolitan forces on entering the town burned whole streets, committing 'the most unheard-of ravages. Some of the details of their cruelties are really too horrible to be cited.' The carnage was only stopped when French and British warships standing off-shore – in spite of neutrality having been imposed on them by their governments – intervened in the name of humanity to stop the slaughter. And then in 1908 came the worst disaster of all, when the same earthquake which flattened Reggio killed 96,000 people.

On landing at Messina, Hare tells us that it is almost useless to ask one's way. 'One is sure to be answered by – "Who knows?" or with the assertion in reply to any remonstrance, that a housewife has no need to know the way anywhere but to her church or her fountain.' Should you care to go along the coast to the lighthouse at Cape Pelorus, 'travellers are beset by the rough, noisy inhabitants of the village, and a dirty begging crowd accompanies them to the lighthouse, and prevents their having any enjoyment'.

As for the travelling in the interior, Bartlett says, with echoes of Charlotte Eaton: 'I shall spare the reader a detailed account of our progress from Syracuse to Girgenti, in which we made full proof of the deplorable filth and misery of the interior of the island. Suffice it to say that we passed the first night at Palazzolo, the second at Biscari, and the third at Terranova. The first was bad, the second worse, and the third so utterly unsupportable, that to escape the onslaught of the vermin I ordered the mules in the middle of the night and departed. No sooner on horseback, however, than the sense of fatigue returned with increased force, and one rides on half asleep, and at every moment, ready to drop, until the rising sun awakens a forced and feverish activity; and so one goes forward the whole day under the blazing heat.'

Thirty years later the hotels in the larger towns of the island were said by Hare to be excellent, but that if the traveller takes the train to Taormina he will suffer much at the hands of railway officials, 'who by night thrust emigrants into first and second class carriages'. He also reports that the recent abolition of the rural police has brought insecurity, 'causing an exaggerated report of brigandage, which has consequently fallen upon the less populated districts, and has deterred most Italian travellers from prolonging their rambles into a country which is nevertheless full of the elements of enjoyment'.

In a later edition he warns travellers, regarding the main cities, 'not to take the same liberties in the suburbs that he may take with impunity at Florence or Rome: though, for that matter, the lonely or the rash visitor may find himself victimised unpleasantly in those of any large town.'

In climbing the volcanic Mount Etna: 'The deepest ashes are very fatiguing, and most visitors are grievously overwhelmed by sickness, induced more by the terrible cold than the noxious gases, before reaching the top, where the guides will often cover them up in the warm ashes till they recover.' At the summit: 'The desolation is supreme – all vegetation has long ceased: there is no sound from beast, bird, or insect. In later times Etna has been supposed to be a place of torment for Anne Boleyn, perverter of the faith in the person of its "Defender"!'

Of all the perils, however, perhaps the greatest was that which at one time threatened in the catacombs of Syracuse. Hare quotes from *Wanderungen in Sicilien* by a German traveller, Gregorovius. 'Twenty years ago a professor, with six pupils, to whom he wished to explain the wonders of the city of tombs, was lost there. They wandered long and despairingly through the horrible labyrinth in search of the entrance till they died of exhaustion, and they were found lying side by side, four miles distant from the gate. Since that time holes for light and air have been pierced in the galleries, through which the dubious daylight shimmers mysteriously into this fearful Hades.'

CHAPTER TEN

THE SOUTH OF FRANCE

Even as early as 1848 Murray had no illusions about the charms of the South of France, nor did he wish his readers to have any, and his comments are repeated in all later editions:

> The Englishman who knows the S. of France only from books
> – who there finds Provence described as the cradle of Poetry and
> Romance, the paradise of the Troubadours, a land teeming with
> oil, wine, silk, and perfumes, has probably formed in his mind a
> picture of a region beautiful to behold, and charming to inhabit.
> Nothing, however, can differ more widely from reality. Nature
> has altogether an arid character; – in summer a sky of copper, an
> atmosphere loaded with dust, the earth scorched rather than
> parched by the unmitigated rays of the sun, which overspread
> every thing with a lurid glare. The hills rise above the surface in
> masses of bare rock, without any covering of soil, like the dry
> bones of a wasted skeleton. Only on the low grounds, which can
> be reached by irrigation, does any verdure appear. There is a
> sombre, melancholy sternness in the landscape of the South. The
> aching eye in vain seeks to repose on a patch of green, and the
> inhabitant of the North would not readily purchase the clear
> cloudless sky of Provence with the verdure of a misty England.
> Neither the bush-like vine nor the mop-headed mulberry, strip-
> ped of its leaves for a great part of the summer, nor the tawny
> green olive, whose foliage looks as though powdered with dust,

will at all compensate in a picturesque point of view for forests
of oak, ash, and beech.

After several hundred more words of this, he treats us to a
disquisition on the character of the people. 'Their fervid temperament knows no control or moderation; hasty and headstrong in
disposition, they are led by very slight religious or political
excitement, on sudden impulses, to the committal of acts of violence
unknown in the North. They are rude in manner, coarse in aspect,
and harsh in speech, their patois being unintelligible, even to the
French themselves, not unlike the Spanish dialect of Catalonia.
From loudness of tone, and energy of gesture, they appear always
as though going to fight when merely carrying on an ordinary
conversation. The traveller who happens to fall into the hands of
the ruffianly porters at Avignon will be able to judge if this be an
exaggerated picture.'

Murray goes on to say that anyone who thinks the climate of
England is bad should try that of the South of France. 'The
variations between summer and winter are marked by the dead
olive, and vine trees killed by the frost; and the torrid influence of
summer by the naked beds of torrents left without water. In many
years not a drop of rain falls in June, July, and August, and the
quantity is commonly very small: the great heats occur between
the middle of July and the end of September, yet even in summer
scorching heat alternates with the most piercing cold; and the
vicissitudes are so sudden and severe, that strong persons, much
more invalids, should beware how they yield to the temptation of
wearing thin clothing, and of abandoning cloaks and great coats.'

If this were the case (and having lived some years in the South
of France I can say that there is at least some truth in Murray's
assessment), why did people go there in such numbers? Especially
when they went on to read that another plague in that part of the
world was that of

mosquitoes, which, to an inhabitant of the North, unaccustomed
to their venomous bite, will alone suffice to destroy all pleasure
in travelling. They appear in May, and last sometimes to November; and the only good which the mistral effects is that it modifies

the intensely hot air of summer, and represses, momentarily, these pestilential insects. They are not idle by day, but it is at night that the worn-out traveller needing repose is most exposed to the excruciating torments inflicted by this cruel insect. Woe to him who for the sake of coolness leaves his window open for a minute; attracted by the light they will pour in by myriads. It is better to be stifled by the most oppressive heat than to go mad. Even closed shutters and a mosquito curtain, with which all beds in good inns are provided, are ineffectual in protecting the sleeper. A scrutiny of the walls, and a butchery of all that appear, may lessen the number of enemies; but a single one effecting an entry, after closing the curtains and tucking up the bed-clothes with the utmost care, does all the mischief. The sufferer awakes in the middle of the night in a state of fever, and adieu to all further prospect of rest. The pain inflicted by the bites is bad enough, but it is the air of triumph with which the enemy blows his trumpet, the tingling, agonising buzzing which fills the air, gradually advancing nearer and nearer, announcing the certainty of a fresh attack, which carries the irritation to the highest pitch.

I have never read a more perfect description of their tactics and torments, and Murray goes on to tell us that the pain and swellings last for several days, and that there is no remedy but patience. 'The state of the blood at that time, however, considerably modifies or increases the amount and duration of suffering. It is said to be the female only which inflicts the sting.'

Another danger is from scorpions, which are sometimes brought into the house with the firewood, and might also be found 'in the folds of the bed-curtains or sheets. Instances, however, of persons being bitten by this foul insect are very rare indeed: from its nature it is fearful, and, when discovered, endeavours to run away and hide itself.'

Having fed us the disadvantages first, in no uncertain terms, Murray brings out a somewhat sweeter pill: 'There is one little corner of Provence which combines remarkable picturesque scenery with a climate so serene and warm, and well protected from the injurious blasts, that its productions are almost tropical in their nature. This is a narrow strip bordering on the blue Mediterranean, extending from Toulon to Nice. It is a favoured region, the true garden of Provence, the real paradise of the Troubadours, sheltered from the injurious mistral . . .'

In such early days the approach to the South of France was on steamboats down the Rhône, being 'almost without exception managed by English engineers', starting every morning from Lyons. The inn at Tain was classified as 'middling', and one downriver at Valence as 'not at all bad, with some pretensions to English comforts, but rather dear. Try here the sparkling St. Peray, an excellent wine, but inferior to Champagne.' There was also a boarding house, kept by two English Protestant ladies.

Later, one could go by railway, and in 1890 the inn at Tain was described as 'a mere cabaret'. If one survived the rigours of the journey, there was, near Avignon, 'a well-managed Hydropathic establishment and pleasant boarding house, in a handsome château. Part of it is of the 14th century. It is under the direction of Dr. Masson, and may be found a pleasant half-way house for invalids going to or returning from a more southern climate.'

In whatever town our traveller stops Murray never fails to inform him of the unpleasantnesses which took place during the French Revolution. At Avignon, Marshall Brune, though Lord Exmouth's passport was in his pocket, 'was murdered by an infuriated mob of Provençal royalists, who, on receiving news of the Battle of Waterloo, and instigated by hatred of Napoleon, rose upon their adversaries, and committed all sorts of atrocities'.

On another page we are treated to an account of the infamous Glacière: 'The tower, so called from an ice-house in a garden near it, stands close to the tower of the Inquisition. Into its depths were hurled no less than 60 unfortunate and innocent persons, females as well as men, by a band of democrats in Oct. 1791. The prisoners were dragged from their cells, and poignarded or struck down; but some of the victims were precipitated from above before life was yet extinct; and to finish the deed, quick-lime in large quantities was thrown down upon the mangled heap of dead and dying.'

Romance, as if the opposite face of the coin to death, was always well represented in Victorian guidebooks: 'Continuing along the Rue de Lices, we shall find the last relic of the *Church of the*

Cordeliers, in which Petrarch's Laura, a lady of the family of De Sade, was buried. The church, destroyed at the Revolution, is now reduced to a fragment of the tower and side walls.'

Arthur Young, at the end of the previous century, described Laura's tomb as 'nothing but a stone in the pavement, with a figure engraved on it, partly effaced, surrounded by an inscription in Gothic letters, and another on the wall adjoining, with the armorial bearings of the De Sade family'. Murray adds that this 'has entirely disappeared, having been broken open, and the contents of the tomb scattered, by the Revolutionists'.

Vaucluse, where John Stuart Mill stayed, was the site of Petrarch's retirement, and 'the Hôtel de Petrarque et Laure is rather a café frequented by Sunday excursionists. Formerly the landlord was a good cook, and, judging from the Strangers' Book, the fried trout and eels, soupe à la bisque, and coquille d'écrevisse, made a far deeper impression on some visitors than the souvenir of Laura; Petrarch himself has mentioned the fish of the Sorgues with praise.'

Going southwest into the Languedoc – then, as now, the 'wrong' side of the Rhône – we may refer to the impressions of Charlotte Eaton, the intrepid lady-traveller quoted earlier. She found that part of France looking dull, uninteresting and neglected: '... the want of wood, of corn, of pasture, of animals, and even of birds; its general desertion both by the proprietor and the peasant, and the absence of life and human habitation, have a most melancholy effect, and accord but too well with the heartless and discontented appearance of the people, who herd together in villages composed of long, narrow streets of miserable hovels, the filth and wretchedness of which I shall never forget. Not a single neat cottage by the way-side, or rural hamlet, or snug farm-house is to be seen; even the château is rare, and when it appears, it is in a state of dilapidation and decay, and the very abode of gloom; not surrounded with pleasure-grounds, or woods, or parks, or gardens, but with a filthy village appended to its formal court-yard. How often did the cheerful cottages, and happy country seats of our smiling country, recur to my mind as I journeyed through the bepraised, but dreary scenes of Languedoc and Provence!'

Nîmes was the birthplace of Nicot, Murray says, a physician

who first introduced tobacco into France (called after him nicotiana, or nicotine); and of Guizot, the historian, 'whose father, an advocate, was guillotined during the Reign of Terror'.

Montpellier is thought little enough of as regards climate since, though 'it bears a name familiar as the type of salubrity and mildness of climate, the place will not in reality answer the expectations of those who seek either a soft air or a beautiful position. Indeed it is difficult to understand how it came to be chosen by the physicians of the North as a retreat for consumptive patients; since nothing is more trying to weak lungs than its variable climate . . . Though its sky be clear, its atmosphere is filled with dust, which must be hurtful to the lungs.'

The sad story is told of how Mrs Temple, the adopted daughter of Young, the poet (no relation of Arthur Young the gentleman farmer) died suddenly at Montpellier, 'at a time when the laws which accompanied the Revocation of the Edict of Nantes, backed by the superstition of a fanatic populace, denied Christian burial to Protestants. Narcissa was buried at Lyons, eventually.' One can imagine the bereaved man travelling from place to place with his daughter's body in the coach, searching for a decent grave for her interment.

Further down the road, the Hôtel du Nord at Béziers was declared by Murray in 1848 to be 'filthy in the extreme and exorbitant'. At that place we are reminded of the fanaticism of the Middle Ages, 'of the horrible slaughter of 1209, which followed the memorable siege by the Crusading army, raised at the call of the Church of Rome, to exterminate the heretical Albigenses, who were numerous in this devoted city. The inhabitants refusing to yield, the crusaders carried the city by storm, led by the Bishop Reginald of Montpellier and the Abbot of Citeaux, who had prepared a list of the proscribed victims. In the confusion of the assault, however, the soldiers were perplexed to distinguish the heretics from the orthodox, whereupon the abbot is said to have exclaimed: "Kill all! The Lord will know his own." The number massacred amounted to 60,000 according to some historians, though the Abbot of Citeaux himself modestly avows that he could only slay 20,000.'

When Henry James visited the region (*A Little Tour of France*), carrying his 'faithful Murray', he slept in a bad bed at Carcassonne, but a worse one at Narbonne, where the hotel was 'crowded from cellar to attic', causing him to spend the night in a room at the local blacksmith's. Breakfasting at the Hôtel de France next morning, 'the dirty little inn and Narbonne at large seemed to me to have the infirmities of the south without its usual graces ... At ten o'clock in the morning there was a table d'hôte for breakfast – a wonderful repast, which overflowed into every room and pervaded the whole establishment. I sat down with a hundred hungry marketers, fat, brown, greasy men, with a good deal of the rich soil of the Languedoc adhering to their hands and boots. I mention the latter articles because they almost put them on the table. It was very hot, and there were swarms of flies; the viands had the strongest odour ... which my companions devoured in large quantities. A man opposite to me had the dirtiest fingers I ever saw; a collection of fingers which in England would have excluded him from a farmers' ordinary.'

After a cursory visit to the cathedral and museum in Narbonne, James seems to like Montpellier rather better as a town. The Hôtel Nevet is 'the model of a good proverbial inn; a big rambling, creaking establishment, with brown, labyrinthine corridors, a queer old open-air vestibule, into which the diligence used to penetrate, and an hospitality more expressive than that of the new caravanserais'.

He spent two days there, 'mostly in the rain, and even under these circumstances I carried away a kindly impression. I think the Hôtel Nevet had something to do with it, and the sentiment of relief with which, in a quiet, even a luxurious room that looked out on a garden, I reflected that I had washed my hands of Narbonne.' Then, as if to boast of his heartlessness, he goes on: 'The phylloxera has destroyed the vines in the country that surround Montpellier, and at that moment I was capable of rejoicing in the thought that I should not breakfast with vintners.' Perhaps he didn't know, or maybe he would not have cared, but in the nearby villages people were hungry to the extent that they had only snails to eat from their ravaged vineyards.

Murray's 1881 version of the Hôtel Nevet is quite different, for it is said to have '200 bed-rooms, dirty and bad smells', whereas in 1848 it was 'a splendid, new, and large edifice, 200 bed-rooms – one of the best hotels in France'. In the Baedeker of 1895 it is the first on the list, and without deleterious comment, while in the issue of 1914 there is no mention of it at all.

The business of hotels could fall off alarmingly after a few adverse remarks in guidebooks, and perhaps some landlords could be forgiven for suspecting that a certain solitary traveller might be an emissary of one of the publishing firms who had come to check his establishment. An unassuming British *voyageur* spotted in the hotel dining-room might cause the waiting maid to spill a tureen of soup at the table, the wine waiter to fall over with his carafe of local wine ('the most one might say about it is that it could be called the best vinegar in France'). The proprietor in trying to be pleasant would be accused in the next edition of obsequiousness, and the early-morning chambermaid would be so rattled as to spill one of the overful pots she was carrying along the corridor – and thereby utterly spoil the reputation of a perfectly good hostelry for the next twenty years because a stray traveller had remarked that the smells were too odious to be endured.

It is fair to say that Murray recognized the possible volatility of his readers' reports when he wrote in *Southern Germany*, 1858: 'The number of good rooms in an inn, especially a country inn, is generally limited: if the traveller gets one of these, and the house is not too full to prevent his being well attended to, he gives it a good character, if it is crowded, and he gets an inferior room, he condemns it. I am sure I have been in the same inn, and during the same summer, under such different circumstances, that I could hardly believe it the same.'

The problem of hotel classification is commented on by Sabine Baring-Gould, a nineteenth-century novelist who also wrote travel books or, rather, what would be today called 'companion guides'. In the preface to *A Book of the Cévennes* he modestly writes that his work is but 'an introduction to the country, to be supplemented by guide-books. For inns, consult the annual volume of the French Touring Club; Baedeker and Joanne cannot always be relied on, as proprietors change, either for the better or for the worse. I have been landed in unsatisfactory quarters by relying on one or other of these guide-books, owing to the above-mentioned reason.'

In very plain prose Baring-Gould describes the scenery and gives some account of local history, as well as telling of such bizarre customs as the following about the Cévennes: 'When the chestnuts have been gathered, then in November they are dried in *sechoirs*. These are small square structures with a door and window on one side, and on the other three or more long narrow loopholes that are never closed. A fire of coals is lighted and kept burning incessantly in the drying-house, and the smoke passes through shelves on which the chestnuts are laid, in stages, and escapes by loopholes. To any one unaccustomed to the atmosphere in these *sechoirs*, it is hard to endure the smoke, and one stands the risk of being asphyxiated. Nevertheless the peasants spend two months in the year in these habitations, amidst cobwebs and soot, swarming with mice and rats, and the smoke at once acrid and moist, for in drying the chestnuts exude a greenish fluid that falls in a rain from the shelves. The natives do not seem to mind the dirt and smell of these horrible holes. Moreover, if there be in a village any one suffering from phthisis, at the end of autumn the patient is taken by the relations in his or her bed, and this is deposited in a corner of the *sechoir*. The sick person is not allowed to leave the drying-house, and it is a singular phenomenon that not infrequently, under the influence of the heat and the sulphurous smoke, the tuberculosis is arrested, and the sufferer lives on for many long years.'

Arles, says Murray, is famous for its beautiful women, 'due to the Greek element which has never been lost. It is odd that not a trace of this should be found in the men.' Augustus J. C. Hare recommends the Hôtel de Nord which, he says, is the best, being 'very good and clean, with obliging landlady'. In 1848 Murray tells us that the man who keeps the Hôtel de Forum was once cook to Lord Salisbury; that the Hôtel du Nord was 'improved, and tolerably comfortable', and that the Hôtel du Commerce on the Quai was kept by the wife of one of the English engineers on the steamboats.

Hare also is not slow to comment on the women, who are perhaps 'the most beautiful of any European city. With dark eyes and raven locks, they are generally majestic in carriage and figure. They are greatly adorned by the becoming costume of Arles –

which is still, happily, almost universal – a black dress and shawl, with full white muslin stomacher, and a very small lace cap at the back of the hair, bound round with broad black velvet or ribbon, fastened with gold or jewelled pins.' By 1930 the costume of the women was only seen on Sundays and holidays.

Henry James devotes two chapters to Arles. 'There were two shabby inns, which compete closely for your custom. I mean by this that if you elect to go to the Hôtel du Forum, the Hôtel du Nord, which is placed exactly beside it, watches your arrival with ill-concealed disapproval; and if you take the chances of its neigh-bour, the Hôtel du Forum seems to glare at you invidiously from all its windows and doors. I forget which of these establishments I selected; whichever it was, I wished very much that it had been the other.'

At a café the next afternoon, James observes that there sat 'behind the counter a splendid mature Arlesienne, the handsomest person I had ever seen give change for a five-franc piece. She was a large quiet woman, who would never see forty again; of an intensely feminine type, yet wonderfully rich and robust, and full of a certain physical nobleness. Though she was not really old, she was antique; and she was very grave, even a little sad. She had the dignity of a Roman empress, and she handled coppers as if they had been stamped with the head of Caesar.'

The main reason why so many English went to the Mediterranean coast of France was that of health, and Marseilles was the gate through which they passed in order to get there. Dickens gave a graphic picture of its summer climate in *Little Dorrit* (1856), and Murray in 1848 was equally explicit: 'From the margin of the old harbour, lined with quays, the ground rises on all sides, covered with houses, forming a basin or amphitheatre, terminating only with the encircling chain of hills. From this disposition of the ground, the port becomes the sewer of the city – the receptacle of all its filth, stagnating in a tideless sea and under a burning sun, until a S.E. wind produces that circulation in its waters which the tide would do on other seas. The stench emanating from it at times is consequently intolerable, except for natives ...'

As a reminder of times past we are told: 'The Lazaret owed its foundation to the fearful ravages of the plague at Marseilles in 1720, which carried off between 40,000 and 50,000 persons, half the population. Amidst the general despair, selfishness, and depravity which accompanied this dire calamity, many individuals distinguished themselves by their noble self-devotion. The streets soon became choked with dead, and of the galley-slaves, supplied at the rate of 80 a-week to conduct the dead-carts, none survived.'

Nor is one allowed to forget that at the Revolution, 'which inflamed to madness the fiery spirits of the people of the south, Marseilles furnished, from the dregs of its own population and the outcasts of other countries, the bands of assassins who perpetrated the greater portion of the September massacres in Paris. The well-known hymn of Revolution, the Marseillaise, was so called because it was played by a body of troops from Marseilles marching into Paris in 1792.'

By 1880 Marseilles had become 'a grand city in site and extent, and, excepting Paris, no town in France has been more improved since 1853, by the creation of streets, quarters, harbours, and public edifices etc.' In spite of all that, the town did not merit the accolade of a stay of some time. Its climate was said to be delightful at certain seasons but, nevertheless, 'in summer and autumn the heat is intense – the streets like an oven, so that it is scarcely possible to move abroad during the daytime, and all rest during the night is liable to be destroyed by mosquitoes.'

Going east along the coast, Murray found in 1848 that none of the hotels at Cannes were any good, though there was a comfortable one at Grasse, 'where an invalid from Nice might put up with advantage during the months of March, as the place is well sheltered'. At Antibes, however, the hotels were so bad that travellers were advised to 'stop outside the gates, and send in for horses; they will thus save time, and their carriage will escape the risk of accidents, in being twice dragged through the most odious streets.'

Hyères, the first place of importance beyond Toulon, became a desirable place to stay later in the century: 'Pure water has been laid on to all parts of the town by a company. The authorities have become more careful in securing cleanliness and drainage. The mildness and dryness of its climate causes Hyères to be chosen as a winter residence for invalids, and renders it one of the best in Europe during the season.' As for Cannes, for those who suffer from the sea-air, 'producing often nervous irritability and want to sleep', the villas on the north side of the town are recommended.

English doctors and bankers were as usual installed in the main towns to care for and cater to the many winter visitors. 'Pattieson's is a good shop for groceries and English stores.' English and Scottish churches mushroomed as on a dank November dawn at home. Today, the condescending wrath towards fish-and-chip shops and Yorkshire-bitter bars set up for those who flock to places like Corfu and Benidorm – who cannot sleep well if the familiar wherewithal is not stowed in their bellies – is a snobbish response to the fact that the hoi-polloi can afford to get off the island at all. If the middle classes (what and whoever *they* are) can have their comforting appurtenances – which they hardly need to export, these days, because the local equivalents serve perfectly well and may indeed be welcomed as 'local colour' – why not the others? The middle classes would of course rather the yobbos stayed at home, playing kickshins and throwing up behind impeccable clap-board cottages lining the village green, instead of acting as evidence for the indigenous foreign population that respectable English tour-ists with the present-day Baedeker or *Blue Guide* might well have come out of the same unruly bucket a couple of generations back.

The English who travelled to or settled on the Riviera in the nineteenth century were, however, certainly responsible for some improvements in sanitation, though the French would undoubtedly have taken these in hand anyway as part of the general trend all over Europe. In this respect Cannes went up many notches in general estimation after 1848. 'The drainage, formerly bad, is now considerably improved; many works have been already carried out, and others, more important, are about to be undertaken.'

An extract from HM Consul's Report, October 1889, at Nice states: 'The Municipality has introduced improvements which con-siderably increase the healthiness of this town, and which, I believe, have so far been carried out in no other towns on the French Riviera. In the first place they have secured, entirely irrespective of the natural supply of water, an immense water supply, which is calculated at little less than 1000 litres a day per inhabitant. The drains are fitted with automatic flushers, placed at intervals of some 300 metres apart; which appear to give excellent results. Street gullies of improved construction have been largely provided, which, when kept full of water (which is done by means of the hose in watering the streets), effectually prevent the escape of foul air, while allowing rain and other surplus water to pass into the drain. These are superior to anything of the kind I have seen in England or elsewhere.'

Dr James Henry Bennet, in *Winter and Spring on the Shores of the Mediterranean*, gives another point of view on the matter of sanitation: 'In the small primitive agricultural towns of the Ligurian coast, and of the south of Europe generally, the want of main drains is not felt. All the inhabitants are usually landed proprietors. Olive and lemon trees, even in the sunny south, will not bear crops of fruit without manure, and where is it to come from in countries where there is little or no pasture unless it be from the homes of the proprietors? Hence, at Mentone and elsewhere, before the advent of strangers, the household drainage was everywhere scrupulously preserved, placed in small casks, hermetically sealed, and taken up to the terraces on the mountain side every few days by the donkey which most possess. There a trench was made around the base of a tree, and the contents of the tub mixed with the soil and the trench closed.' For another page or so Bennet goes on to talk about drainage and cesspools, manure pumps, and dysentery.

Equally to the point perhaps is the advice given in the handbooks on hiring furnished apartments, in which 'the general system is that the agent is paid by the owner. Visitors ought to see that all agreements are made in writing, and to mark particularly that charges for water, gas, porter, be included in the rent; and that a clause be inserted, that if any necessary articles of furniture be wanting, they can procure them at the owner's cost, and that he pays for the inventory. All crockery, china, glass, linen, etc. should be gone over piece by piece, since, if on giving up possession there be the smallest crack or stain, the lodger will have to pay for the article as if it were new. Tenants are naturally expected to have all linen washed before leaving; but the cleaning of curtains and woollen covers is the affair of the owner.'

In a more general manner Murray tells us: 'When Nice first became the resort of British residents, the salubrity and advantages of its climate were perhaps overrated, but at present there is too great a tendency in a contrary direction, in comparing it with other places adopted as a residence for invalids.' Hare says that the place 'is much frequented as a sunny winter residence, but is ravaged in spring by the violent mistral, which fills the air with a whirlwind of dust'.

Eustace Reynolds Ball in *Mediterranean Winter Resorts* wrote: 'Considered purely in the light of an invalid station, there are several objections to Nice. Being a large city and the centre of fashion and gaiety during the season, its numerous attractions and amusements, offer too many temptations to the invalid visitor, and may lead him to neglect precautions, which may have a serious result.' He quotes a Dr Yeo's remarks that 'whatever defects the climate of the Riviera possesses, these are specifically concentrated and aggravated at Nice.'

Let us continue to Mentone, where I spent the year of 1952, recovering from tuberculosis. In 1875 Dr Bennet wrote: 'Until latterly but few of the tribe of health loungers chose Mentone as a residence. The Mentonians were at first all real invalids, glad to escape from the gaieties of Nice, as well as from its dust and occasionally cold winds. Many, however, are becoming attached to this picturesque Mediterranean nook. It is thus beginning to attract mere sun-worshippers, and a foreign population is gradually growing up, of the same description as that of Nice and Cannes... The inhabitants of Mentone are exceedingly gracious and cordial to strangers, and are doing their utmost to render the place agreeable to them.'

These 'health and invalid guides' discuss problems of sickness and disease in a way that suggests there were tens of thousands of hypochondriacs (or seriously ill people) in Britain who, having the money, were ready to go to the Riviera in the hope of a cure. People vitiated by a lifetime's service in India, or those blighted by consumption in the damp climate of England (where the disease was endemic) or those needing to recover after the gruelling task of overseeing their factories in the industrial north, would look on the South of France as the sure place of restoration.

Reynolds Ball says: 'In indicating the class of cases which receive benefit from a winter residence on the Riviera, one must first mention the affectations of the respiratory organs. Bronchitis, emphysema, laryngitis, the early stages of phthisis (especially those cases in which no important haemorrhages have taken place), all receive conspicuous benefit; and recognising the therapeutic value of absolutely dry air in all catarrhal affectations, great improvement is speedily manifest in cases of bronchial, nasal, post-nasal, pharyngeal and laryngeal catarrh.'

Those suffering from rheumatism and gout were said to do extremely well; rheumatism of the joints was almost unknown among the locals, although muscular rheumatism was occasionally met with. 'The mildness of the climate and persistent sunshine, encouraging the action of the skin, produces an excellent effect upon the disease of the kidneys and liver, and cases of diabetes received marked benefit.'

In Mentone, according to Black's 1906 guide, the Villa Helvetia is 'a convalescent home for ladies not younger than 18 nor older than 40, who are received for 20 shillings a week, which includes everything except laundress and fire in the bedroom.' In San Remo, just along the coast in Italy, the Villa Emily is also a home for 'invalid ladies of limited means. They pay 25 shillings a week, which includes doctor's fees, comfortable board and lodging, and wine or beer.' The sanatorium at Gorbio did not take tubercular patients, and a full-page advertisement in Reynolds Ball's guide, paid for by the town council of Beaulieu-sur-Mer, says, in case guests would be upset by the early morning coughing, 'Consumptives refused in all hotels.'

Hare notes that English doctors, 'seldom acquainted with Mentone, are apt to recommend the Western Bay as more bracing, but it is exposed to mistral and dust, and its shabby suburbs have none of the beauty of the Eastern Bay'. That was the side I lived on for a year, whereas Katharine Mansfield, who stayed in Mentone for a few months during the First World War in the hope of ameliorating her tuberculosis, chose the area suggested by Hare, and died of her affliction.

Dr D. W. Samways, in his *Guide to Mentone*, relates the following: 'In one hotel was a young German lady, distinctly phthisical, who had lost a sister the previous year from the same malady. A young engineer also arrived, with indications of early pulmonary mischief. An American lady, somewhat seriously ill, completed the list of patients. After two winters in Mentone the German lady was sufficiently well to live in Berlin again, and later on I heard she had become engaged to be married. The engineer never needed to return, and I saw him in good health some years later. The American lady remained for several seasons in Mentone, but did not recover, though she considerably prolonged her life.'

Some of those convalescents who took walks in the environs were given a warning by Murray in 1881: 'A very general complaint has been made against visitors trespassing in the olive-grounds and vineyards, in search of flowers, by which damage to a considerable extent is inflicted on the peasantry.'

Dr Bennet asks his readers not to pay children and donkey-women 'for seeking and bringing them flowers', but Murray has something more serious to say on the matter: 'We may add that the depredations of strangers are not confined to flowers, but extend to lemons etc. Let them be made aware that the laws in France as to trespass are very stringent in such cases, the punishment extending to fine and imprisonment.'

One may wonder what happens to those invalids who came to the Riviera and die, either in a hotel, or in a furnished apartment. On this matter Reynolds Ball informs us: 'Any actual cost incurred by making good any damage caused by the illness and death in putting the bedroom into a proper sanitary condition – repapering, whitewashing, renewing curtains, etc., must of course be paid for by the representatives of the deceased.

'But any charge for "moral damages" by way of indemnity for supposed loss of custom, can, and should, be resisted. Speaking generally, if a sum exceeding 500 fr. be demanded, legal advice should be sought with a view of resisting the claim, or, at all events, the advice of the nearest British Consul should be taken.'

He cites the arrangements to be made at Montreux, in Switzerland, where 'the proprietors have decided on a uniform tariff of charges for death occurring in any of the hotels of that town. A sliding scale has been adopted as follows: – For death from natural causes, the relatives of the deceased will pay from 200 to 300 francs; for a death due to a non-contagious disease, 300 to 400; while for a death resulting from a contagious disease, 400 to 500 francs.'

CHAPTER ELEVEN

SUNNY SPAIN

The first real guidebook to Spain in English, by Richard Ford, was published in 1845. Soon after his return from Italy in 1840 he was asked by John Murray to write the *Hand-book for Travellers in Spain*. The first edition, of eleven hundred pages in two thick volumes, weighs three pounds on my bathroom scales. Early travellers must have found it a work of literature as well as guidance, with all the quirks, prejudices and foibles of an English gentleman of that time. Solid good sense padded such matter out, as did accounts of Peninsular battles (the Peninsular War being still within living memory), accurate topographical description, historical anecdote, as well as informed opinions on Spanish life and people.

Ford's preface half-apologized for the length of his 'handbook': 'In presenting these and other things of Spain, let not any occasional repetition be imputed to carelessness or tautology, for matter descriptive and critical more than sufficient to have made another volume, has been cancelled in order to economise space, already too confined for so large a subject. By repetition alone are impressions made and fixed; and as no hand-book is ever read through continually, each page should in some wise tell its own story; and when so many sites have witnessed similar events, the narrative and deductions cannot materially differ.'

From the beginning he hopes to set our minds at rest, due to what he considers the many misrepresentations regarding Spain: 'few . . . have been more systematically circulated than the dangers and difficulties which are there supposed to beset the traveller. This, the most romantic and peculiar country in Europe, may in reality be visited throughout its length and breadth with ease and safety, for travelling there is no worse than it was in France or Italy in 1814, before English example forced improvements.'

The first difficulty, of course, is that of passports which, as he usually did about all that is fundamentally wrong in Spain, Ford blames on the French, who, 'during their intrusive occupation, introduced the severe machinery of police and passports, and all those petty annoyances which impede the honest traveller, who, conscious of meaning no harm, is too apt to overlook forms and regulations, which the dishonest take especial care to observe, regulations which have neither name nor existence in England'.

As for getting to Spain, a postscript to the preface informs the traveller: 'By arrangements just concluded Madrid may now be reached in six days from London; the Peninsular Steamer from Southampton arrives at Corunna in about 72 hours, whence a Royal Mail coach runs to the capital in three days and a-half.'

He remarks that the voyage offers many opportunities to lovers of sea views, though he is hardly reassuring to sufferers from seasickness. 'No one who has never crossed the Bay of Biscay, where the storms seldom cease, can form any idea of what a sea is – those vast mountain-waves which roll unchecked and unbroken across the whole of the mighty Atlantic.'

On landing at Cádiz the traveller will be inconvenienced by the tedious quarantine precautions, although: 'It is carrying a joke some lengths, when the yellow cadaverous Spanish *health* officers suspect and inspect the ruddy-faced Britons, who hang over the packet gangway, bursting from a plethora of beef and good condition ... The boatmen, who crowd to land passengers, rival in noise and rascality those of Naples. The common charge is a peseta per person; but they increase in their demands in proportion as the wind and waves arise ...'

A Spanish customs officer is likened to 'a gentleman who pretends to examine baggage, in order to obtain money without the disgrace of begging, or the danger of robbing. They excuse themselves by necessity, which has no law; some allowance must be made for the rapacity of bribes which characterises too many

Spanish *empleados*; their regular salaries, always inadequate, are generally in arrears, and they are forced to pay themselves by conniving at defrauding the government; this few scruple to do, as they know it to be an unjust one, and say that it can afford it; indeed, as all are offenders alike, the guilt of the offence is scarcely admitted. Where robbing and jobbing are the universal order of the day, one rogue keeps another in countenance, as one goitre does another in Switzerland.'

After some advice on food and accommodation (the best hotel in Cádiz being run by an Englishman), Ford goes on: 'None, however, going to make any lengthened stay should omit consulting Mr. Brackenbury, the consul, whose kindness and hospitality are hereditary and proverbial. His golden sherry deserves special notice.' 'Thank you, very much,' Mr B. must often have said, after publication of this advice, speeding another thirsty visitor on his way.

Behaviour, naturally, comes high on the list of Ford's exposition: 'It is incredible how popular an Englishman will become among Spaniards, if he will assimilate himself to their forms of society; a few bows are soon made, and the taking off of one's hat, especially to ladies, in a fine climate, is no great hardship . . . The better rule is, on landing at Cádiz, to consider every stranger in a long-tailed coat to be a marquis, until you find him out to be a waiter, and even then no great harm is done, and you dine the quicker for the mistake. You are always on the safe side. When Spaniards see an Englishman behaving to them as they do to him and to other gentlemen, from not expecting it, a reaction takes place. "I have met the Englishman; he is as perfect a gentleman as one of us." '

Setting off from Cádiz for other parts of the peninsula, it is a common mistake to suppose 'that the Spanish highroads are bad; they are in general kept in good order. The war in the Peninsula tended to deteriorate their condition but the roads of the first class were so admirably constructed at the beginning, that, in spite of all the injuries of war and neglect, they may, as a whole, be pronounced superior to many of France. The roads of England have, indeed, latterly been rendered so excellent, and we are so apt to compare those of other nations with them, that we forget that fifty years ago Spain was much in advance in that and many other respects.'

If you expect to be well lodged on the road you will be disappointed, the inns being not only bad, but often very bad, and even the best in the country are 'only indifferent when compared to those to which Englishmen are accustomed at home, and have created on those high roads of the Continent which they most frequent.'

Ford's comments on inns continue for pages, many of the buildings having 'at a distance quite the air of a gentleman's mansion. Their white walls, towers, and often elegant elevations, glitter in the sun, gay and promising, while all within is dark, dirty, and dilapidated.'

The traveller's reception is hardly ever as he would wish: '. . . no one greets him; no obsequious landlord, bustling waiter, or simpering chambermaid, takes any notice of his arrival. He proceeds, unaided, to unload or unsaddle his beast . . .'

As for which inn to choose at the end of the day: 'The safe rule is to go to the one where the diligence puts up – The Coach Inn. We shall not be able often to give him the exact names of the posadas, nor is it requisite. The simple direction "Let us go to *the* inn," will be enough in smaller towns; for the question is rather, *Is* there an inn, and where is it? than, Which is the best inn?'

In spite of earlier reassurances about public security, the pages later devoted at length to the matter may well have caused a frisson of romantic alarm in the bosoms of many readers. Travelling with a baggage waggon is 'of all others that which most exposes the party to be robbed'.

When the caravan arrives in the small villages it attracts immediate notice, and if it gets wind that the travellers are foreigners, and still more English, they are supposed to be laden with gold and booty. In the villages near the inns there is seldom a lack of loiterers, who act as spies, and convey intelligence to their confederates; again, the bulk of the equipment, the noise and clatter of men and mules, is seen and heard from afar, by robbers who lurk in hiding-places or eminences, who are well provided with telescopes, besides with longer and sharper noses. The slow pace and impossibility of flight render the traveller an easy prey to well mounted horsemen. We do not wish to frighten our readers with much notice on Spanish robbers, being well assured that they are the exception, not the rule, in Spanish travel. It is not, however, to be denied that Spain is, of all countries in Europe, the one in which the ancient classical and once universal system of robbing on the highway exists the most unchained.

First and foremost come the '*ladrones*', the robbers on a great scale. These are the most formidable; and as they seldom attack any travellers except with overwhelming force, and under circumstances of ambuscade and surprise, where everything is in their favour, resistance is generally useless, and can only lead to fatal accidents; it is better to submit at once to the summons which will take no denial. Those who are provided with such a sum of money as the robbers think according to their class of life, that they ought to carry about them, are very rarely ill-used; a frank, confident, and good-humoured surrender generally not only prevents any bad treatment, but secures even civility during the disagreeable operation. The Spaniard is by nature high-bred and a 'caballero', and responds to any appeal to qualities of which his nation has reason to be proud; notwithstanding these moral securities, if only by way of making assurance doubly sure, an Englishman will do well when travelling in exposed districts to be provided with a bag containing fifty to one hundred dollars, which makes a handsome purse, feels heavy in the hand, and is that sort of amount which the Spanish brigand thinks a native of this proverbially rich country ought to have with him on his travels. The traveller should be particularly careful to have a watch of some kind, one with a gaudy gilt chain and seals is the best suited: not to have a watch of any kind exposes the traveller to more certain indignities than a scantily filled purse.

Some consolation is intended by the remark that Spanish robbers may well think twice before attacking armed English travellers, particularly if they appear on their guard. The robbers dislike fighting. They hate danger, from knowing what it is; they have no chivalrous courage, or abstract notions of fair play. They have also a peculiar dislike to English guns and gunpowder, which, in fact, both as arms and ammunition, are infinitely superior to the ruder Spanish weapons. Though three or four Englishmen have nothing to fear, yet where there are ladies it is always far better to be provided with an escort.'

Travel was certainly slow, and indeed leisurely, for Ford tells us that to make a general tour of Spain 'would be a work of much time and difficulty', and 'could scarcely be accomplished in under a year and a half; indeed we ourselves devoted three years to the task'.

On the way to Seville we are told to beware of the inn rooms where, in summer, 'legions of fleas breed in the mattings; the leaf of the oleander is often strewed as a preventive. Bugs, or French ladybirds, make bad beds resemble busy ant-hills, and the walls of *ventas*, where they especially lodge, are often stained with the marks of nocturnal combat, evincing the internecine *guerrilla*, waged against enemies who, if not exterminated, murder innocent sleep; were the bugs and fleas unanimous, they would eat up a Goliath, but fortunately, like true Iberians, they never pull together, and are conquered in detail . . . From these evils, however, the best houses in Seville are comparatively free.'

Ford does not genuflect to any tenets of 'political correctness' – happily unformulated in his day – when dwelling on the character of the people in southern Spain. They are, he writes, 'as impression-able as children, heedless of results, uncalculating of contingencies, passive victims to violent impulse, gay, clever, good humoured, and light-hearted, and the most subservient dupes of plausible nonsense. Tell them that their country is the most beautiful, themselves the finest, handsomest, bravest, the most civilized of mortals, and they may be led forthwith by the nose. Of all Spaniards the Andalucian is the greatest boaster; he brags chiefly of his courage and wealth. He ends in believing his own lie, and hence is always pleased with himself, with whom he is on the best of terms. His redeeming qualities are his kind and good manners, his lively, social turn, his ready wit and sparkle: he is ostentatious, and, as far as his limited means will allow, eager to show hospitality to the stranger, after the Spanish acceptation of that term, which has no English reference to the kitchen.'

Ford goes on thus for some time, until his analysis takes on a more political, not to say racial, aspect: 'If the people are sometimes cruel and ferocious when collected in numbers, we must remember that the blood of Africa boils in their veins; their fathers were the children of the Arab, whose arm is against every man; they have never had a chance given them – an iniquitous and long-continued system of misgovernment in church and state has tended to depress their good qualities and encourage their vices; the former, which are all their own, have flourished in spite of the depressing incubus. Can it be wondered that their armies should fly when every means of efficiency is wanting to the poor soldier, and when unworthy chiefs set the example? Is there no allowance to be made for their taking the law into their own hands, when they see the fountains of justice habitually corrupted? The world is not their friend, nor the world's law; their lives, sinews, and little properties have never been respected by the powers that be, who have ever favoured the rich and strong, at the expense of the poor and weak; the people, therefore, from sad experience have no confidence in institutions, and when armed with power, and their blood on fire, can it be expected that they should not slake their great revenge?'

Ford's amusing sketch of a Spanish bookseller reads like a more inspired entry in modern-day Driff's *Guide to Second-Hand Bookdealers* in Great Britain. In Spain such a character was a 'queer uncomfortable person for an eager collector to fall foul of . . . He acts as if he were the author, or the collector, not the vendor of his books. He scarcely notices the stranger's entrance; neither knows what books he had, or what he has not got; he has no catalogue, and will scarcely reach out his arm to take down any book which is pointed out; he never has anything which is published by another bookseller, and will not send for it for you, nor always even tell you where it may be had.'

On the subject of Spanish painting, which he doesn't think much of, Ford is strongly opposed to exporting them to hang 'in the confined rooms of private English houses'. Nevertheless: 'A Spanish Venus, at least on canvas, is yet a desideratum among amateurs. Those of Titian and Paduanino, which are in the royal collection of Madrid, blush unseen – they, with all other improper company of that sort, Ledas, Danaes, and so forth, were all lumped together, just as the naughty epigrams of Martial are collected in one appendix in well-intentioned editions; the peccant pictures were all consigned into an under-ground apartment, into which no one was admitted without an especial permission.'

One could be sure, of course, that 'the fair sex' would not gain entry to that too spicy collection, for in Spain, 'those ladies who have an azure tendency are more wondered at than espoused. Martial, a true Spaniard, prayed that his wife should not be *doctissima*; learning is thought to unsex them. The men dislike to see them read, the ladies think the act prejudicial to the brilliancy of the eyes, and hold that happiness is centred in the heart, not the head.'

As if to get back to reality, or at least to everyday life, Ford describes the beggars of Spain who 'know well how to appeal to every softening and religious principle. They are now an increased and increasing nuisance. The mendicant plague rivals the moskitos; they smell the blood of an Englishman: they swarm in every side; they interrupt privacy, worry the artist and antiquarian, disfigure the palace, disenchant the Alhambra, and dispel the dignity of the house of God, which they convert into a lazar-house and den of mendacity and mendicity. They are more numerous than even in the Roman, Neapolitan, and Sicilian states.'

John Bull, ever destined to become their victim, 'is worshipped and plundered; the Spaniard thinks him laden with ore like the asses of Arcadia, and that, in order to get on lighter, he is as ready as Lucullus to throw it away. The moment he comes in sight, the dumb will recover their speech and the lame their legs; he will be hunted by packs as a bag-fox, his pursuers are neither to be called nor whipped off. They persevere in the hopes that they may be paid a something as hush-money, in order to be got rid of; nor let any traveller ever open his mouth, which betrays that, however well put on his capa, the speaker is not a Spaniard, but a foreigner. If the pilgrim does once in despair give, the fact of the happy arrival in town of a charitable man spreads like wild-fire; all follow him the next day, just as crows do a brother-bird in whose crop they have smelt carrion at the night's roost. None are ever content; the same beggar comes every day; his gratitude is the lively anticipation of future favours; he expects that you have granted him an annuity.' Ford suggests certain phrases – in Spanish – on hearing which the beggar should immediately break off his importunities.

We are seriously warned against falling ill in Spain, for whatever malady you have will be followed by another far worse should you fall into the hands of the native doctor. 'The faculty at Madrid are little in advance of their provincial colleagues, nay, often they are more destructive, since, being practitioners at court, the heaven on earth, they are in proportion superior to the medical men of the rest of the world, of whom of course they can learn nothing. They are, however, at least a century behind the practitioners in England.' One is reminded of the Spanish doctor in Le Sage's *Gil Blas*: the more people he kills the more esteemed be becomes.

Of all the pleasures of the Spaniard one of the most addictive is the bullfight and, on the torrid afternoon in question, everyone makes for the Plaza de Toros. 'Nothing can exceed the gaiety and sparkle of a Spanish public going, eager and full-dressed, to the *fight*. They could not move faster were they running from a real one. All the streets or open spaces near the outside of the arena are a spectacle. The merry mob is everything. Their excitement under a burning sun, and their thirst for the blood of bulls, is fearful. There is no sacrifice, no denial which they will not undergo to save money for the bull-fight.'

More than three pages are devoted to the pleasures of smoking. '. . . whether at the bull-fight, lay or clerical, wet or dry, the Spaniard during the day, sleeping excepted, solaces himself when he can with a cigar. Can it be wondered at that the Spanish population should cling to this relief from whips and scorns, and the oppressor's wrong, and steep in sweet oblivious stupefaction, the misery of being fretted and excited by empty larders, vicious political institutions, and a very hot climate. Tobacco, this anodyne for the irritability of human reason, is, like spirituous liquors which make it drunk, a highly-taxed article in all civilised societies.' This seems little different, in fact, to the punishing taxes of today, when we also have many nanny-minded moralists continually inveighing against the pleasures of the weed. Ford reminds us, in conclusion, that Sir Walter Raleigh, the patron of Virginia, 'smoked a pipe just before he lost his head, which, I think, was properly done to settle his spirits'.

Cigar-making seemed to be one of Spain's main industries. 'The cigar manufactories are the only ones in really full work. The many thousand pairs of hands employed at Seville are principally female: a good workwoman can make in a day from ten to twelve bundles, each of which contains fifty cigars; but their tongues are busier than their fingers, and more mischief is made than cigars. Very few of them are good-looking, yet these *cigareras* are reputed to be more impertinent than chaste, and undergo an ingeniously-minute search on leaving their work, for they sometimes carry off the filthy weed in a manner her most Catholic majesty never dreamed of.'

Ford tells us that the Inquisition, which has so cowed and lacerated the Spanish soul, was first derived from France, and then 'remodelled on Moorish principles, the *garrote* and furnace being the bowstring and fire of the Moslem, who burnt the bodies of the infidel to prevent the ashes from becoming relics. The subject of the Inquisition in Spain, however, is no laughing matter: In the changes and chances of Spain it may be re-established, and as it never forgets or forgives, it will surely revenge. No king or constitution ever permits in Spain any approach to religious toleration; the spirit of the Inquisition is alive; all abhor and brand with eternal infamy the descendants of those convicted by this tribunal; the stain is indelible, and the stigma, if once affixed on any unfortunate family, is known in every town, by the very children in the street.'

While in Andalucia – on the way to Gibraltar – the traveller will of course visit Granada, there to wander around the Alhambra, one of the marvels of Islamic art and architecture in Spain. Concerning the depredations of *foreign* vandals (as opposed to the destruction carried out by the French occupiers in the Peninsular War), the 1892 edition of Murray makes the following remarks: 'Too much cannot be said against the vulgar habit of cutting names and tearing off pieces of plaster and tiles. The guides have the strictest orders not to let travellers remain alone, and if they see them injuring in any way the building to report to the authorities immediately. The name-carving mania is all the more reprehensible when (as on the fountain basin in the Court of Lions) names of persons incapable of such pranks are deliberately forged.'

Gibraltar itself, as a town, is said to be 'stuffy and sea-coaly, the houses wooden and druggeted, and built on the Liverpool pattern, under a tropical climate; but transport an Englishman where you will, and like a snail, he takes his house and his habits with him. The traveller who lands by the steamer will be tormented by *cads* and *touters*, who clamorously canvass him to put up at their respective inns. They are second-rate and dear. At Griffith's hotel is one Messias, a Jew (called Rafael in Spain), who is a capital guide both here and throughout Andalucia. The other posadas are mere punch and pot-houses, nor is the cookery or company first-rate, but the hospitality of the Rock is unbounded, and, perhaps, the endless dinnerings is the greatest change from the hungry and thirsty Spain. As there are generally five regiments in garrison, the messes are on a grand scale; more roast beef is eaten and sherry drunk than in the whole of Spain: but there is death in the pot, and the faces of "yours and ours" glow redder than their jackets; a tendency to fever and inflammation is induced by carrying the domestics and gastronomics of cool damp England to this arid and torrid "Rock".'

We are told that no one should omit to cross the Straits and set foot on African soil. 'The contrast is more striking than even passing from Dover to Calais.' At Tangiers one can put up at the house of a Scottish woman, 'or at Joanna Correa's; one Ben Elia also takes in travellers, for he is a Jew . . . obtain a soldier as an escort, and ride in twelve hours to Tetuan; lodge in the Jewish quarter. The daughters of Israel, both of Tetuan and Tangiers, are unequalled in beauty: observe their eyes, feet, and costume; they are true Rebeccas.'

Moving further up the coast of the Spanish peninsula, Ford has little good to say about the people. 'The Valencians are perfidious, vindictive, sullen, and mistrustful, fickle, and treacherous. Theirs is a sort of *tigre singe* character, of cruelty allied with frivolity; so blithe, so smooth, so gay, yet empty of all good; nor can their pleasantry be trusted, for, like the Devil's good humour, it depends on their being pleased; at the least rub, they pass like the laughing hyena, into a snarl and bite: nowhere is assassination more common; they smile, and murder while they smile.'

As for their physical appearance: '. . . they are as dusky as Moors, and have the peculiar look in their eyes of half cunning, half ferocity of the Berbers. The burning sun not only tans their complexions, but excites their nervous system; hence they are highly irritable, imaginative, superstitious, and mariolatrous; their great joys and relaxations are religious shows.'

Perhaps some of this can be put down to their work in the

surrounding rice-fields where 'the sallow amphibious cultivator wrestles with fever amid an Egyptian plague of moskitos, for man appears to have been created here solely for their subsistence. The mortality in these swamps is frightful; few labourers reach the age of 60. The women are seldom prolific, but the gap is filled up by Murcians and Arrogonese, who exchange life for gold, as there is a fascination in this lucrative but fatal employment; so closely and mysteriously do the elements of production and destruction, plenty and pestilence, life and death, tread on the heels of each other.'

The Catalans are said to be discourteous and inhospitable to foreigners, 'whom they fear and hate. They were neither French nor Spanish, but *sui generis* both in language, costume, and habits; indeed the rudeness, activity, and manufacturing industry of the districts near Barcelona, are enough to warn the traveller that he is no longer in high-bred, indolent Spain.'

Nevertheless, when you get to know them, 'they are true, honest, honourable, and rough diamonds ... Catalonians, powerfully constituted physically, are strong, sinewy, and active, patient under fatigue and privation, brave, daring, and obstinate, preferring to die rather than to yield. They form the raw material of excellent soldiers and sailors, and have always, when well commanded, proved their valour and intelligence on sea and land.' Ford's handbook is often as much a guide to himself as to Spain, and later guides, as we shall see, discontinued this prejudicial if not prejudiced analysis of the Spanish provincial character, apart from a few general and unexceptionable remarks which left the traveller to find things out for himself.

In the edition of 1892, still said to have been written by Ford though it was thirty-four years after his death (though 'revised and corrected'), the above comments on the Catalans had been much reduced, while the strictures against the Valencians had disappeared altogether.

In the half-century after Ford's day twelve thousand kilometres of railways were built or put under construction, 'principally by means of French capital, and at enormous cost. They are, perhaps, the worst constructed and worst managed lines in the world, but they keep excellent time. Every train is bound to carry a first-class non-smoking compartment, but the privilege is not commonly enjoyed without hard fighting, unless the non-smoker has already taken possession at the starting-point of the train. Railway guards, and indeed all officials except the very lowest, invariably travel first-class, and sometimes occupy nearly half the available seats in the carriages. Luggage robberies on railways are not uncommon; it is therefore better not to put valuables into the trunks which go in the van.'

In 1892 the most convenient way to Spain was still by boat to Gilbraltar or Cádiz, though a year or two later Baedeker could tell us that the 'quickest connection is, of course, by railway via Paris'. Regarding the time necessary to see Spain, Murray now informs us that a complete tour may be made in five months 'by those to whom *time* is an important consideration'.

A. & C. Black's guidebook for 1892 considers three months to be enough, remarking in the preface that: 'The improvements affected in the country during the last decade, in the directions of travelling facilities, hotel, police, and sanitary arrangements, are hardly credible. The hotels in the principal cities are now equal to those of any other country; while the complete network of well-appointed lines of railway enables the traveller to visit the finest and most interesting localities in a short space of time, with comfort and with safety.'

Passports had been abolished in 1862, though foreigners were still liable 'to be called upon by local Spanish authorities to declare their nationality, and object of their journey'. After assuring us of the efficiency of the post office, Black's says, 'Letters are never opened save during exceptional *pronunciamiento* moments and electioneering time. It is also a mistake to put "Esquire" after the name when receiving letters *poste restante*, because the Spanish clerk who searches for the letter in the rack will think that is your surname.'

Regarding toilet facilities on the trains and at stations Murray says that some are very poor, and others 'often mere hovels. The extreme filthiness of every place to which railway servants and passengers of every class have access in common is much to be deplored.' Even in 1913 Baedeker said that railway stations inside Spain were still 'very primitive. The waiting-rooms are generally closed, or unusable, or altogether lacking. Refreshment rooms are rare and poor. It is advisable, therefore, to be provided with food and wine for consumption in the railway carriage.'

To depart from the railway routes still meant travelling by 'the odious diligence', with distances measured in leagues which, 'especially in the wilder and mountainous districts, are calculated more by guesswork than measurement'.

Black says, 'Pedestrianism is unknown in Spain, with the exception of such areas as Asturias, Galicia, and the Pyrenees.' Bicycle tours were, however, possible in many districts favoured by long stretches of excellent roads. Volume Three of *The Cyclists Touring Road Book* of 1887 has a section on Spain for those of its 25,000 members who might wish to go there, and in the introduction it tells them: 'As far as there is any rule of the road, it is the opposite to that which obtains in England.' Baedeker for 1913 says that, for cyclists, 'Riding is practically impossible in summer on account of the heat; and the endless monotony of the Castilian plateau makes cycling very wearisome.'

'Since the introduction of the railway system,' Murray explains, 'there has been a marked development in the construction of high-roads also; thus, whilst the total length of roads existing in Spain in 1855 was only 5920 English miles, it may be calculated that more than double that number are at the present time open. But even this amount is quite disproportionate to the wants of a country like Spain.'

As a cyclist or a pedestrian you would find it difficult to procure good topographical maps of the country. Baedeker in 1908 says, with rare humour: 'Of the *Spanish Topographical Map* in 1080 sheets, on a scale of 1:50,000, projected in 1875, only 125 sheets have appeared, dealing merely with the centre of the Peninsula. At this rate a century must elapse before the completion of the work.'

Motoring was coming into vogue before the First World War, but Spain 'cannot be recommended, chiefly on account of the inferiority of the roads, though those in the northern part of the country, as well as those around Madrid, are very fair'.

Regarding money, Baedeker reminds us: 'Every shop-counter is provided with a stone slab for the testing of silver coins, and the traveller also should learn to know their true ring, as false coins are by no means uncommon. A handful of change should never be taken without examination, since even railway officials will sometimes try to take advantage of the unsuspecting stranger by passing base money mingled with the good.'

There was no longer much fear of brigands, though Baedeker's notes on law and order are worth reading. '*Public Security* in the towns of Spain is on the same level as in most other parts of Europe. For excursions into the interior, especially in S. Spain, it is advisable to make previous inquiries at the barracks of the gendarmes as to the safety of the route. Isolated cases of highway robbery still occur at intervals. The *Guardia Civil* is a select body of fine and thoroughly trustworthy men, in whom the stranger may place implicit confidence. On the other hand it is seldom advisable to call in the help of the ordinary police. In the case of a riot or other popular disturbance, the stranger should get out of the way as quickly as possible, as the careful policemen, in order to prevent the escape of the guilty, are apt to arrest anyone they can lay their hands on.'

Begging, as the national pest of Spain, seemed little altered from Ford's day. The Baedeker of 1913 tells us that: 'Beggars accost the stranger on the streets, follow him into shops, cafés, and hotels, and sit in swarms at all church-doors. In S. Spain they even besiege the railway ticket-offices and the passing trains at wayside stations.'

In the section on 'Intercourse with the People' we are told that in educated circles, 'the stranger is at first apt to be carried away by the lively, cheerful, and obliging tone of society, by the charming spontaneity of manner, and by the somewhat exaggerated politeness of the people he meets. He should, however . . . above all refrain from expressing an opinion on religious or political questions. The national pride of the Spaniard and his ignorance of foreign conditions render a collision in such cases almost inevitable.'

We are told that, on the other hand, the Spaniard of the lower classes 'is not devoid of national pride, but he possesses much more common sense and a much healthier dislike of humbug than his so-called superiors. The tactful stranger will not find it difficult to get in touch with him. Two points, however, must be carefully remembered. In the first place it is necessary to maintain a certain courtesy of manner towards even the humblest individual, who always expects to be treated as a "caballero". In the second place the traveller, while maintaining his rights with quiet decision, should avoid all rudeness or roughness, which simply serves to excite the inflammable passions of the uneducated Spaniard. Common intercourse in Spain is marked by a degree of liberty and equality which the American will find easier to understand than the European.'

Perhaps one reason why not so many people visited Spain was because the traveller had to rely more on himself than in almost any other country in Europe. 'Full and accurate information as to means of communication, the postal arrangements, the hours at which galleries and museums are open, and the like can seldom be obtained even in the hotel-offices. Waiters, porters, and other servants are of absolutely no use in this matter, partly owing to their illiteracy and partly to their complete indifference to anything beyond their own particular sphere. Enquiries in the street, unless of the very simplest nature, should be addressed only to well-dressed people. It is desirable to avoid all contact with the members of the lowest classes who haunt the footsteps of the stranger in towns like Burgos, Avila, Toledo, Granada, and Córdova, offering their advice and services as guides. In dealing with guides, cabmen, and the like it is advisable to come to a clear understanding beforehand, even where there is a fixed tariff.'

Baedeker carries an accurate and detailed section on bullfighting, which is finally disapproving. Cock fighting was also popular in Spain, 'especially among the less reputable classes, but it is attended by so much disgusting brutality that the tourist is advised to have nothing to do with it'.

The 1913 Baedeker is still one of the best guidebooks to Spain, which I profitably carried on my meanderings in the 1950s and 1960s. I still prefer it to modern editions, whose coloured illustrations leave nothing either to the intellect or the imagination, and which don't even give idiosyncratic opinions for the rootless cosmopolitan such as myself to wonder at.

CHAPTER TWELVE

THE ROAD TO THE EAST

Until Thomas Cook's first organized parties set out for Egypt in 1869 it was not easy to go much beyond the beaten tracks of Western Europe. An independent tour for yourself and family, or for yourself alone, to less civilized or wilder places, demanded a great deal of money, as well as enterprise and energy. In the early part of the century, such a journey resembled an expedition, as related by Alexander Kinglake in his *Eōthen*, a popular book on eastern travel.

Murray's handbooks for the East began to appear in the late 1840s, providing help and instruction to those gentleman-scholars and others who, having seen Rome, wanted to visit the classical sites of Greece, the holy places of Palestine, or the Egyptian wonders in the Valley of the Nile.

To reach such countries by steamship from England, via the Mediterranean, soon became comparatively easy, but those who decided to go overland found many difficulties in their path, though Murray (and gradually improving maps) helped them to find their way. Even so, when Harry de Windt wrote *Through Savage Europe* sometime before the Great War, and was asked: 'Why "savage" Europe?' he replied, 'Because the term accurately describes the wild and lawless countries between the Adriatic and Black Seas.' He might well have said the same of the area today.

The traveller setting out overland some sixty years before de Windt, and hoping to get to Constantinople relatively unscathed, would need Murray's *Southern Germany and Austria* of 1858, as well as *Greece* and *Turkey*, both of 1854. From these three volumes he would derive much practical information, as well as an adequate amount of interesting matter to read, leading him to agree with Thackeray as he jogged along that: 'Much delight and instruction have I had in the course of the journey from my guide, philosopher, and friend, the author of "Murray's Hand-book" '.

Even as early in his journey as southern Germany, our traveller 'must by no means expect to meet with splendid hotels. Except in the chief towns, the inns are generally built on low vaults; the entrance serves for man and beast; and an oppressive odour of the stable often pervades them. The extreme disregard to cleanliness and sweetness, which is most annoying and disgusting to Englishmen, merits the utmost reprobation. The Germans themselves do not seem to be aware of it: let it be hoped that their increased intercourse with the English will introduce a taste for cleanliness, and a greater appreciation of it. In the bed-rooms, the small provision made for washing, usually confined to a small shallow pie-dish, a caraffe or tumbler of water, and a handkerchief for a towel, proclaim the nature of German habits in this respect, and shows how easily the desire for ablution is satisfied.'

By now one could pass fairly quickly through the country by train. 'The middle and wealthy classes travel almost exclusively in the second class, of which fact the traveller may easily satisfy himself by observing the very small number of first-class places in each train, and that even these are usually unoccupied, unless the conductor happens to have filled them with his friends.'

It was more than likely that the traveller's route lay through Bavaria, in which case he would have been interested in the following observations on beer, which the Bavarian is said to like inordinately, and to which 'he seems even more addicted than the natives of other parts of Germany... The conversation of the people constantly runs upon the amount and the quality of the annual brewing; it is a subject of as important discussion as the vintage or harvest in other countries... A genuine beer-drinker will contrive to swallow 10 to 12 measures, each holding much more than a quart English. Notwithstanding this attachment to beer, it may be said that drunkenness is not prevalent – at least it is not offensively visible – the principal reason being that it is not easy even for a Bavarian to swallow sufficient to produce intoxication.'

Should the traveller stop off for a few days at Nuremberg, he may take a ride on the first railway completed for locomotives in Germany, to the nearby town of Fürth, where about a quarter of the population of 15,000 are Jews, who 'being interdicted by an illiberal law from settling, or even sleeping, in Nuremberg, have made the fortune of Fürth by their industry and perseverance. They possess a college of their own here, a separate court of justice, 2 Hebrew printing establishments, and several schools and synagogues, and enjoy privileges denied them in other parts of the Continent. The town may be considered a German Birmingham . . .'

On coming to Austrian territory the traveller is treated with great civility, and 'asked for his passport, and requested to declare if he had any contraband articles. Those expressly forbidden, and not admitted even on payment of duty, are playing-cards, almanacs, tobacco, snuff, cigars, and sealed letters. All *books interdicted* by the censor are at once confiscated; those about which a doubt exists are retained to be examined by the censor . . . As a general rule, it is worth the traveller's while, on entering a new territory, to give the douaniers a couple of francs, by which he will obtain civility and despatch.'

The traveller is reminded: 'The same offences that would subject him to police interference in his own country would of course be attended with similar consequences in Austria; and if he were to get up in a coffee-room in Vienna and abuse the Austrian government, there is no doubt that he would find a gentleman from the police waiting at his own door in readiness to conduct him to the frontier. But to a mere traveller the police regulations are not more oppressive than in most other continental countries, and the officers by whom they are administered are usually distinguished for the civility and politeness with which they treat strangers, especially Englishmen, provided they themselves are treated as gentlemen.'

Apart from the usual scenery and art treasures to be seen in Austria, a visit to one of the many salt-mines is highly recommended. In the works where the commodity is processed: 'The increase of temperature causes the thin iron pan to heave and twist, and . . . Sometimes a hole is burned in the bottom, or a crack is produced; and as it is not possible to put out the fire merely on account of it, a man is sent into the pan to seek out the leak. This is a hazardous enterprise, as he runs the risk of being nearly stifled by the vapour, and of being boiled alive if he lose his footing. For this purpose he is shod with a pair of high pattens, not unlike two stools, upon which he wades through the boiling brine.'

Austrian inns are said to be rather better than those in Germany, as are the restaurants. On arriving at one in some remote area in the mountains, 'the new comer must not expect to be ushered in by a trim waiter with napkin tucked under his arm. He will most probably have to find his own way, under a low archway, by a passage which, though boarded, serves for the ingress and egress of horses and carriages, to the public room, which he will perhaps have to share with the people of the village; unless, as sometimes happens, there is an inner or better apartment for guests of distinction. It is generally a low apartment, with vaulted roof, supported on massive buttresses; at the door he will find a little cup for holy water; not far off hangs a crucifix, sometimes with a figure as large as life, and the walls are ornamented with stags' horns, or a chamois head, probably trophies of the rifle of mine host.'

The scene thus set is not unlike that of the opening of a 1930s horror movie, for after describing the furniture the writer goes on: 'Several sleepy-looking peasants will usually be seen seated on benches around the tables of unpainted wood, half enveloped in the smoke of their pipes, nodding over several huge beer-glasses with pewter lids. In the corner stands an unwieldy stove, the general point of attraction in cold weather. If the stranger, in search of some member of the establishment, extend his researches, he may perhaps find his way into the kitchen, in the centre of which, below a gaping chimney, is a raised platform paved with stones all scorched and black. Upon this culinary altar a wood fire is blazing, over it hangs a caldron, while around it, 2 or 3 busy females will be assembled, each tending some department of cookery, and too busy to notice the stranger.'

Perhaps our traveller is induced to tap his stick on the wall, for eventually the waitress makes her appearance, and very pleased he must have been to see her: 'She is a bustling, active damsel (often the landlord's daughter), with ruddy cheeks, and a good-humoured smile for everybody, very trimly dressed, and bearing about her the symbols of her office, a bunch of keys on one side, and a large leathern purse on the other. Through her active mediation the traveller's wants (provided they are not extravagant) are soon attended to, and in half an hour the trout and chamois are smoking on the board, and, with the never-failing friendly salutation of "I wish you a good appetite," he is invited to commence his repast. Sometimes mine host himself appears and seats himself by the stranger's side, as it would be considered rude to leave him alone during dinner in this country – a piece of old-fashioned politeness which an Englishman, if not prepared for it, might call imperti-nence. As he rises from the table, the guest is probably wished a "good digestion"; and for the douceur of a 5-Kreutzer piece when settling his bill, the waitress will smother his hand with kisses – for here the expression "I kiss your hand," in return for a favour, is not confined to the word, but is followed by the act; and as he leaves the house a hearty greeting of "*glückliche Reise!*" from the whole household, will follow his departing steps, provided he has conducted himself properly.'

Murray lavishes praise on the welcome which travellers receive in out-of-the-way inns of Austria and the Tirol, which he likens more to the reception of a friend than of a passing guest: '. . . there seems an anxious and disinterested study on the part of the inmates to make the stranger comfortable, and not to contrive how to get the most out of him, as in Switzerland.' He emphasizes that there is no cringing or obsequiousness, 'and the traveller must not return the attempts made to please him with complaints or dissatisfaction, else there is a chance of his being left supperless'.

The bedroom, however, is not as good as Murray would have wished, for it is often 'destined for 10 or 15 tenants at one time, and the beds not always provided with clean sheets, unless a little coaxing be employed to put the Kellnerinn into good humour, and thus obtain the concession of this point. As a general rule, however, the cleanliness of the inns of Tyrol, Austria, and parts of Styria, is most praiseworthy, as will forcibly occur to the mind of the traveller as soon as he crosses the frontier of Italy, and sighs with regret for the clean sheets which he has left behind.'

In Vienna the hotel charges were stated to be higher than in most other German capitals. Those of the first class were: '*Hotel Munsch*, very good and comfortable, but charges high and portions small; *Kaiserin Elizabeth*, kept by a most obliging and attentive host; well conducted and moderate for Vienna; *Erzherzog Karl*, a fashionable hotel, much frequented by the English, and dear, but excellent cuisine, and in a central situation, near the theatres; *Stadt London*, good, clean, civil people, fair cuisine, "Times" taken.'

After some molly-coddling in the capital our traveller will pursue his leisurely way along the great mountain range towards the Balkans, no doubt agreeing with Murray that: 'The strong religious feeling of the people is very remarkable; but who can live among the high Alps and not be impressed more than elsewhere with the dependence of man upon the Ruler of the elements? The pine riven by the lightning, the cottage burned by it, the winter's avalanche remaining through the summer unmelted in the depths of the valley, the line of desolation it has caused in its course, marked by the prostrate forest with the stumps only standing like straw in a stubble-field, the hamlet buried by the landslip or swept away by the mountain torrent, are subjects of every-day occurrence.'

Perhaps the favourite pastime of rifle-shooting started the occasional avalanche, for such a sport is found 'nowhere to the same extent as in Tyrol, whose inhabitants may be called the Kentuckians of Europe. Bred to the use of the weapon from their boyhood, and priding themselves above measure in the skilful exercise of it, and in accuracy of aim, they furnished an admirable corps of sharp-shooters.'

In the 1890 edition of the handbook Murray has some amendments to the above: 'Up to the last few years the Tyrolese were supposed to be amongst the best shots in the world, but the English marksman has now completely eclipsed him in both precision and distance', a competition, I suppose, only finally decided between the trenches of the Great War.

The Tirolese were also said to take delight in gymnastic exercises, for a Sunday afternoon or a fête day 'usually terminates in a wrestling match, which, in some parts of the country, is coupled with a species of pugilistic encounter not unlike an American gouging-match. Almost every Tyrolese peasant wears a very thick ring of silver or iron on the little finger of the right hand, and a fist so armed inflicts cruel wounds. Such savage combats not unfrequently terminate in the loss of an eye, ear, or nose, such acts of violence not being considered unfair or contrary to the laws of the sport. The old men are umpires, and take a pleasure in stimulating the combatants.'

The greatest passion of the Austrian mountaineers is music and the dance. 'They appear born with a taste for music: a violin or a guitar is a part of the furniture of every cottage, and not unfrequently a piano. The enthusiasm, almost approaching to frenzy, with which the dance is kept up, in spite of the heat and crowd, from noon till night, is truly surprising. The partners often seize each other by the shoulders, in an attitude not unlike hugging.'

Further east the Styrian inns are 'generally comfortless, the people disobliging; and one feature, which strikes the traveller more than any other, and is, as far as I know, unexampled in Europe, is the extraordinary precautions taken against house-breaking, by the invariable use of strong iron stanchions in the smallest windows of the most trifling cottages, whilst iron shutters and bars are common, even in small villages. Highway robbery, though less frequent than formerly, is by no means unknown, and military posts are established for the protection of travellers on the great road from Laibach to Trieste. The use of ardent spirits (Slivovitz) is fearfully universal.'

The Bohemian inns, except in Prague, the large towns and the spas, are 'dirty, and very inferior to those in Austria Proper. In part of Moravia and Galicia they are filthy hovels, perfectly wretched . . .'

Baedeker tells us that in Prague there are ten synagogues, the one in the Altneuschule being 'a strange-looking, gloomy pile of the 12th century, the oldest synagogue in Prague, having been founded, according to tradition, by the first fugitives from Jerusalem after its destruction. The large flag suspended from the vaulting, and extending across the whole synagogue, was presented by Ferdinand III, in recognition of the bravery of the Jews during the siege of Prague by the Swedes in 1648.'

Murray says that the Jews of Prague were settled in the locality *before* the destruction of Jerusalem, making it the oldest Hebrew settlement in Europe. 'In 1290 the Jews were almost exterminated by the fanaticism of the ignorant populace, stirred up by rumours of their having insulted the Host – a prevalent accusation – which caused an almost universal massacre of them throughout Germany. Indeed the history of the Jews in Prague is a dark chapter of that of Christianity. It is one uninterrupted narrative of tyranny, extortion, and blood on the one side, and of long-suffering on the other. Till the end of the last century, Charles IV, Rudolf II, and Joseph II appear the only rulers who held out any protection to this devoted race.'

For part of his journey to the east the traveller may have referred to Captain Spencer's *Turkey, Russia, the Black Sea, and Circassia*, 1854. In this he would have learned that before the 1848 Revolution against the Austrian tyranny, the cities of Hungary 'could boast of palaces and public buildings, which would be admired for the beauty of their architecture even in the meridian of London and Paris; stagnant moats, which shed around their pestilential exhalations, were filled up and converted into public promenades; a magnificent suspension bridge, thrown across the Danube, connected Pest and Buda; while hospitals and benevolent institutions, richly endowed, had been established to relieve the wants of the poorer part of the population. If we penetrated into the rural districts, they also exhibited all the indications of prosperity – comfortable farm-houses, villages, and roadside inns, everywhere met the view, together with an improved system of agriculture.'

A few pages later Spencer described the country on a visit in 1850, after the uprising had, with Russia's help, been ruthlessly put down. 'The scene of ruin and desolation which everywhere met our view was perfectly appalling . . . we beheld traces of the barbarian hordes of half wild Croats, Wallachs, and Serbs, and we may add Austrians and Russians, who had so lately rode roughshod over the entire land, and by imperial authority massacred every human being of Magyar origin who fell into their hands; and even at this time, when it might be supposed that the worst passions of man's nature would have been satiated by indulgence, there was scarcely any abatement in the cruelties exercised by the government towards this unfortunate people. The brutality of the soldiers was unrestrained, the vexatious insolence of the police unendurable –

the sufferings of the unhappy prisoners who filled the dungeons of the fortresses and all the strong places were such as revengeful tyranny alone delights to inflict.'

Murray, in his guide of a few years later, tells us: 'Police regulations are, in respect of passports, at least as stringent as in any other part of the Austrian dominions.' He goes on to say: 'The greater part of English travellers in Hungary are contented with a visit to Pest, which is most easily effected by descending the Danube from Vienna by steamer in 10 to 12 hours.'

Should you disregard this advice and go out of the main cities, Murray has other observations to pass on to you: 'The Hungarian inns are on the whole the worst I have found in Europe. They are generally of one storey, planted in the midst of a court-yard ankle-deep in mud, with an arcade running round them; broken steps and uneven pavement lead up to them. Landlord and waiter are seldom at hand to receive a traveller when he presents himself; the attendance is slow and bad: but these are trifles. I am not over nice, but I must confess the public dining-room, with its tobacco fumes, dogs, the practice of spitting to excess, and not unfrequently the horrid smell of garlic, and, what is worse, the total absence of all attempt to purify the apartment, filled me with disgust. But you are no better off in the bed-rooms: they are equally bespitten, and as seldom cleaned. The spider nestles for ever in the corners, and his tapestry is the only drapery which adorns the bare walls. As for the beds, I shudder to think of them. With all the discomforts of those of Germany they have this in addition, that they are usually filthy. The sheets are sewn on to the coverlid, and how often they serve it is impossible to say. You must especially *order* clean sheets, and your desire will then be complied with. A bell is almost unknown, even in the chief towns. If you want anything, you must open your window or door and call out to the waiter. You need not expect an answer; but go down stairs, and you will find him in the passage curling his moustachios.'

A stout travelling carriage is absolutely necessary for getting around: 'Except on one or two roads, Hungary affords nothing but common carts. Leather sheets are desirable, and sleeping in a carriage is often preferable to a bed. No Hungarian gentleman thinks of travelling without his sheets, pillow, pillow-case, and leather sheets. Mattresses are required by those about to penetrate from Hungary into the far east. Mosquito-curtains will be found of the greatest service to those who descend the Danube, and who value skin, sleep, or comfort, since myriads of those venomous insects are engendered on the marshy shores of the river.'

As for food, a chicken may be put on the traveller's table within half an hour of arrival, 'but in other respects the larders of the country inns are very badly provided; therefore let the traveller furnish a basket with cold meat, etc., and take several bottles of good wine from whatever starting point he may set out from.'

One of the main highways into the Balkans was the Danube, on which river steam navigation had been started by two English shipbuilders in 1828. Even so, they had 'commenced the undertaking unaided by others, and, sharing the usual discouragements which attend strangers in a foreign land, they would have been compelled to abandon their plan, had it not received the encouragement of two enlightened noblemen'. The earliest boats were 'vessels of a peculiar construction, used for the conveyance of pigs from Serbia to Vienna. Many of the engines are by well-known British engine-makers.'

To get downriver from Vienna to the Black Sea took five days on the faster steamers, which were 'built after the American fashion, with a spacious deck saloon, and sleeping cabins behind. Provisions are not included in the fare, but there is a very tolerable restaurant on board, and the dinner-hour is 12 o'clock. The sleeping accommodation is not good, fleas are very numerous; there is a small ladies' cabin, generally very crowded; and round the gentlemen's cabin is a sofa or divan, serving instead of beds; but in summertime it often happens that there is not room for half the passengers, and the remainder must therefore sleep on the floor or on deck. The decks of the steamers are often crowded with merchandise, and the convenience of passengers is sacrificed to the accommodation of goods, inasmuch as they have barely room to stir. Two or three other inconveniences must be mentioned. The mosquitoes, gnats, etc., abound, especially in the lower part of the river; and to escape this plague it may be prudent to take a mosquito net. The marshy land at the mouth of the Danube is *most unhealthy* at certain seasons, *teeming with fever and ague*, which those who merely pass up and down without stopping do not always escape. The Hungarians almost surpass the Americans in the filthy habit of spitting, which is not always confined to the deck.'

If our traveller deviates from the river, to look for adventure in other parts of the Austrian dominions, the railway to Lemberg will take him through the land of the Slovaks, who are 'a quiet, inoffensive, industrious people, but are said to be obstinate, avaricious, fond of flattery, and no great lovers of cleanliness'.

It may be as well to avoid Stuhlweissenburg where the 'palace of the bishop, and some of the buildings connected with it, are handsome, but the whole town is disagreeably placed in the centre of a huge bog'.

A romantic story is related concerting the seventeenth-century castle of Murany, the residence of 'the young and beautiful' widow Maria Szecsi. She was a Protestant and, in defence of that cause, garrisoned her mountain fastness with a detachment of troops commanded by her brother-in-law. 'The castle was amply furnished with provisions and ammunition; the troops brave and faithful; their commander, a staunch Protestant. Murany was therefore deemed impregnable, and the defenders laughed and made merry when, in 1644, they saw it invested by an imperial army under the Palatine Vesselenyi. The Palatine, however, soon managed to acquire possession of it, – not indeed by force of arms, but simply by marrying its fair occupant, gaining thus, at the same time, both the lady and the castle.'

Venturing into the wilder parts of Wallachia, one travelled in the common cart of the country, 'made entirely of wood, without a particle of iron, very light, on low wheels, easily upset, and as easily righted. They are ... capable of holding only one person, and, on account of the rude jolting, are only to be endured, by those accustomed to them, when filled with hay to sit or lie upon. 4 horses are harnessed to them, and they always go at full gallop, driven by a rough peasant on the near wheeler. The situation of a traveller in rainy weather, seated close behind, and on a level with the heels of 4 wild horses, is not agreeable; in a few minutes he becomes plastered over with mud.'

One of the crossing points into the Turkish Empire was at Belgrade which, to quote Captain Spencer, 'with its picturesque old castle, its domes and minarets, first announces to the traveller on the Lower Danube that he has entered the territory of the unchanged and unchanging Land of the Crescent'.

Murray's *Turkey*, 1854, says: 'The traveller will find here a very good khan and a large German hotel. The once celebrated fortress of Belgrade is now only a picturesque ruin. This citadel, and a few other fortresses in Serbia, are garrisoned by Turkish troops, but Serbia is virtually independent.'

Constantinople can be reached from Belgrade, we are told, in 143 hours, though it had been performed 'in 6 days by couriers riding day and night, and in 12 days by ordinary travellers, who require 6 horses for himself, baggage, and tatar'. The cost was said to be £25, including £2 bakshish. 'A Turkish shawl, sash, woollen overalls, leather trowsers, and two or three large cloaks, will be found convenient clothing, except in winter, when the "shaggy capote" is almost indispensable in the snowy passes. A pair of pistols worn in a belt may be advisable, rather in conformity with custom than for use.'

The Danubian principalities of Wallachia, Moldavia, Serbia, Bosnia, part of Croatia, Herzegovina, Montenegro, Bulgaria and Thrace were all under the control of the Turks. On one of his journies Captain Spencer passed through the town of Jassy, in a region of constantly shifting frontiers inhabited by 'Boyards and Turks, Greeks, Armenians, Slavonians, and Jews'. Said to be beautifully situated it is, like everywhere else in the area, unhealthy. 'There are, however, some signs of improvement at Jassy, since we see here and there an elegant mansion recently erected, and others in the hands of the builder.' Of the various races, all are said to be

adhering as strictly to their own language and peculiar costume, as if their very existence depended upon the cut and form of their garments. Each of these nationalities also occupies a separate district in the town. The Jews are so numerous as to form about a third of the whole population, rather good-looking than otherwise, more especially the women, whose appearance was much improved by their half oriental dress. The velvet tiara, set with pearls and precious stones, is said to be of the same form as that worn by the court beauties in the days of King Solomon; which proves that the fair daughters of Israel in those days were so far coquettish as to invent a mode of head-dress well adapted to their peculiar style of beauty, as it certainly makes a pretty face look still more captivating; and I was assured by my Jew banker, whose guest I was during my stay at Jassy, that one of these head-dresses is not unfrequently worth five hundred pounds sterling, and descends as an heir-loom in the family.

Spencer goes on to tell us the same old story:

These poor people, the Jews, to whose industry and enterprise as merchants, traders, and shopkeepers, the state is indebted for a great part of its revenue, occasionally suffer severely from the fanaticism of the inhabitants, who are credulous enough to believe the most absurd reports that can be conceived. Still, the Jews of these countries, however averse they are in general to fighting, do not submit to be led like sheep to the slaughter; they are always prepared, if necessary, to repel force by force. Unhappily, these contests with the Christians of the Greek Church, both here and in Russia, are too frequent and sanguinary; and, singular enough, their rallying cry, *Gewalt! Gewalt!*, is in the German language; and when this is heard, the whole Hebrew population, men, women, and children, arm themselves with some weapon of defence, and rush to the scene of action.

Pursuing our slow way towards Constantinople and the Golden Horn, we would perhaps tarry awhile at Nissa where 'the traveller is struck with the sight of a tower composed of skulls, erected to commemorate a victory over the Serbs by the Turks'. At Sofia, the hot baths were famous for their medicinal qualities, and: 'Good accommodation may be found in a private Greek house.' But the khan at Adrianople was 'large and very dirty; a clean room, however, may be procured by means of bakshish to the innkeeper. An hotel according to European customs has of late been opened, but it can scarcely be considered preferable to the old khan.'

Those who went down the Danube to the Black Sea could take

ship to Constantinople, and if they had not delayed, would have made the journey from England in about twelve days. A more leisurely method was to go all the way by sea on a P & O steamer in some fifteen days, the ship calling at Malta where, Murray says, 'The higher classes of native Maltese are not surpassed by those of any country in general intelligence, in highly cultivated tastes, or in the accomplishments and personal character of individuals. But for many years it had been so much the practice of English residents to treat the Maltese with indifference or contempt, that there is very little opportunity for a stranger to form any opinion except from such examples as may be found in most places where a large fleet and garrison are stationed.'

A journey to the Mediterranean on a steamship from Liverpool took on the nature of a cruise, one line issuing a ticket, out and home, for thirty pounds. 'A gentleman and his wife can obtain a reduction. This affords a most agreeable trip, particularly for an invalid, and occupies about six weeks or two months. Some of these are splendid vessels, and in the autumn there is often pleasant society.' Should you go overland by rail as far as Trieste, and then on by boat: 'The steamers are good, and each carries a doctor and stewardess.'

Travelling conditions and speeds were improving all through the nineteenth century, and by the end one could take the overland train to the Rumanian port of Constanza on the Black Sea, where 'comfortable and well managed' steamers went to Constantinople, the trip taking about four days. When the railway was opened to Salonika you could travel through Thrace, which shortened the journey even more.

Just before the First World War the Orient Express went into service 'between London and Constantinople' via Paris, Vienna, Budapest, Belgrade, Sofia and Adrianople. A copy of the timetable is given in the 1907 edition of Murray's handbook, and Hachette published a special guide *De Paris à Constantinople* in 1912. This covered much of the Balkans and western Turkey, and it is hard to imagine anyone setting out on the journey without a copy, the latest Murray being by then out of date. The Orient Express did the 3200 kilometres from Paris in sixty hours, 'without changing either train or carriage', though a high supplement was payable on the first-class fare of the ordinary train.

Bradshaw's *Through Routes to the Capitals of the World*, 1903, gave the route as via Paris in seventy-two hours, for the price of twenty-two pounds and eleven shillings, pointing out in the preface: 'Travel is becoming more luxurious and more expensive. For the better accommodation provided and the greater speed attained the passenger has to pay.'

Half a century earlier, Murray had recommended the carrying of two pistols in the belt for the overland journey to the East. On the matter of public safety in 1903 Bradshaw comments: 'A revolver is usually a tiresome encumbrance, never likely to be of service to those who are not well-practised shots. Where one must be carried, let it be a good one. In the few cases when one does want a revolver one wants it very badly, so let it be handy – not in the hip pocket, but in the side-pocket of the overcoat or jacket; not under the pillow, but down in the middle of the berth or bed, near the right hand; and at need do not hesitate to fire through the clothes, and before the weapon can be seen.'

CHAPTER THIRTEEN

GREECE AND EGYPT

Should a tour of Greece be taken in on the way to Egypt, Palestine and Turkey, Murray's handbook of 1854 would be essential reading, since Baedeker's *Greece* did not appear in English until 1889. Murray's commonsense is early to the fore: 'In Greece and the East generally, even more than in other countries, let the traveller bear in mind this important *hint before starting* – he should never omit visiting any object of interest whenever it happens to be within his reach at the time, as he can never be certain what impediments may occur to prevent him from carrying his intentions into effect at a subsequent period.'

After giving advice on protection against vermin Murray makes suggestions on the equipment to be taken: 'A *large and stout cotton umbrella* is required as a protection not only from the rain, but also from the sun. A *green veil, and blue or neutral-tinted spectacles*, are very useful as a safeguard against the glare of the sun. A *pocket-telescope, a thermometer, drawing materials, measuring tape*, and the like, are luxuries to be provided or not, according to the taste and pursuits of each individual tourist.'

The section on kitting out quotes Edward Lear as saying: 'Arms and ammunition, fine raiment, presents for natives, are all nonsense, simplicity should be your aim', though Murray goes on to inform us that those who stay some time in the East, or sail in their own yachts, 'will often wish to leave some token of remembrance with officials. For this purpose the best articles to provide are a few pairs of English pistols, knives, pocket-telescopes, toys for children, and ornaments for ladies. Prints of the Queen, the Ministers etc., are very acceptable to the British Consular Agents, who are generally natives.'

A few pages of hints concerning health tell us that: 'The abundance of fruit is a great temptation to foreigners, but nothing is more pernicious, or more likely to lead to fatal consequences.' As for malaria: 'No Eastern traveller should be without a small *bottle* of quinine pills, and a few simple directions for their use.'

Locomotion is by horse. 'One hour is, on average, equivalent to about 3 English miles; though in level parts of the country, and with good horses, the traveller may ride much faster', but 'the usual rate of progress does not exceed from 20 to 25 miles a-day'.

Though hotels existed in Athens and other large places, charging about ten francs a day for full board, it was different in the countryside, where: 'The keepers of coffee-houses and billiard-rooms (which are now very general) will always lodge a traveller, but he must expect no privacy here. He must live all day in public, and be content at night to have his mattress spread, with some twenty others belonging to the family or other guests, either on the floor or on a wooden divan which surrounds the room. When particular honour is to be shown to a guest, his bed is laid upon the billiard table: he never should decline this distinction, as he will thereby have a better chance of escape from vermin.'

The traveller can take some comfort on reading that: 'The stranger is almost invariably received with much natural courtesy; and in the domestic arrangements, manners, and language of his hosts, he will find much to remind him of their forefathers. The description in Homer of the cottage of Eumaeus is not inapplicable to the hut of a Greek peasant of the existing generation; while the agricultural implements and usages of the present day are not far removed from those of the times of Hesiod.'

On the inhabitants, after a few words each about the Ghegs, Toskes, Liapes, and Tjames, we are told that the genuine Skipetar (or Albanian) is 'generally of the middle stature, and of lighter complexion than the Greeks; very spare and muscular, and particularly slight around the waist. The lower classes are filthily dirty, often wearing the same coarse woollen skirt and kilt till they fall to pieces. The peasant women are generally handsome and well formed when young, but hard fare, exposure, and the field labour which they undergo, soon nip their beauty in its bud.'

As for the Greeks, they are 'often called assassins, robbers, etc.', says one of Mr Murray's correspondents quoted in the book, 'yet I knew the commander of the police well, when in a whole winter at Athens – the population being 20,000 – there was no case of *housebreaking* or murder. Indeed, my kitchen was cleared of its contents, being an outhouse, and a householder killed in a village; but the one, as most other pilferings, was the work of Bavarians, and the other the crime of a British subject – a Maltese. Greeks are generally called rogues, yet in commerce no Greek merchant of consequence has failed; and both an astute English merchant and a canny Scotch agent have often told me a bill, with three good Greek names to it, is security never known to fail.'

Murray tells us that the Greek character has suffered much from centuries of slavery: 'All the vices which tyranny generates – the abject vices which it generates in those who quail under it – the ferocious vices which it generates in those who struggle against it – have occasionally been exhibited by Greeks in modern times. Despite their many faults we call to mind their misfortunes and the blood that is in them, and still love the Greeks. Their forefathers were the intellectual aristocracy of mankind.'

Should the British traveller wish to learn more of the country he might with advantage meet 'Mr. Black, professor of English etc., and husband of Lord Byron's "Maid of Athens", who gives lessons in Modern Greek and other languages, and may be applied to for general information with regard to the country where he has been established amidst all its vicissitudes for many years.'

There is no street plan of Athens in Murray, and the traveller may be forgiven for getting lost on his way to the Acropolis. 'The minor streets are hardly deserving of the name, being merely narrow lanes displaying a marked contempt for all regularity.'

Forty-four lines of Milton and eighteen lines of Byron are given the traveller to read while pausing with wonder on the steps of the Acropolis. Perhaps it will not surprise him to note that, concerning the nature of democracy among the Ancient Greeks, 'The chief authority for the population of ancient Attica is the census of

Demetrius Phalerus, taken in B.C. 317. According to this census, there were 21,000 Athenian citizens, 10,000 resident aliens, and 400,000 slaves.'

The Acropolis suffered in repeated wars, during which the ten Doric columns of the Parthenon were 'together with the whole of the central building and the adjoining columns of the peristyle, thrown down by the explosion of a magazine of gunpowder, ignited by the Venetian bombardment in 1687'.

According to Baedeker: 'The Turks entrenched themselves on the Acropolis and concealed their store of powder in the Parthenon. The latter accordingly became the target of the Venetian artillery-men, and on Friday, Sept. 26th, [1687] at 7 p.m., a German lieutenant had the doubtful honour of firing the bomb which ignited the powder and blew the stately building into the air.'

Some distinguished travellers had a fine time archaeologically looting while in Greece, and the museums of Europe have much to thank them for, depending on your point of view, if not your nationality. With an eye, as it were, to the main chance, the Venetian commander, Morosini, 'after the capture of the city' – back to Murray – 'attempted to carry off some of the statues in the western pediment; but, owing to the unskilfulness of the Venetians, they were thrown down as they were being lowered, and were dashed in pieces'.

Then of course there is the issue of the Elgin Marbles, on which Murray says: 'At the beginning of the present century, many of the finest sculptures of the Parthenon were removed to England.' More recent archeological investigations (1835) had revealed 'frag-ments of columns of a sculptured frieze, exactly answering to four pieces in the British Museum brought over by Lord Elgin . . .' as if that might in some way make up for his depredations.

One of the caryatides found in an excavation at the Erechtheum in 1846 was 'restored to its former place, and a new figure cast in cement was sent out from England in place of the sixth, which was, and is, in the British Museum'.

There was no making amends, for Baedeker in his second English edition says rather tartly: 'In 1787, the French agent *Fauvel* managed to secure a few fragments of the Parthenon sculptures for the French ambassador. But to the British ambassador *Lord Elgin*

belongs the discredit of instituting a systematic removal of the art-
treasures of the Acropolis. In 1801 he procured a firman authorising
him to remove "a few blocks of stone with inscriptions and figures",
and with the aid of several hundred labourers, he removed the
greater part of the metopes, the pediments, and the frieze. The
priceless sculptures and their conveyance to England cost about
£36,000. In 1816, after various abortive negotiations, during which
the value of the sculptures had been set in a proper light, they were
purchased by the British Government; and they now, under the
name of the "Elgin Marbles", form the most valuable possession
of the British Museum.'

So much for that, but the Germans were no babes at the game,
either. Schliemann looted Troy, where excavations were carried on,
says Murray, showing commendable understatement, 'with such suc-
cess'. Most of the treasures went to Athens, where Schliemann had
married a Greek lady, some of the treasures going around her neck.

The Prussians were busy excavating at Pergamon, also in
modern Turkey, from 1879 and, according to Hachette's *Eastern
Mediterranean*, 'The principal sculptures were removed to Berlin.'
I saw them there in 1970, and very impressive they were, for whole
buildings had been taken from their rightful home.

Baedeker tells us in 1894 that a journey to Greece 'no longer ranks
with those exceptional favours of fortune which fall to the lot of
but few individuals. Athens, thanks to modern railways and
steamers, has been brought within four days of London.'

Even so, conditions had changed little since Murray's handbooks was written forty years previously, because at places in the
interior: 'The inns are usually miserable cottages, with a kitchen
and one large common sleeping-room; nowadays some of them
also possess a few separate rooms, which are, however, destitute of
furniture, glass windows, and fire-places. The traveller must bring
his own coverings with him, as the rags presented to him for bed-
clothes are almost always full of vermin.' The point is made that
the civilized traveller will find so much dirt and vermin 'that their
deep enthusiasm for treading classic soil and their deep admiration
for Greek scenery become seriously impaired'.

Hospitality from the locals had its drawbacks in that 'consideration for the feelings of his host limits the traveller in various ways, and this is increased by the fact that the modern Greek has generally very little idea of the value of time. The only return the stranger can make for his reception is a gratuity to the servants. In small houses, however, where the traveller has been received without the formality of introduction, the sum of 4–5 dr. is expected for the night's lodging, while, on the other hand, the visitor may take his ease almost as freely as at an inn.'

Should the traveller prefer to avoid such complications and cruise among the islands: 'The small coasting steamers are usually very poorly appointed, and the cabins often swarm with vermin. The want of order on almost all the Greek steamers is particularly disagreeable. In spite of the nominal prohibition, the steerage passengers, who are often more picturesque at a distance than agreeable at close quarters, occasionally invade the after-deck, and the notice forbidding smoking in the saloon is sometimes more honoured in the breach than in the observance.'

Baedeker goes on to say that those who do not know modern Greek 'should not attempt to travel in the interior without a guide', then gives a facsimile of the necessary contract for engaging one: 'In concluding the agreement, which is best done in a café over a cup of coffee, the traveller should preserve an air of indifference and should avoid all indications of hurry.'

Taking walks of more than a day or two is practically impossible 'owing to the climate, the difficulty of obtaining food and shelter, and the badness of the roads. Travellers should never quit the main roads without a guide, partly on account of the savage dogs.' As a protection against this menace the traveller to remote parts is recommended to carry a stout cane or long riding whip, which will sometimes be found useful in repelling them, 'though stone-throwing is perhaps still more effective'.

Public safety is said to be 'all that can be desired. Since the bold acts of brigandage in 1870 (an Italian and three English gentlemen were shot by the bandits) the Greek government has exerted itself strenuously to extirpate this national evil; and only a few isolated cases have occurred near the Turkish frontier.'

Baedeker's *Lower Egypt*, 1885, informs us that since the publications of the French scholars attached to Napoleon's Expedition, Egypt has 'attracted the ever-increasing attention of the scientific; its historical and archeological marvels have been gradually unveiled to the world; it is the most ancient, and was yet at one time the most civilised country of antiquity; and it therefore cannot fail to awaken the profoundest interest in all students of the history and development of human culture.'

Murray's handbook of 1858 was written by Sir I. Gardner Wilkinson, who puts the cost of travelling via Marseilles and then to Alexandria by steamer at twenty-seven pounds. Rather than take the French boat, the English vessel is considered 'far preferable on the score of living, civility, cleanliness, a greater certainty of arriving at the promised time, and the smaller number of extra charges. Complaints are also made of the great confusion on arriving at Alexandria from the admission of so many natives, touters from the hotels and others, on board the French boats.'

Items useful for a journey to Egypt are said to include: 'Iron bedstead to fold up; pipes, Wire for cleaning pipes, put into a reed; Mouth-pieces and pipe-bowls; Washing-tub; Flags, for boat on Nile; Small pulley and rope for flag; Fireplaces. In the boat going up the Nile have a set put together in a large fireplace with a wooden back; Gun, pistols; Powder and shot; For observations, a sextant and artificial horizon; An iron rat-trap for the boat.'

Notes on health tell us that: 'Bathing in the Nile is by no means prejudicial in the morning and evening; and, except in the neighbourhood of sandbanks, there is no fear of crocodiles. It is unnecessary to say much respecting the plague, which seldom now visits Egypt; and if it should appear, any one may escape it by leaving the country on the first alarm.'

Most guidebooks go into the practicality of Europeans donning oriental dress, Murray telling us that is by no means necessary, and indeed that anyone wearing it 'who is ignorant of the language, becomes ridiculous . . . a person is never respected who is badly dressed, of whatever kind the costume may be, and nowhere is exterior appearance so much thought of as in the East.'

When the ship reaches the vicinity of Alexandria it is not easy to get into port, Murray says, due 'to the complicated channels which are beset with shoals and reefs. But on making the coast late in the evening, the steamer lays to till daylight, and early in the morning the pilot comes off; for no captain thinks of entering the harbour without him; the buoys laid down by the English in 1801, to mark the passage, having been removed as soon as they left the country.'

The stranger is told that if he escapes the rapacity of the boatmen who, like everyone at Alexandria, are *never satisfied*, however well paid, 'he is immediately pressed on all sides by the most importunate of human beings, in the shape of donkey-drivers. Their active little animals may be called the cabs of Egypt; and each driver, with vehement vociferations and gesticulations, recommending his own, in broken English or bad Italian, strives to take possession of the unfortunate traveller, and almost forces him to mount.'

After expatiating on the difficulties of hiring a carriage comes the remark that: 'It is not only the natives who are rapacious and exacting; the Europeans in Egypt may vie with any of them, and their example is seldom beneficial to the Egyptians.'

Bradshaw, of 1903, mentions the 'boys (most arrant knaves) driving donkeys at a railway pace', and tells us that on landing 'either proceed per omnibus waiting at the pier or jump on a donkey; take your things with you (the boys are very clever, but not to be trusted), and proceed to the hotel'. He adds that we must not let ourselves be 'tormented to death' by claims for bakshish.

Baedeker says that the Customs examination is fairly strict, the articles chiefly sought for being tobacco, weapons and diamonds. 'No fee need be given to the officials.'

For the rail trip to Cairo Murray advised that you 'take a few sandwiches, or a fowl, and wine, for the journey, rather than pay a high price for them at the railway-station on the road'. Regarding the canal between the two cities, which it took 250,000 men a whole year to dig, Murray says: 'Another proof of bad management in its execution was the great loss of life among the workmen; no less than 20,000 being said to have perished by accidents, hunger, and plague.'

The best hotel at Cairo was, of course, Shepheard's, under the proprietor Mr Zech, a hotel still 'most frequented by travellers', in

Bradshaw's guide. If you took a house at Cairo, it was as well, said Murray, 'not to trust too much to the honesty of servants'. He recommends several, however, who are reliable, including Mahmood, 'formerly in the service of the Duke of Northumberland and Colonel Felix'.

Should you care for a bath, none of the establishments 'are remarkable for size or splendour. They are all vapour-baths; and their heat, the system of shampooing, and the operations of rubbing with horse-hair gloves, contribute not a little to cleanliness and comfort, though it is by no means agreeable to have to undergo the operation of being shampooed by the bathing-men.'

There were said to be five thousand Jews in Cairo, out of a population of 200,000, and in the Jewish quarter 'many of the houses of the two opposite sides actually touch each other at the upper stories. The principal reason for their being made so narrow is to afford protection in case of the quarter being attacked, and to facilitate escape when the houses have been forced.'

The population of Cairo had decreased in recent years, and Murray expressed the wish that this had been the case with the dogs as well, because 'a small number would suffice for all the purposes for which they are useful, and the annoyance of these barking plagues might be diminished to great advantage. Their habits are strange; they consist of a number of small republics, each having its own district, determined by a frontier line, respected equally by itself and its neighbours; and woe to the dog who dares to venture across it at night, either for plunder, curiosity, or a love of adventure. He is chased with all the fury of the offended party, whose territory he had invaded; but if lucky enough to escape to his own frontier unhurt, he immediately turns round with the confidence of right, defies his pursuers to continue the chase, and, supported by his assembled friends, joins with them in barking defiance at any further hostility. Egypt is therefore not the country for a European dog, unaccustomed to such a state of canine society: and I remember hearing of a native servant who had been sent by his Frank master to walk out a favourite pointer, running home in tears with the hind leg of the mangled dog, being the only part he could rescue from the fierce attacks of a whole tribe of town mongrels.'

The attraction for which no number of asterisks would have been sufficient was a visit to the Pyramids, beginning with that of Cheops. 'The ascent is by no means difficult, though fatiguing to some unaccustomed to climbing, from the height of the stones, while others ascend with the greatest ease; and I have known one, an officer of the Cyclops, reach the top in 8 min. Ladies, who are often dragged up, rather than assisted, by the Arabs, will find a great advantage in having a couple of steps, or a footstool, to be carried by the Arabs, and put down where the stones are high; and this would be not less useful in descending than in going up the pyramid.'

Baedeker is a little more explicit. 'The traveller selects two of the importunate Beduins by whom he is assailed, and proceeds to where the ascent begins. These strong and active attendants assist the traveller to mount by pushing, pulling, and supporting him, and will scarcely allow him a moment's rest until the top is reached. As, however, the unwonted exertion is fatiguing, the traveller should insist on resting several times on the way up, if so disposed. Ladies should have a suitable dress for the purpose . . . At the summit of the Pyramid the patience is again sorely tried by the onslaught of vendors of *spurious* antiquities and dishonest money-changers, all parley with whom should be avoided.'

Bradshaw tells us, unnecessarily, that 'the tourist, especially if alone, will be pestered by the Arabs and Arab boys who live near Gizeh, proffering their services as guides, attendants, etc., and punctuating every sentence with a call for "bakshish".' One should, however, take no notice of them, but 'if too pressing or annoying, application should be made to the Sheik, who when appealed to will exert his authority and free the individual, or the party, from further trouble on this point whilst within his neighbourhood. It is advisable to give something to each person whom one allows to render a service, but there should be no indiscriminate scattering of largesse.'

The population of Egypt was said to be about two million, while the Thomas Cook handbook of fifty years later gave it as nearly ten million. Settled conditions after 1882, when the country was

administered by the British, perhaps accounted for the steep rise.
The Baedeker of 1885 puts the population in ancient times at seven
million. 'This number is quite reasonable in itself, as it is estimated
that the country could support 8–9 million inhabitants.' The latest
census gives a population of 55 million.

The local people are seen, in the mid-Victorian Murray, from
the point of view of those who hold the purse-strings: 'The traveller,
apart from his ignorance of the language, will find it exceedingly
difficult to deal with the class of people with whom he chiefly
comes in contact. The extravagance of their demands is boundless,
and they appear to think that Europeans are absolutely ignorant of
the value of money. Every attempt at extortion should be firmly
resisted, as compliance only makes the applicants for bakshish
doubly clamorous. Payment should never be made until the service
stipulated for has been rendered, after which an absolutely deaf ear
should be turned to the protestations and entreaties which almost
invariably follow. Thanks, it need hardly be said, must never be
expected from such recipients. Even when an express bargain has
been made, and more than the stipulated sum paid, they are almost
sure to pester the traveller in the way indicated. The Egyptians, it
must be remembered, occupy a much lower grade in the scale of
civilisation than most of the western nations, and cupidity is one
of their chief failings; but if the traveller makes due allowance for
their shortcomings, and treats the natives with consistent firmness,
he will find that they are by no means destitute of fidelity, honesty,
and kindliness.'

An authority on the country, Wallis Budge, wrote a short guide
to the monuments of the Nile for the benefit of Thomas Cook &
Son's tourists in 1886. In twenty years, this work had become a
thousand-page *Hand-book for Egypt and the Sudan*, fully the equal
of Murray or Baedeker. In the preface Budge states, of course, that
travellers in Egypt 'owe the ease and comfort which they now enjoy
in journeying through the country entirely to the efforts of Messrs.
Thos. Cook & Son, who were the first to organise the tourists
system, and to make Egypt and its wonderful antiquities accessible
to all classes. They have spared neither pains nor money in perfect-
ing their arrangements for tourists, and their officers are ever watch-
ful to place promptly at the disposal of those who travel under

their care the advantages of rapid and comfortable transit which are becoming more and more numerous owing to the steady development of the country under British influence.'

The last word on begging is a notice, printed verbatim in the handbook, issued by Lord Cromer, and the United States and German Consul General: 'The attention of the Egyptian authorities has been frequently drawn (in 1906) both by visitors and by residents of the country, to the evils resulting from the indiscriminate bestowal of "bakshish" to the inhabitants of the Nile villages, and other places visited by tourists during the winter season. The intention of the donors is no doubt kindly, but the practice – more especially in view of the yearly increase of visitors to Egypt – cannot fail to be detrimental to the moral sense and the social well-being of the poorer classes of the community. At the present time many of the poorer inhabitants of those towns on the Nile which are most visited by tourists live almost entirely on what they can obtain by "bakshish" during the winter months; the easy means thus afforded of obtaining a small livelihood prevents their adopting any form of labour; and children are brought up to regard the tourist season as the period during which they may, by clamorous begging, enable their parents and themselves to lead a life of idleness for the remainder of the year. The unhealthy tendency of such a system is obvious.'

After more of such advice the section concludes with a plea: 'Tourists should especially abstain from throwing money from the decks of steamers on to the landing stages or on to the banks of the Nile for the purpose of witnessing the scramble for the coins; such exhibitions are mischievous as well as degrading.'

The writer of the handbook naturally wants tourists to look favourably on Egypt, and to appreciate the benefits the country has to offer, and with this end in view we are told that whoever visits the country for the first time 'will certainly be delighted . . . but it is probable that he will not admire the natives with whom he will come in contact until he knows them fairly well'. He strains to give a balanced view by saying that the Egyptians in general 'have never been accustomed to travel, and they look upon those who wander from country to country as beings who are possessed of restless though harmless devils'. The Egyptian whose character has not been tainted by cupidity 'is a very estimable individual. He is proud of his religion, but is tolerant to a remarkable degree', but 'it must never be forgotten that the strictest Muhammadans despise the Christian faith in their hearts, although Christians are treated with civility'.

Now comes a paragraph, again from Cook's handbook, which will no doubt find agreement with many people today.

The abolition of corporal punishment, by Lord Dufferin, early in 1883, has had effects which were not contemplated by him. *As soon as the whip was abolished the people refused to work*, and Lord Cromer says that the period which followed its abolition 'caused him greater anxiety than any other' during his lengthened Egyptian experience. Another result was that *life and property became insecure*, and Nubar Pasha was obliged to appoint 'Commissions of Brigandage,' that is, to introduce martial law. The Egyptian had also learned that no one can be punished for a crime unless he is proved guilty, and that proof of guilt which will satisfy the law courts is hard to get. The result has been that large numbers of guilty people have escaped punishment, and through the country the people have little respect for the Law. The inability of the governors to use the whip is the cause of the present state of unrest among a certain class of Egyptians, and it is clear that only corporal punishment will reduce this class to order and obedience.

In 1858 our traveller arranged his trip up the Nile, says Murray, by first hiring a dahabeyeh, which boat was provided with 'at least two or three cabins and a bath; and the largest have a front cabin sufficiently spacious to accommodate a party of 8 or more persons at dinner. The price depends of course on the size of the boat and the number of men; but a large one, capable of accommodating 3 or 4 persons, generally lets for about 50 to 70 pounds a month. All furnished boats are supplied with divans and other furniture, a canteen, kitchen, fireplace, and all requisites for the journey except provisions.'

The boats are said to be very clean, 'so that it is no longer necessary to have them sunk before going on board'. Then follows advice on destroying flies, still one of the plagues of Egypt, but much attention is paid to strict discipline in the boat, and obedience to orders, as long as they are reasonable and just. 'But I am far from advising that constant use of the stick which is sometimes resorted to most unnecessarily: firmness and the determination of being obeyed seldom fail to command respect and obedience; for, when they know you *will* be obeyed, they will seldom disregard an order.'

It is just as well that 'however much they may try to impose on one over whom they think to get the upper hand, they never harbour any feelings of revenge. In short, my advice is, to be strict and just, without unnecessary violence, in order to have the satisfaction of being indulgent.'

A system of rewards was suggested, in the event of the crew behaving well. On going up the river, 'give them a sheep at some of the large towns, or a certain quantity of meat at least, as a *reward for past exertions*; but some travellers have spoilt them through a want of discrimination, and they now begin to look on it as a right, whether they deserve it or no. This should be resisted; and they should be made to understand that they are to have no reward till they have earned it. They are allowed a sheep no longer; but instead of it a small sum may be given to a crew if they have had *much towing* and have *worked well*; though certainly not if the wind has done all the work for them.'

At the end of the journey, when the crew is paid off, 'they also expect about 24 piastres each if they have given satisfaction; if not, they should be dismissed with no more than 6 piastres each, and, if at all unruly, they should have nothing but an introduction to the police'.

Before setting out for the south a few items of interest may be culled from the various guidebooks on Lower Egypt. At the village of Bebayt-el-Hagar, we are told in Murray's that the author 'had the satisfaction of shooting the great enemy of the village, a large wolf, which in broad daylight was prowling about the field that now occupies part of the enclosure of the temple. It had been a great annoyance to the people, and had been in the habit of entering the village at night, and carrying off sheep, poultry, and whatever it could find; so that its death caused great joy among those who had suffered from its unwelcome visits.'

In the Wadi Natrun there were several monasteries, to which

Arabs were not admitted, though if they had been they would not
have made away with so many priceless Coptic manuscripts as did
visiting Europeans. The Revd H. Tattam departed with 'upwards of
50 volumes; among which was a treatise on Eusebius, not previously
known, and on his return in 1842 he obtained four times that
number of manuscripts, all indeed that were not used by the monks'.

He presumably received every civility during his stay with them,
'particularly from the superior of St. Macarius; and I have reason
to believe that the other Monasteries are equally hospitable. The
room allotted to a stranger at Dayr Suriani is large and well lighted;
but I recommend him to remove the mats before he takes up his
abode there, otherwise he is not likely to pass a comfortable night,
under the assaults of some hundreds of bugs; and he will run a risk
of carrying away many score in his baggage, which may continue
to torment him' – though I suppose the conscience did not torment
those who carried away such loot in their baggage, a not so novel
way in those days of financing one's expeditions.

Wallis Budge relates that the Revd Tattam sold his manuscripts
to the Trustees of the British Museum in 1838, who the same year
sent him back to Egypt, 'to obtain the manuscripts which were
still there, and of these he was so fortunate as to secure about 314,
which arrived at the British Museum in 1843. In 1845 M. A.
Pacho went and lived with the monks for six weeks, and in the
end succeeded in obtaining the remainder of the manuscripts, about
190 in number; 172 of these came to the British Museum in 1847,
10 were sold to the Trustees in 1851, and M. Pacho kept back and
sold several to the Imperial Public Library in St. Petersburg in
1852. At the present time there are no manuscripts of importance
in the Natron Valley, and only those who are interested in archeol-
ogy are recommended to visit it.'

Setting off down the Nile in his well-appointed boat, our traveller
will be captivated by the town of Benisooef, which presents 'the
ordinary scenes common to all large towns on the Nile; among
which are numerous boats tied to the shore – buffaloes standing or
lying in the water – women at their usual morning and evening
occupation of filling water-jars and washing clothes – dogs lying

in holes they have scratched in the cool earth – and beggars importuning each newly-arrived European stranger with the odious word "bakshish." This is followed by the equally odious "Ya Hawagee," by which the Franks are rather contemptuously dismissed; and the absurd notion of superiority over the Christians affected by the Moslems is strikingly displayed in these as in many other instances. The "Faithful" beggar, baredly covered with scanty rags, and unclean with filth, thinks himself polluted by the contact of a Christian, whose charity he will not condescend to ask in the same terms as from a *true believer.*'

The people of the Nile do not have the same prejudices against dogs as those of Lower Egypt, though. 'Some of the fancies of the Moslems respecting what is clean and unclean are amusingly ridiculous, and not the least those respecting dogs. Three of the sects consider its contact defiles; the other fears only to touch its nose, or its hair if wet; and tales about the testimony of dogs and cats against man in a future state are related with a gravity proportionate to their absurdity.'

Beyond Keneh, the author encounters the crocodile, a rather timid animal, 'flying on the approach of man, and, generally speaking, only venturing to attack its prey on a sudden; for which reason we seldom or never hear of persons having been devoured by it, unless incautiously standing at the brink of a river, where its approach is concealed by the water, and where, by the immense power of its tail, it is enabled to throw down and overcome the strongest man; who, being carried immediately to the bottom of the river, has neither the time nor the means to resist.'

While one village abominates the crocodile, the next place may venerate it, which 'was the cause of serious disputes with the inhabitants of Ombos, where it was particularly worshipped; and the unpardonable affront of killing and eating the god-like animal was resented by the Ombites with all the rage of a sectarian feud. No religious war was ever urged with more energetic zeal; and the conflict terminated in the disgraceful ceremony of a cannibal feast, to which (if we can believe the rather doubtful authority of Juvenal) the body of one who was killed in the affray was doomed by his triumphant adversaries.'

Thus we come to the great Gem of Thebes (or Gems, for the

traveller is informed that he may spend weeks in this area with profit) and, on arriving, 'horses and asses are readily obtained for visiting the ruins with guides, some of whom are intelligent, and well acquainted with all that travellers care most to see. Though many guides are deserving of recommendation, I am, from my own experience during many visits to Thebes, bound to speak well of the civility, honesty, and other good qualities of one of them called A'wad.'

In 1886 Luxor was still a rundown village, 'unlit at night, and not in a prosperous condition', according to Budge. Thomas Cook, in December of that year, inaugurated his line of steamers from Cairo, and from then on large numbers of tourists transformed the place, until it became 'a town suitable for travellers to live in'. Cook's improved the waterfront, encouraged local business ventures, and rebuilt the old Luxor Hotel. Trade increased, the streets and alleys were cleaned up, and 'the natives began to build better houses for themselves, and European wares began to fill the bazaars'. A few years later, 'Mr. Cook founded a hospital, and hundreds of sick and suffering gladly and promptly availed themselves of the medical assistance which be provided gratis.'

A minor industry grew up in the manufacture of spurious antiquities, and the traveller is warned against buying them, although 'those who understand them and know how to make a judicious choice, not giving a high price for the bad, but paying well for objects of real value, may occasionally obtain some interesting objects. The dealers soon discover whether the purchaser understands their value; and if he is ignorant they will sell the worst to him for a high price, and false ones, rather than the best they have. Indeed a great portion of those sold by dealers are forgeries; and some are so cleverly imitated that it requires a practised eye to detect them.'

Before describing the wonders of the area Murray protests against 'the manner in which some travellers visit its monuments, particularly the tombs of the kings, which are frequently lighted by *torches*. No one should be mean enough to spare a few wax candles for this purpose; and it is mere selfishness to obtain a great light by torches, with the certainty of blackening the sculptures by their smoke. A man should have some consideration for those who come after him.'

During his peregrinations the traveller is recommended to have with him 'a small supply of eatables, and, above all, of water in *goollehs*. Each of these porous water-bottles may be slung with string (as on board-a-ship), to prevent the boat-men, or whoever may carry them, from holding them by the neck with their dirty hands; and moreover, they should not be allowed to touch the water, and should be made to bring their own supply if they want it.'

Perhaps the strictures against flaring torches that blot out sculptures and paintings acquires some importance when we read the account of the Great Temple at Medeenet Haboo: 'The sculptures on the walls of these private apartments are the more interesting, as they are a singular instance of the internal decorations of an Egyptian palace. Here the king is attended by his harem, some of whom present him with flowers, or wave before him fans and flabella; and a favourite is caressed, or invited to divert his leisure hours with a game of draughts; but they are all obliged to stand in his presence, and the king alone is seated on an elegant *fauteuil* amidst his female attendants – a custom still prevalent in the East.'

This scene is described somewhat differently by Wallis Budge. 'The walls of the rooms are decorated with scenes in which the king is seen surrounded by naked women, who play tambourines, and bring him fruit and flowers, and play draughts with him.'

The Baedeker of 1892 judges the scene from the strict Victorian point of view, as if Mrs. Grundy, the guardian of morality, is looking over his shoulder. 'Rameses III is here represented in his harem. The nude maidens with whom he is playing chess, or who hand him one a fig, another a pomegranate, another a melon, another a flower which he smells, appear from the shape of their faces and from the arrangement of their hair to be captive princesses rather than his own children. This supposition is farther strengthened by the occurrence here of several representations of a distinctly immodest character. The vicious propensities of this king are gibbeted with biting scorn on other monuments. He himself appears to have looked with peculiar pride on his harem, which was rich in beauty of all kinds, and to have immortalised its memory in his Memnonium. At all events his reign marks the beginning of an epoch of luxury and immorality, upon which decay followed close.'

Travellers who wanted to stay in their boat as far as Khartoum would have been disappointed, for Baedeker's 1892 volume allows them to go only as far as Wadi Halfa: 'It is much to be hoped that the time will soon come when the way will be open as far as Khartoum, which fell into the hands of the Mahdists on Jan. 27th 1885, when the brave Gordon met his death. The possession of Khartoum and the security not only of the Nile-route thither but also of the desert-route from Berber to Suakin are necessary conditions for the gradual civilisation of the Sudan.'

For a description of Khartoum we have to wait for Wallis Budge's handbook, which appeared after the Mahdi revolt had been put down in 1895. The expedition of Kitchener's troops up the Nile, their transport and supplies, had been organized by none other than Thomas Cook & Son, which firm had the necessary experience (and fleet of boats) for moving large numbers of people.

At the Battle of Omdurman, which preceded the liberation of nearby Khartoum, 'the Dervish loss was 11,000 killed, 16,000 wounded, and 4000 were made prisoner'. The Dervish army was 'mown down', Budge goes on, 'by the awful rifle fire of the British and Egyptian troops, and the shell-fire from the gun-boats.' He tells us later that 'of the wounded Dervishes from 6000 to 7000 were treated in the hospital which was improvised in Omdurman. Visitors to the battlefield may even this day find weapons and small objects belonging to those who were killed there.'

An architectural description of the Mahdi's Tomb concludes with: 'The dome was badly injured in the bombardment of Omdurman on September 2nd., and since the building was the symbol of successful rebellion, up to a certain point, and fanaticism, and had become a goal for pilgrimages, and the home of fraudulent miracles, it was destroyed by charges of guncotton by the British. For the same reasons the Mahdi's body was burnt in the furnace of one of the steamers, and the ashes thrown into the river.' In case anyone should imagine that to have been the normal practice of the British towards their enemies he adds that it was done 'on the advice of Muhammadan officers and notables; the Mahdi's head is said to have been buried at Wadi Halfa'.

All this would seem to be justified by the fact that: 'In Khartoum itself business is increasing, and under the just and equitable government which the country now enjoys will continue to do so.' Dervish rule of the Sudan, it is pointed out, reduced the population from eight million to two million in ten years, a fate much like that endured by Pol Pot's Cambodia in the present century.

CHAPTER FOURTEEN

THE HOLY LAND

Murray strikes exactly the right tone in the preface to his two-volume 1868 guide: 'The Bible is the best Hand-book for Palestine; the present work is only intended to be a companion to it.'

Even so, he loses no time in passing judgement on the people the traveller can't avoid meeting: 'Their dress, their manners and customs, and their language, are all primitive. No European nation, with the exception perhaps of the Spaniards, bears the least resemblance to them. Like Spain, too, the best specimens of humanity are found among the lower classes. The farther we go from government offices, the more successful shall we be in our search after honesty, industry, and patriarchal hospitality. The Arabs are illiterate, and ignorant of all Frank inventions; but there is a native dignity in their address and deportment, which will both please and astonish those who have seen the awkward vulgarity of the lower classes in some more favoured lands. Whether we enter the tent of the Bedawy or the cottage of the *fellah*, we are received and welcomed with an ease and courtesy that would not disgrace a palace. One is apt to imagine, on hearing the long series of enquiries after the health, happiness, and prosperity of the visitor who drops in, and the evasive replies given, that there is some hidden grief which politeness would fain conceal, but which the heartfelt sympathy of the host constrains him to search into. It is disappointing to discover, as every one will in time discover, that this is all form. Still there is something pleasing in these inquiries, compliments, and good wishes, empty though they may be.'

The further we get from Europe, i.e. civilization, the more romantic is travelling shown to be, though Murray is too astute to allow such feelings to become overwhelming. 'An Arab when eating, whether in the house or by the wayside, however poor and scanty his fare, never neglects to invite the visitor, or passing wayfarer, to join him. And this is not always an empty compliment; indeed there are few Arabs who will not feel honoured by the traveller's tasting their humble fare. The invitation, however, is generally declined by a courteous phrase.'

The politeness of an Arab shopkeeper can be embarrassing: '. . . when the price is asked, he replied, "Whatever you please, my lord." When pressed for a more definite answer, he says, "Take it without money." Our feelings of romance, however, are somewhat damped when we find the price ultimately demanded is four or five times the value of the article. An Arab always tells you that his house is yours, his property is yours, he himself is your slave; that he loves you with all his heart, would defend you with his life, etc., etc. This all sounds very pretty, but it will be just as well not to rely too much on it. Nothing, however, is lost by politeness; and so one may seem to believe all that is said. It has been sometimes the practice of travellers to rule their Arab servants and muleteers by bullying and browbeating; but this is a great mistake. I need not say that such conduct is beneath the dignity of an English gentleman. Unvarying courtesy, accompanied with as unvarying *firmness*, will gain the desired object far more effectually. This is especially the case with the Bedawin, who can often be persuaded by a kind word when they could not be driven by a rod of iron. At the same time, any approach to undue familiarity will be attributed by the Arab to weakness of character, perhaps in some cases to fear, of which he will not be slow to take advantage.'

With regard to Arabs in general, they 'are and have been for centuries "lords of the soil," and they constitute the great majority of the community. They are proud, fanatical, and illiterate. They are taught by the faith they hold to look with contempt on all other classes, and to treat them not merely as inferiors but as slaves. They are generally noble in bearing, polite in address, and profuse in hospitality; but they are regardless of truth, dishonest in their dealings, and immoral in their conduct. In large towns the greater proportion of the upper classes are both physically and mentally feeble, owing to the effects of polygamy, early marriages, and degrading vices; but the peasantry are robust and vigorous, and much might be hoped for from them if they were brought under the influence of liberal institutions, and if they had examples around them of the industry and enterprise of Western Europe.'

With regard to the Jews of Palestine the handbook tells us that they are 'in one sense the most interesting people of the land. 18 centuries ago they were driven from the home of their fathers, and yet they cling to its "holy places" still. They moisten the stones of Jerusalem with their tears; "her very dust to them is dear," and their most earnest wish is that the dust of their bodies should mingle with it. The tombs that whiten the side of Olivet tell a tale of mournful bereavement and undying affection unparalleled in the world's history.'

Totally different from these, he tells us, are the Jews of Damascus and Aleppo, who must be considered as much natives as any of the inhabitants of Syria. 'They are Arabs in language, habits, and occupations, in so far at least as religion will permit. Some of them are men of great wealth and corresponding influence. For generations they have been the bankers of the local authorities, and have often fearfully realized the strange fluctuations of Eastern life – now ruling a province, now gracing a pillory – at one time the all-powerful favourites, at another the disgraced and mutilated outcasts.'

The Turks, who are few in number, and foreigners in race and language, are 'hated by every sect and class, wanting in physical power, destitute of moral principle, and yet they are the despots of the land. They obtain their power by bribery, and they exercise it for extortion and repression.'

Murray sums up with one final – as he thought – nail in the coffin of the Ottoman Empire that the observant Englishman must be sure to notice: 'There is not a man in the country, whether Turk or Arab, Mohammedan or Christian, who would give a para to save the empire from ruin; that is, if he be not in government pay, in which case of course his salary and the empire would go together.

The patriotism of the Syrian is confined to his own house; anything beyond it does not concern him – selfishness reigns supreme. The consequence is, that there is not a road in the whole country except the one recently made by a French company; the streets of the great cities and villages are in winter all but impassable, and in summer reeking with the stench of dead dogs and cats and other abominations. Dogs are the only scavengers; anything which is too corrupt or filthy for them to eat, rots where it lies. One would imagine, in traversing Syria, that the whole country had recently been shaken to its centre by an earthquake, there are so many broken bridges, ruinous mosques, and roofless caravanserais. It is emphatically a land of ruins, and ruins are increasing in number every year.'

As for the best seasons for visiting Syria and Palestine, in a country without railways or coaches, and with only one road, 'progress must necessarily be slow, and the summer's sun and winter's rain are alike to be avoided'. The traveller is reminded that 'there are no inns along the great thoroughfares, with cheerful chamber, well-aired bed, and tempting *cuisine* to make one forget the fatigues of a day's ride, or to afford a pleasant asylum from drenching rain and muddy road'.

Tent-life is the only solution, which is 'very romantic; it reads well in a poetical traveller's journal, and there are few who have tried it but will look back to it as to a sunny spot. But it requires fine weather; it is no pleasant task to pitch your tent and spread your bed in mud: there is little romance in canvas when the rain is pouring through it.'

For those who are old, or a traveller in ill health, a long journey on horseback may prove too much, therefore the easiest mode of conveyance is 'a light arm-chair, without legs (which are apt to get entangled among rocks), securely fastened on two long poles, like a sedan-chair. Two easy-paced mules attached to this machine carry the occupant with considerable comfort.'

Murray perhaps has toilet paper in mind when he says that, among the provisions: 'There are a few things I recommend the more fastidious, and especially ladies, to take with them for their own use; and I advise them also not to trust such precious commodities to the exclusive care of servants, whether English or Arab.'

A tour in the region was, in those days, still rare enough for the following comments: 'Every traveller should have his note-book to record incidents and describe scenes to which memory will look back with pleasure in after years. Descriptions written on the spot will "photograph" scenes and events on the mind. As to the propriety of publishing I say nothing. Every one must exercise his own good taste and wisdom in that respect. But a "journal" has a real and absorbing interest, apart from all thought of Albermarle Street or Paternoster Row.'

There was, of course, the matter of security, for the roads in Syria weren't always safe from bandits, and Murray recommends that a small revolver may be carried, which 'should be worn in a leather belt so as to be visible, especially when the traveller sees fit to indulge in solitary rides or walks. The robbers of Syria are generally amateurs, who take up the profession when opportunity offers. They will seldom venture on a party of Franks if there be any show of arms among them; but a few peasants, when they meet a timid traveller, will first beg, then demand, and finally take a *bakshish*. By cool self-possession and a determined manner one can generally overawe them. There should be no blustering or hurry in such cases, for noise seems to rouse an Arab's "pluck"; but the traveller should be careful to show all whom it may concern, by the ease and dignity of his bearing, that, while he may enjoy a *joke*, it would scarcely be safe to carry it too far.'

For visiting remote districts an escort was necessary, 'composed of members of that tribe to which the country we propose to visit belongs. Even friendly tribes have no right to conduct strangers through the territories of others. It not unfrequently happens that adventurous chiefs will undertake such a task, and, for the sake of the pay, run the risk of a sound drubbing, if not worse. When an attack is made under such circumstances, and especially if it be by the Bedawin of the desert, no attempt at resistance should be made. Leave the matter wholly to your escort, and act as if you had no interest in it whatever. It may be well to explain to the enemy that you had no intention of breaking the laws of desert life; that you had engaged a sheikh to escort you under the impression he was the proper person; that he had become guarantee for your safety; and now it was his affair, not yours, if he had trespassed on the territory of others. A calm and conciliatory bearing, aided *in the end* by a small present, will in nine cases out of ten clear away all difficulties.'

Such delicate negotiations with desert tribes will be conducted through an interpreter, since it is 'useless to burden a Handbook with a collection of words and phrases'. There is, however, no better propagandist for the trip to the Holy Land than Murray:

A spring tour in Syria is to the invalid an admirable sequel to a winter in Egypt. The soft and balmy air of the desert, with its cool nights and bracing mornings, gradually prepares him for a return to more northern climes. The noble scenery of the Sinai peninsula, with its holy associations, occasions sufficient excitement to release the physical frame from the depressing influence of melancholy. Then follow the rough rides over Syrian mountains; the constant variety of scene; the engrossing interest of place – all rose-tinted by a dash of danger and romance. Others besides the invalid might reap lasting benefit from such a ramble. The city merchant who has been cramped up for years within the dingy confines of a counting-house, and who has grown dyspeptic and gouty on London fog and turtle-soup; the 'West-end' politician, whose physical man has been dried up by late 'Houses,' later assemblies, and the harassing cares of party; – these, if they wish again to know what life and liberty are, should try a tour in Syria. After the murky magnificence of the London house, or the solemn splendour of the country mansion or baronial hall, Syria would be a new world. The pure air from morning till night and from night till morning; the constant exercise; the excitement of novel scenes and novel circumstances; the relief of thought; and the relaxation of overstrained mental powers – all tend to make a new physical man, while they contribute in no small degree to give a healthy tone to the intellect.

The usual land route into the country for British and American travellers was said by Murray to be from Cairo to Suez and across the Sinai peninsula. In 1858 the three principal stations on the road to Suez provided the following high cholesterol fare: 'Breakfast, consisting of tea or coffee, bread and butter, a plate of eggs or a chicken; dinner, consisting of rice, a chicken or pigeon, potatoes, English cheese, and fruit; supper, consisting of tea, bread and butter, a plate of eggs or a chicken. N.B. The use of a bed, as well as wines and all other extras, must be paid for separately according to tariff.'

Suez was the last civilized outpost, and to reach Jerusalem meant a journey of some four hundred miles over mostly uninhabited ashy-looking waste, only the occasional oasis, monastery or ruin to vary the scenery, which was desolate and spectacular in turn. The first notable stopping place was the Monastery of St Catherine at the foot of Mount Sinai, but to get there from Suez 'it will be necessary to engage some of the Tor Arabs, who will supply camels, and act as guides through their desert'. Before starting it was necessary to make sure that every camel had its full and proper load, 'if not, the Arabs will put a few things on each, and go away pretending they are loaded, their object being to get as many engaged as possible'.

Another trick practised by the Arabs was pointed out: 'It sometimes happens that a traveller is stopped on the road by what is said to be a party of hostile Arabs, and obliged to pay a sum of money, as he supposes, to save his life, or to secure the continuation of his journey in safety.' It is obvious, however, that: 'If no resistance is made on the part of those who conduct the traveller, the attacking party are either some of their own, or of a friendly tribe who are allowed to spoil him by the very persons he pays to protect him; for an Arab would rather die than suffer such an affront from a *hostile* tribe in his own desert. If then his Arabs do not fight on the occasion, he may be sure it is a trick to extort money . . . he should, therefore, use no arms against the supposed enemies, but afterwards punish his faithless guides by deducting the sum taken from their pay; and it is as well, before starting, to make them enter into an agreement that they are *able* as well as *willing* to protect him.'

Hints of danger were not exaggerated. Richard Burton, in *The Land of Midian*, 1879, had, with reason, a poor opinion of the Bedouin law of honour: 'They will eat bread and salt with the traveller whom they intend to murder.' Cook's guidebook *Pales-*

tine and Syria, 1911, tells us that near the beginning of their journey Professor Palmer, Lieutenant Charrington and Captain Gill were killed by Arabs on 11 August 1882.

Two groups of the same tribe would sometimes argue over who was to escort the traveller, 'and after he had gone some distance on his journey, he and his goods are taken by the opposition candidates, and transferred to their camels. The war is merely one of words, which the inexperienced in the language cannot understand; but he fully comprehends the annoyance of being nearly pulled to pieces by the rivals, and his things are sometimes thrown on the ground, to the utter destruction of everything fragile.'

In spite of these possible perfidies, the author concludes: 'An extra supply of coffee and tobacco, to give the Arabs occasionally, will be found useful.'

By the time of the first English edition of Baedeker's *Palestine and Syria*, 1876, the dragoman system had come into operation, and many of the above difficulties were taken care of by him. All the same: 'It is customary for the traveller to enter into a written contract with the dragoman, and to get it signed by him and attested at the consulate', otherwise 'it is often a matter of great difficulty to induce them to make the slightest deviation from the usual routes, which in all probability have been followed by the caravans for many centuries.'

Baedeker tells us that though there is no danger on the more frequented routes of the area, 'in the valley of the Jordan, and more particularly to the east of Jordan, danger from nomadic Beduins might perhaps be apprehended but for the custom of travellers in these parts to provide themselves with a Beduin escort'. Certain sums are specified which must be paid, and 'in return for these fees, a number of Beduin village sheiks, settled near Jerusalem, have undertaken to protect the interests of travellers, make compensation for thefts, etc., and the traveller who neglects to avail himself of this kind of insurance will profit little by appealing to his consul. Far higher demands are of course made for escorting travellers beyond Jordan, where the Turkish supremacy is but nominally recognised, and where, especially in the border districts, the petty sheiks affect to disdain francs and shillings, and often demand English sovereigns for their services.'

Nevertheless, the bordering deserts were 'infested with marauders of all kinds, but once in the interior of the territory of a desert-tribe, and under the protection of one of its sheiks, the traveller will generally meet with much kindness and hospitality. Predatory attacks are occasionally made on travellers by Beduins from remote districts, but only when the attacking party is the more powerful. To use one's weapons in such cases may lead to serious consequences, as the traveller who kills an Arab immediately exposes himself to the danger of retaliation from the whole tribe.'

In unsafe districts at night a guard should be posted outside the tents, and objects of value placed either under the traveller's pillow or as near the middle of the tent as possible, 'lest they should be within reach of hands intruding from the outside. The traveller should likewise be on his guard against the thievish propensities of beggars.'

With regard to the ownerless ill-looking dogs which the traveller encounters in the villages and towns, they are often 'a source of some alarm, but they fortunately never bite. Each town and village is infested with as many masterless dogs as its refuse can support. Unowned dogs will sometimes follow caravans if they are fed, in which case they will generally make themselves useful by their watchfulness at night.'

In the Baedeker of 1912 the above remarks are substantially the same, and though there had been some improvement in communications, a dragoman was still necessary for most places beyond Damascus and Jerusalem. Protection on the road to Jericho is discussed by a writer in 1909 in the magazine *Travel and Exploration*, and he tells the following story:

A few years ago two tourists, considering that the armed escort was an obsolete and futile custom, decided to dispense with them on their excursion to Jericho. Reaching their destination after an uneventful journey, they were not unnaturally jubilant. The arrival of two unaccompanied tourists reached the ears of the sheik (whose livelihood depended on his fees for escorts), and he laid his plans promptly. When the tourists reached the Wady Kelt on the return journey, they were waylaid and, though not injured in any way, all their clothes were taken from them. In this sorry plight the two victims were fain to fashion themselves some sort of covering out of a copy of *The Times* (the only possession left them by the sheik's hirelings), and thus quaintly garbed they slunk into Jerusalem at nightfall, sadder and wiser men.

An earlier issue of the same magazine relates that violence wasn't only to be expected from local marauders near Jericho, because 'an enterprising German society is making extensive excavations under special firman, and hundreds of native women are employed to uncover the secrets of forty centuries. The zeal of these scientific Germans would be more admirable if it were tempered with a little more courtesy. Not since spies first came to Jericho has the stranger been regarded with such suspicion. The overseers resent the presence of a camera within a hundred yards. One unhappy tourist, ignorant of these restrictions, was suddenly accosted last season, his Kodak wrenched from his grasp and dashed upon the ground.'

Anyone wanting to lodge in Jericho would be faced with an inn described by Baedeker as 'a dirty mud-hut surrounded by hedges. The beds are bad, the rooms small and close, and vermin abundant. The inhabitants of Jericho appear to be a degenerate race, as the hot and unhealthy climate has an enervating effect. The traveller should be on his guard against thieves.'

In 1876 Baedeker relates that an unusual system of accommodation prevailed in the area south of Damascus, because 'every village possesses its public inn, where every traveller is entertained gratuitously, and the Hauranians deem it honourable to impoverish themselves by contributing to the support of this establishment. As soon as a stranger arrives he is greeted with shouts of welcome, and is conducted to the inn. A servant or slave roasts coffee for him, and then pounds it in a wooden mortar, accompanying his task with a peculiar melody. Meanwhile the whole village assembles, and after the guest has been served, each person present partakes of the coffee. Even at an early hour in the morning we have been pressed to spend the whole day and the following night at one of these hospitable village inns. Now, however, that travellers have become more numerous, the villagers generally expect a trifling bakshish from Europeans. A sum of 10–20 piastres, according to the refreshment obtained, may therefore by given to the servant who holds the stirrup at starting. The food consists of fresh bread, eggs, sour milk, raisin-syrup, and in the evening a dish of wheat boiled with a little leaven and dried in the sun, with mutton.' This is reprinted verbatim in the 1912 edition.

Hotel accommodation in the main cities was often of an indifferent nature, as well as being expensive. In Damascus the Hotel Dmitri was said by Baedeker to be tolerable, but 'the management is chiefly in the hands of an insolent set of waiters'. The city was not known for its tolerance of Christians, 6000 of whom had been massacred in 1860, only sixteen years before. There were booksellers in the bazaar, 'whose fanaticism is so great that they despise even the money of the "unbeliever", and often will not deign to answer when addressed by him'.

A. & C. Black's guidebook of 1911 tells us that in Damascus 'a European stranger cannot, even at the present day, wander about the streets alone without risk of insult, especially in the neighbourhood of a mosque'. In a Saharan town of Algeria, not so many years ago, stones began landing around me when I got to within a hundred yards of one such temple.

The traveller can't even console himself in another direction, when in the afternoon he may 'encounter a crowd of women enveloped in their white sheets and closely veiled, waddling from shop to shop, carefully examining numberless articles which they do not mean to buy . . . but in this jealous and fanatical city it is imprudent and even dangerous to be too observant of the fair sex'.

Women, Christian though they might be, were not wanted at the Monastery of Mar Saba near Jerusalem, which seems just as well, since: 'The divans are generally infested with vermin. The accommodation is very poor, but bread and wine are to be had, and there are kitchens for the use of travellers who bring their dragoman and cook.' At Hebron, the accommodation at several Jewish houses was said to be tolerable, but the Muslims in that place 'are notorious for their fanaticism, and the traveller should therefore avoid coming into collision with them. The children shout a well-known curse after "Franks", of which of course no notice should be taken.' The Baedeker of 1912 gives the same warning, to which is added: 'Travellers are earnestly warned against that arrant beggar, the son of the deceased old sheikh Hamza', though why is not stated.

Black's guide recommends a day's excursion to the town: 'The unique historical associations of Hebron, its striking topography, and the intense jealousy with which the shrine of the great Jewish patriarch is guarded from Jews and Christians alike, make this excursion one of peculiar interest, and it should not be omitted by those who can only devote a week to Jerusalem.' King Edward VII (then Prince of Wales) had been a visitor there in 1862, furnished with a special permit from the Sultan, though 'in the face of the bitterest opposition from the inhabitants'. Since then, 'nearly a score of distinguished travellers have been permitted to visit this sacro-sanct spot'. Baedeker says that a dragoman is unnecessary, but Black's guide disagrees: 'Travellers who value their comfort should take one, in view of the unfriendly attitude of the inhabitants.'

At Nablus there was for a long time only the camping ground for accommodation, though by 1912 one of the two hotels had been established by the Hamburg-Amerika shipping line. The camping ground still existed, however, and Baedeker recommends: 'The commandant should be requested to furnish one or two soldiers as a guard for the tents, as the inhabitants are fanatical and quarrelsome.'

Cook's guide tells us: 'The people have a bad reputation for their discourteous treatment of strangers, and even today Christian visitors are sometimes greeted with cries of Nazarene! accompanied by pelting of stones.' Henry S. Lunn, in his *How to Visit the Mediterranean*, 1896, gives a more final verdict: 'The Moslems, noted for their fanatical and turbulent character, offer no inviting prospect for residents alien in race and creed.'

One also had to endure the 'plaintive cry of the lepers. Unhappily, these poor creatures intrude their misfortunes before the gaze of the stranger, who is often sorely tried at witnessing the distorted faces and wasting limbs, and to hear the horrible and husky wail peculiar to themselves.'

And so to Jerusalem, the star of all places for Jewish and Christian pilgrims, first and foremost the City of David, and nearer to God than any other. Baedeker's guidebook provides a magnificent fold-out panorama, fit for framing, which shows the main sights and almost every building. We are reminded that 'Jerusalem' comes from the Hebrew, meaning 'Vision of Peace', and that to most travellers it is 'a place of overwhelming interest, but at first many will be sadly disappointed in the Holy City, the venerable type of the heavenly Zion. It would seem at first as though little were left of the ancient city of Zion and Moriah, the far-famed capital of the Jewish empire; and little of it indeed is to be discovered in the narrow, crooked, ill-paved, and dirty streets of the modern town. It is only by patiently penetrating beneath the modern crust of rubbish and rottenness which shrouds the sacred places from view that the traveller will at length realise to himself a picture of the Jerusalem of antiquity, and this will be the more vivid in proportion to the amount of previously acquired historical and topographical information which he is able to bring to bear upon his researches.'

Baedeker suggests at least a week to see the main sights, while Black's, perhaps in consideration of the Sabbath, thinks six days should be enough. Murray makes no comment on the matter, assuming that the intelligent reader can decide for himself.

Accommodation was possible at the Mediterranean Hotel, where the landlord was Moses Hornstein, said to have a Scottish wife; and at the Damascus Hotel, owned by his brother: 'Food generally good; rooms small, but sufficiently large for ordinary travellers who are seldom in-doors.' Murray's earlier edition also recommends the Hornstein hotels, the first being 'a large and commodious house. The reports are favourable of the landlord's civility and attention to the comforts of his guests.'

By 1912 there were more hotels, and Black's guide commends an English pension run by a Mr Hensman, said to be a 'favourite resort of the clergy', where English cooking was the rule. Thomas Cook used the Grand New Hotel for his clients.

Several hospices catered for Roman Catholic travellers, though: 'In the height of summer many of the inhabitants camp outside the gates for the sake of the purer air, but the traveller should not attempt this in the spring, as the weather is then often bitterly cold, unless he is compelled to do so from want of accommodation within the city.'

Regarding bankers: 'Valero, in David Street, is a good Jewish house . . . Small change, with which the traveller should always be well supplied, may be obtained at the bazaar, but as reckoning in piastres is puzzling at first, he should be on his guard against imposition.'

Among medical men, Dr Chaplin, of the Jewish Mission, is recommended, followed by 'Dr. Sandreszki, a skilful operator, physician of the German institutions'.

In 1912 Baedeker gives the population of Jerusalem as 70,000, including 45,000 Jews and 15,000 Christians. Of the Jews, the number 'has greatly risen in the last few decades, in spite of the fact that they are forbidden to immigrate or to possess landed property. The majority subsist on the charity of their European brethren, from whom they receive their regular *khaluka*, or allowance, and for whom they pray at the holy places.'

In order to visit the Moslem Haram esh-Sherif, 'the permission of the Turkish authorities and the escort of a soldier is necessary, but on Friday and during the time of festivals, entrance is entirely prohibited to strangers'. Access to Jewish and Christian sites was unimpeded.

Cook's handbook, forty years after the above, tells us: 'It is only recently that Christians have been at liberty to enter any of the Mosques. The restrictions have now, however, been removed, and some of the principal Mosques, which bold travellers of an earlier date risked their lives to enter, may be visited by any one who makes the proper application to the consul, and pays the proper fees.'

Cook reminds the visitor that 'although he may not believe in the religion of the Moslems, he should respect their institutions so far as to adopt those customs which are deemed by them to be due to their religion. It will be well to observe these things, not only as a matter of good taste, but also from prudential motives, as there is still a strong feeling against this invasion of holy places by infidels – as the Christians are called – and Mohammedan fanaticism is a passion which it is unsafe to arouse.'

One ought not to leave Jerusalem, however, without an example of Christian fanaticism, and I quote from Murray's handbook of 1868: 'A description of the Church of the Sepulchre could hardly be considered complete without some account of the scenes enacted at the time of the miracle (*imposture?*) of the Holy Fire. On the Easter-eve of each returning year it is affirmed that a miraculous flame descends from heaven into the Holy Sepulchre, kindling all the lamps and candles there, as it did of yore Elijah's sacrifice on Carmel. The Greek patriarch or his representative alone enters the tomb at the prescribed time; and the fire soon appearing is given out to the expectant and excited multitude through a hole in the northern wall. The origin of this extraordinary scene is involved in mystery. It is singular, too, and worthy of notice, that at a few of the Moslem saints' tombs a supernatural fire is said to blaze on every Friday, superseding all necessity for lamps.'

Murray continues: 'The imposture of the Holy Fire is unquestionably one of the most degrading rites performed within the walls of Jerusalem. It is not too much to say that it brings disgrace on the Christian name. It makes our boasted Christian enlightenment a subject of scorn and contempt to both Jews and Mohammedans. Its effects upon those who sanction or take part in it are most melancholy. It makes their clergy, high and low, deliberate imposters; it rouses the worst passions of the poor ignorant pilgrims who assemble here from the ends of the earth: and it tends more than aught else to convert the pure, spiritual, elevating faith of the Lord Jesus into a system of fraud and degrading superstition.

'The fostering of fanaticism, superstition, and imposture is not the only evil result of the Holy Fire. Scarcely a year passes in which some accident does not occur at the exhibition – an unfortunate woman is crushed to death, or an old man is trampled over by the crowd; or oftener still one or two are stabbed in the quarrels of rival sects. In the year 1834 a fearful tragedy occurred . . .'

The description of it is given over to Lord Curzon, from his *Monasteries of the Levant*:

The guards outside, frightened at the rush from within, thought that the Christians wished to attack them, and the confusion soon grew into a battle. The soldiers with their bayonets killed numbers of fainting wretches, and the walls were spattered with blood and brains of men who had been felled, like oxen, with the butt-ends of the soldiers' muskets. Every one struggled to defend himself, and in the mêlée all who fell were immediately trampled to death by the rest. So desperate and savage did the fight become, that even the panic-struck and frightened pilgrims appeared at last to have been more intent upon the destruction of each other than desirous to save themselves.

For my part, as soon as I had perceived the danger I had cried out to my companions to turn back, which they had done; but I myself was carried on by the press till I came near the door where all were fighting for their lives. Here, seeing certain destruction before me, I made every endeavour to get back. An officer of the Pasha's, equally alarmed with myself, was also trying to return; he caught hold of my cloak, and pulled me down on the body of an old man who was breathing out his last sigh. As the officer was pressing me to the ground, we wrestled together among the dying and the dead with the energy of despair. I struggled with this man till I pulled him down, and happily got again upon my legs – (I afterwards found that he never rose again) – and scrambling over a pile of corpses, I made my way back into the body of the church . . . The dead were lying in heaps, even upon the Stone of Unction; and I saw 400 wretched people, dead and living, heaped promiscuously one upon another, in some places above 5 ft. high.

A final comment from Murray wonders whether or not it isn't 'high time for enlightened Russia to step in, and put an end, by the high hand of her authority, to this most disgraceful and degrading imposture'.

CHAPTER FIFTEEN

TURKEY

We will begin our section on travel in the Turkish Empire by quoting from an article in *Blackwood's Magazine* of 1847, which describes a party of English travellers disembarking on the coast near Smyrna. 'When I landed at that nest of pirates, Valona,' the anonymous author says, 'was I to look upon that wretched rabble as Turks? Men dressed in every variety of shabby frock-coat and trousers; and above all, men who were undisguised in the exhibition of vulgar curiosity. When, then, I saw these people flocking together on their jetty to meet us, I at once recognised them as mongrel and degenerated. The whole community are piratical; the youth practically, the seniors by counsel. They manage their evil deeds with a singleness of purpose that neglects no feasible opportunity, and with a caution that restrains from doubtful attempts, and almost secures them from capture. Incontinent they launch their boats, – terrible vessels that hold twenty or thirty armed men besides the rowers, and cleave their irresistible course towards the motionless and defenceless victim. On such occasions it is only by rare hap that any individual survives to tell the tale and cry for vengeance. The bloody work is no sooner over than its traces are obliterated and the community restored to the appearance of inoffensiveness: the boats are pulled up on shore, the crews dispersed.'

The town isn't mentioned in Murray's handbook for Turkey of 1854, and though if the Turks in general get a somewhat better reference for their would-be employers, it isn't by much. On reaching Constantinople: 'Those that mean to confine their excursions to Stamboul and its vicinity want no weapons, but those that mean to go inland had better provide themselves with some portable efficacious arms, such as the smaller size of Colt's revolvers.'

The traveller is told, with regard to the climate, that the 'thin, pure and exciting air, is salubrious, but also very dangerous, and persons of a full habit, or those that are intemperate, are liable to acute diseases of an alarming character. Catching cold very frequently leads to bronchitis and pneumonia; intemperance produces dysentery.'

Access to the city seemed easier in those days to what it was to become later. 'On arriving in the Bosphorus the kaiks are by far the safest boats, if one gets into them and out of them with proper care; and the Maltese, anywhere but in Malta, are among the greatest scoundrels in the Levant. The stranger, if conscious of having no goods liable to duty (and it would be strange if he had), should refuse to be taken to the Custom-house, where he would be detained to no purpose.'

If he does go through the Customs, however, he must, when finished, engage a *hamal* (porter) to carry his luggage. 'The stranger should name the hotel he wishes to go to, and the hamal will conduct him. If more than one hamal seizes the luggage, they should be left to fight it out among themselves.'

Murray states that, as a general rule, 'before the hamals are sent away it is necessary to have a preliminary settling with the landlord. The hotels, or rather the boarding-houses which are called hotels, are full to overflowing, and for one guest who leaves the house, deterred by the prices, the landlord may have two or three next day. In any case the stranger should refuse to settle the price with the landlady if the husband be absent. He should rather wait for the return of the master of the house, for, greedy and grasping as the Greeks are (most of the hotel-keepers are either Greeks or Maltese), the women are by far more greedy and grasping, and decide their bargains with an unblushing hardness which utterly confounds the wanderer.'

After more sermonizing on the incompetence and rapacity of the people, Murray goes on to say: 'Though in the first instance it is necessary to go to an hotel, a prudent stranger will not remain here, but look out for some furnished lodgings.' The only way to find them is to walk the streets, though the houses which display notices that rooms are to let are always full. However, should he at last find one he may be unlucky enough to be given dinner, which he will eat alone, 'in the worst room of the house, served on a dirty tablecloth, by a grumbling servant, while the children of the house come in and look at the barbarian taking his meal'.

Having settled the price of all this: 'The next proposition, which the stranger should resolutely decline, is to take the rooms by the month. Some trifling difference in the price is held out as a bait, but it should not be swallowed. If taken for a month the landlord will also insist on prepayment, and every complaint of rudeness, filth, and neglect, is after that met with the cool rejoinder, "You are perfectly at liberty to go if you don't like the house." '

If the traveller is lucky enough to get a room he should move in immediately, 'for the landlords do not scruple to let the same room twice in a day, and he who comes first occupies it, while the man who comes too late is in a very awkward position, especially if he had given up his room in the hotel. A slow or careless person may most unexpectedly find himself on the pavement, with his traps loaded on the shoulders of two hamals, whose language he does not understand, but whose impatient gestures ask, as plain as words can tell, "Where in the name of all that is absurd, are we to go?" '

As for getting information from the landlord or waiters of a hotel, 'they know nothing, and, generally speaking, are not even able to tell the traveller in which direction to go to the British legation'.

For those wanting to venture beyond Constantinople the guide-book says that travelling on horseback at the rate of twenty-five miles a day 'involves hardships, exposure, and fatigue'. Even so, you are 'in immediate contact with nature. A burning sun may sometimes exhaust, or a summer-storm may drench you, but what can be more exhilarating than the sight of the lengthened troop of variegated and gay costumes dashing at full speed along to the crack of the Tartar whip?'

If our traveller be rich, intrepid, valiant and not disposed to consider his personal comfort – indeed he may be delighted to disregard it – he could take the road to Baghdad, perhaps as an army officer retracing his leisurely steps to his regiment in India.

A steamship from Constantinople to Trebizond on the Black Sea would put him on the old Tartar road to Mosul, in modern-day Iraq. Not only that, but if he knew his classics he might choose to follow, though in reverse, the celebrated March of the Ten Thousand – Greek mercenaries commanded by Xenophon on their retreat from Persia where they had served under Cyrus in 401–399 BCE.

The guidebook tells us that, after Mosul: 'There is no danger whatever on the journey when the Beduin tribes are quiet; but if the traveller learns on inquiry that they are at war, either with each other or with the Sultan's authorities, he should consult the Turkish officers and modify his plans accordingly.'

When the traveller is deep into Mesopotamia we are treated by Murray in the handbook of 1854 to a passage which deserves to be quoted in full, for there could surely have been no more amazing piece of advice.

If of an adventurous disposition, and not averse to run a certain degree of risk, the tourist might extend his sphere of observation by paying a visit to the great Bedouin tribe of Shammar. The first step is to get the consul at Moussul to send for some small sheikh of the tribe, who would not venture within a Turkish pasha's grasp to meet a long account of plundered caravans unless he had the protection of a consulate. But with that assurance he arrives with 2 or 3 attendants on broken-down old mares or trotting dromedaries. He is remarkable for a scanty and unclean wardrobe, brilliant eyes and teeth, and a very dignified and gentlemanly deportment. A present must be made to him – a fur cloak for winter or a brace of Turkish pistols – to secure his good-will, conciliating him further by hints of additional largesse in the event of a safe return, and the traveller may then set out on his novel expedition.

The desert once gained, there will be abundant sources of gratification for the lover of nature. As he rides over the boundless waste of short grass, unbroken by the smallest attempt at cultivation, he will also observe the sharp look-out kept by the Bedouin escort. All around the horizon is a vast solitude, and the little party creeps across it like lonely pilgrims through a deserted world.

Suddenly is heard the word 'horsemen', uttered by some one perched on the back of a camel: at once all is excitement; the sheikh scans the horizon, and announces strangers, though none are visible to less practised eyes. The escort is on the alert; the sheikh receives his spear from the hands of his henchmen; the camels are left in the charge of a boy; led horses are mounted; the priming of pistols and guns is looked to, and the whole party is ready to fight or retreat according as the enemy may be in strength or not. The sheikh gallops up a small height to reconnoitre; comes back at full speed; shouts 'enemies', and in a greater force than their own.

Not a moment is lost; sauve-qui-peut is the order of the day; and the Arabs disperse, leaving the traveller to make terms as best he can, probably a permission to return on foot and naked to the town. The wild-looking sons of the desert, mounted on rough but high-bred mares, comes down upon him like a whirlwind, with a loud unearthly yell, shaking their lances over their heads; and the interview is soon over, the tourist finding himself again alone on the broad plain, with or without a shirt, as the case may be. If any resistance has been made by him, any man or mare killed or wounded, the traveller's adventures here terminate for ever in the thrust of a lance.

It is more likely, however, that the horsemen in the distance prove to be friends, for the Bedouins seldom venture to cross a dangerous district unless assured of the absence of all tribes with whom they have feuds. Under the direction of the sheikh the camp is pitched near some lonely spring, disturbing possibly thereby a troop of wild asses, which gallop off to drink at some safer place.

After a few days' journey of this kind are described in the distance numerous black specks which gradually assume the form of an encampment, the home of your Bedouin guides. As the party approaches it will be joined by scouts, who come careering towards it with intricate feats of horsemanship, spear in rest, to excite the admiration and respect of the unknown visitor.

On arriving, the guest is taken to the largest tent, where he dismounts, and exclaims, '*Salaam aleikum!*' Its inmates gravely respond, in a sonorous voice, '*Aleikum salaam!*' When seated on the best carpet he is regaled with a small cup of black unsugared coffee, rendered still more unpalatable by an odious infusion of bitter-herbs. Presently a huge bowl of rice, cooked with butter, probably rancid, and lumps of mutton, certainly tough, is placed on the ground, and every one thrusts his fingers into it and helps himself. Each partaker of the feast retires when his appetite is satisfied, and leaves his place to another until the last remnants of the fare are devoured by a troop of naked and hungry children, and the bones by the lean curs of the encampment.

All idea of privacy must be given up, as the tent of the stranger will be open to all visitors, who would be much offended if he were to say 'Not at home' to the least of them. With the exception of this intrusive disposition, the Bedouins will be found gentle, considerate, and anxious to please their guest. In the morning he may ride out on a hawking party.

While the tourist is enjoying this rich treat, some plundering enterprise may perhaps be planned by the sheikh against the Aneyzeh tribe, which is in a state of perpetual foray and reprisals with the Shammar.

If the traveller should wish to push his study of the desert so far as to run this additional risk, he must see that he be well mounted for a forced retreat, and he must equip himself in a Bedouin costume to avoid the danger of being captured with a view to a heavy ransom. Early in the morning the party will be on their mares, and, taking with them a few thin wheaten cakes for food and each a sheepskin cloak to sleep on, they start in a straight line to a point on the horizon at a good pace, that their enemies may be taken by surprise. All those whom they meet on their way, if of friendly tribes, are invited to join the expedition, which they are always ready to do, and the number of the party will probably soon be thus increased to about a hundred horsemen.

When the ground becomes uneven, a scout is sent to every

height to reconnoitre, and towards nightfall a concealed position is sought for a bivouac. No fires are lit, no tents are pitched, but each man throws himself on the ground to eat his dry bread and sleep beside his picketed mare, one being, however, on guard.

An hour or two before daylight the word 'mount' is passed from mouth to mouth, and the mares are again put to their mettle. The arrival at the doomed encampment is timed so as to meet the flocks and herds just when they are being driven out in the morning to graze, and before they are scattered about on the pastures, that they may thus be swept off in a body.

The war-chant is commenced. The mares prick their ears and snort with excitement. Those who have been told off to drive the captured cattle and carry off the booty separate from the main body, which gradually quickens its pace, the war-song becoming louder and louder, till a full gallop and a yell bring the assailants round some sheltering mound, and they charge in among the tents.

A scene of disorder ensues which baffles description. The men of the plundered tribe spring out of their tents; some hurl their javelins at the horsemen, others fire their long rifles at them and quickly load, while the women shriek and fling stones; the cattle gallop in all directions with their tails in the air, and the hostile parties of drivers and fighters show the greatest activity in getting the herd together on the move, and in dispersing those who attempt to prevent its being taken away.

If the Shammar be worsted, the sooner the traveller gets his mare into a gallop, in the direction whence he came, the better will it be for him; but, if successful, a few minutes will suffice to get the cattle on their way home, covered by a strong force in the rear, the Aneyzeh firing distant shots to harass them for some miles. The wounded are carried off, the dead left on the field, and, if prisoners have been taken, their ransom is transacted by regular embassies, as well as the conditions for the restoration of a part of the booty when the plundered tribe can afford it. Such incidents are of so frequent occurrence that the traveller will find no lack of opportunity for witnessing them, if it be his wish.

If any English traveller was foolish enough to join such an

enterprise; and some no doubt were, or it would not have been written about; and if he survived to tell the table, which he obviously did, he would then pursue his lucky and exhilarated way to Baghdad, where he would, we are told, 'Meet with a little Anglo-Indian society, which will materially enhance the enjoyment of his stay there.'

Such an adventure as the above may have been possible in the Turkish dominions of the 1850s, but by the beginning of the twentieth century a great deal had changed, proved by the fact that there were more guidebooks to the region, though Baedeker was published in German only. A volume was devoted to Constantinople in the *Medieval Towns* series, and a special edition, already mentioned, of the *Blue Guide* (in French) commemorated the opening of the Orient Express route. Apart from Black's, there was Murray's updated handbook to the Bosphorus and Dardanelles area, and fifty excellent pages in Macmillan's *Eastern Mediterranean*, 1905.

The Bradshaw of the day tells us that getting through the customs at Constantinople was less easy than formerly, but that: 'A bakhsheesh of 5 piastres will expedite matters.' Murray informs us: 'Rifles, revolvers, foreign cigars, and tobacco are prohibited. Books, newspapers, and all printed matters are submitted to the censor; if not returned within a day, application should be made for them through the Consulate. Books such as the "Hand-book" and the "Continental Bradshaw" have, on occasion, been seized.' Should this be the case, the traveller need not despair, because 'Otto Keil, booksellers to H.I.M. the Sultan stock all books on the East, including Murray's Handbooks', according to an advertisement in Black's guide.

With regard to accommodation Murray says in his preface that 'great changes have taken place in TURKEY within the last few years. Travellers who intend to make a long stay may sometimes take furnished lodgings, and have their meals at clubs, hotels, or restaurants. All the furnished lodgings are bad, and very few respectable. The sanitary arrangements and the attendance are wretched.'

The traveller is warned against wearing a fez on his arrival in the East, which is 'a very unwise thing to do, as by donning the native head-gear he *ipso-facto* loses his foreign prestige'. He is also told that: 'There is no postal delivery at Constantinople; letters must be called for at the Post Office at which they are expected to arrive.'

As for getting about, we read in Black's: 'With two or three exceptions, the streets of Constantinople are but little better than narrow, crooked, wretchedly-paved, and dirty alleys.' As a guide or dragoman, Hutton, of the *Medieval Towns* series, strongly recommends: 'Eustathios Livathinos as a most pleasant companion. Jacob Moses has also much experience.'

We are also told in Black's that: 'The Jews are pretty numerous, and are, with some exceptions, the poorest and most wretched of all the races inhabiting Constantinople. Many of the Greeks, Armenians, and Jews are employed under the Government; but the majority of them are merchants, shop-keepers, artisans, hawkers, labourers, etc. They are officially styled "rayah" or "the herd", a term which the Turks apply to the non-Mussulman subjects.' The *Guide Bleu* says that 'the Jews make up the part of the population of the Ottoman Empire the least hostile to foreigners'.

One's conduct has to be continually monitored nevertheless, because on visiting the Aya Sophia Mosque, which Baedeker's double asterisk makes a 'must': 'Visitors should be careful not to touch anything.' *The Mediterranean Traveller*, 1905, published for tourists from the United States, tells its readers: 'All foreigners in Turkey are under constant suspicion and surveillance, and are greatly hindered in their personal and business affairs.'

A section in Black's dealing with theatres and music halls states that the theatre at Shehzdeh Bachi 'should not be visited by ladies'. How you would pay your entrance fee would seem a problem, in any case, because the same book tells us: 'There is practically no such thing as legal tender in Turkey, and payment may be made in coins of any current denomination.'

Taking boats from one shore to another is no relaxing matter. 'These craft are very crank, and the greatest care should be taken in getting in and out of them. They are not provided with thwarts for passengers, but the latter have to sit down on the cushions in the well, where if they only sit still they are safe enough.'

If the theatres are morally out of bounds perhaps the traveller will take note of the following in Murray: 'The devotional exercises of the Dancing Dervishes are held on *Tuesday* and *Friday*, after the Sultan returns from the mosque. Those of the Howling Dervishes may be witnessed at Skutari.'

Another feature of the town are the dogs, of which Murray gives the best account. 'There are two popular errors concerning the dogs that throng the streets of Constantinople; the one, that they are ferocious; the other that they are scavengers, and thus instruments of cleanliness. The Constantinople dog is a mild, sociable creature, never aggressive, and always thankful for small mercies. But he is anything but an instrument of cleanliness; on the contrary, he contributes in no small measure to the uncleanliness of the streets, and his scavenging is limited to rummaging for edible morsels in the heaps of rubbish which householders throw out before their doors for the dustman to clear away in the morning. The dog's existence is precarious; depending on the produce of dust heaps aforesaid, on the scraps and offal of the butchers, and on the stale loaves which bakers cut up and distribute.'

Murray then describes how the canine population operate the same strict demarcation system as in Cairo, concluding: 'The principal inconvenience of the dogs to mankind is their nocturnal barking and howling. The number of them, however, has perceptibly diminished of late years; the waste spaces in which they used to bask and breed have been enclosed or built over, and gradually the Constantinople dog is being improved away.'

Perhaps the following rules were drawn up by the police based on their knowledge of the dogs' passion for guarding their territory: '*Police regulations* in Constantinople do not differ much from those in other European cities. But the police, who are all Moslems, are wanting in knowledge and tact, and they are not always to be relied on in case of a difficulty. It is, however, easy to keep out of trouble. In the frequented parts of the city a foreigner runs no risk whatever of molestation, if his own conduct is discreet. If, however, he penetrates into the quarters inhabited exclusively by Mussulmans, he should be always accompanied by a dragoman. The children in these quarters are prone to hooting and throwing stones, and any resentment of these offences is certain to lead to difficulty. If the traveller strays into one of those quarters, the best thing to do is make his way out of it as soon as possible. Should a traveller get into trouble, the only course to follow is to exercise the utmost patience, and on arriving at the police station, to send a note to the Consulate.'

One would not in any case want to be caught in any of the above areas after reading about fires in Constantinople, which are said to be 'of frequent occurrence and often very destructive, desolating whole quarters of the city. Great precautions are now taken both to prevent them, and to check their progress. The fire-engines are in the hands of firemen who are paid by enjoying some special privileges; but the engines are small boxes, which are carried on the shoulders of four men; these run head-long, crying "fire!" at the tops of their voices. Having reached the place of conflagration, they wait to be hired by people whose houses are in danger. There is another set of firemen who prove eminently useful on such occasions. They are soldiers armed with axes and long poles, with iron hooks at the end. These tear down the wooden houses, and so isolate the fire, as effectually to put an end to its ravages. Still, a fire in Constantinople is an awful scene; 2000 houses and shops have been known to burn in the space of a few hours. It is indeed impossible to describe the confusion and horror of the sight. Men, women, and children escaping from their abandoned homes, each dragging or carrying on his shoulder whatever he happened to catch at the moment. The police are powerless for good. Evil-intentioned men rush into the houses and rob them, under the pretence of being friends of the family. They have been known to spread the conflagration by carrying burning coals into dwellings yet unreached by the flames.'

CHAPTER SIXTEEN

RUSSIA

After the delights and perils of Turkey our traveller may decide to visit Russia on his long way home, thus completing the circuit of his Grand Tour. From Constantinople a boat will carry him through the Black Sea to Odessa. As for getting through the Russian Customs, we learn: 'In order to encourage the officials in discovering contraband goods the following general rule is issued: "In the event of goods liable to duty and confiscation being found while the search is being carried out, all the searchers who took part in the discovery will receive a reward from the first half of the reward fund."'

The Customs ordeal seems to have been more onerous than in other places: 'Whether,' says Baedeker's *Russia*, 1914, 'at the railway frontier station or at a seaport the examination of passengers' luggage is generally thorough. Unprinted paper only should be used for packing, to avoid any cause of suspicion.

'The only things that are passed DUTY FREE are *Used Objects* indispensable for the journey. Travellers should avoid works of a political, social, or historical nature; bound books are subject to duty. Passengers are particularly warned against offering gratuities. Prohibited goods, such as gunpowder and playing cards, are confiscated.'

Having obtained clearance, supposing he had any luggage left, our traveller in 1888 would find good hotels and restaurants in Odessa, and boulevard cafés at which to take his ease. There was also an English Club, and a German Club, Murray says, 'where amateur theatricals are frequently performed in German; the Nobility Club, of which the members are principally Jews'. In the town he would also find an Anglican church, a British Consul-General and a British Seaman's Institute, Home and Reading Room, facilities which no doubt gave the feeling of being back in civilization. By 1912 two hundred steamers a year harboured there, though Baedeker's *Mediterranean*, 1911, says: 'The excesses of the revolution of 1905 were nowhere more ghastly than at Odessa.'

As soon as our traveller departs from the cosmopolitan comforts of the Black Sea coast and goes north through the Ukraine into Russia proper he will come up against the realities of the Russian character as described in several guidebooks. Depending on his religion he may reflect on the following from Murray: 'Alien *Jews* may only visit Russia with the sanction of the Minister of the Interior, which must be sought by petition. Exception to this rule is, however, made in favour of foreign Jews distinguished by their position in society, or by their extensive business transactions.'

Railway travel in Russia was slow, though the carriages were said to be the most comfortable in Europe. There was sometimes 'a certain amount of disorder in the taking and keeping of seats. On entering a train all the seats will at first appear to be occupied, but an application to the station-master will soon cause a removal of the cloaks, bedding, &c., with which the carriage is packed. However, these artifices are not peculiar to Russia alone. Cases of theft are unfortunately not unfrequent, particularly in the south. It is dangerous to leave valuables in a carriage while taking refreshments at a station.'

In *Things Seen in Russia* by W. Barnes Steveni (one of a series, with many photographs of the time which now makes the books very collectable) we may read that: 'There is probably no country in Europe where railway travelling is so cheap as in Russia . . . but third-class travelling is *dear at any price*, on account of the stifling atmosphere of the carriages and the undesirable and lively company of all kinds, especially those that never pay their fare! These workmen travel enormous distances in special trains at ridiculously low fares, probably cheaper than in any country in Europe.'

From the same source we learn that matters of the stomach are well taken care of, since before the start of the journey passengers may 'meet at the beautiful buffets for which the Russian stations are noted, to gossip and regale the inner man with Pekoe tea flavoured with lemon, and eat caviare, meat pies, and other delicacies. As a rule, Russian buffets on the principal railways surpass anything I have seen in England as regards cheapness and variety of food.'

Steveni's observations on the Russian character are worth quoting: 'I have noticed that the larger the village, the more corrupt and spoilt the inhabitants; for human beings in this respect appear to be like apples – the more they are crowded together, the sooner they become rotten.'

He goes on to say that there were a hundred and twelve million peasants in Russia, and that, 'If this be the case, there is latent in the Russian people a force which will some day not only affect its destinies, but probably the destinies of Europe, for such a mighty power cannot always be suppressed or ignored.' He calculated that there is room for six hundred million people in the Russian Empire and, 'As the population doubles every fifty to fifty-five years, the population in 1985 – without counting probable annexations of more territory – will amount to 400,000,000 souls.' Which goes to show how demographic speculation can be so wide of the mark; the population in 1979 was about 262,500,000: and in any case, who could have foreseen the many calamities which were to fall upon the unfortunate Russian people?

Steveni considers that, as far as survival goes, 'the Russian peasant's idea of hygiene are so primitive that, were it not for the plentiful and regular use of the steam bath he would contract so many diseases that the race would rapidly die out'.

He occasionally reflects on their morals, and deplores the fact that women do so much work in the fields. 'It is not infrequently happens that while the women are busy ploughing or reaping, sometimes several miles away from their villages, some of the little urchins or mites that have been left behind, all alone, set fire to the house or outbuildings. As most of the houses are built of wood and thatched with straw, the entire village before long is ablaze, and the old and infirm and young are burnt to death before they can be rescued from the flames. If one wishes to understand the mind of the Russian peasants, his ideals and outlook on life, we must not turn to books of travel or to the works of modern novelists, but instead study the works of William Langland and Chaucer.'

Baedeker's reflections on the character of the Russians are also interesting, for the people have been 'influenced not only by a long history of subjugation to feudal despotism, but also by the gloomy forests, and unresponsive soil, and the rigorous climate, and especially by the enforced inactivity of the long winters. In disposition they are melancholy and reserved, clinging obstinately to their traditions, and full of self-sacrificing devotion to Tzar, Church, and feudal superior. They are easily disciplined, and so make excellent soldiers, but have little power of independent thinking or of initiation. The normal Great Russian is thus the mainstay of political and economic inertia and reaction. Even the educated Russian gives comparatively little response to the actual demands of life; he is more or less the victim of fancy and temperament, which sometimes leads him to a despondent slackness, sometimes to emotional outbursts. Here we have the explanation of the want of organisation, the disorder, and the waste of time which strike the western visitor to Russia.'

Baedeker divides the people of Russia into four classes: '. . . nobles and officials, clergy, citizens or townspeople, and peasants. Alongside of admirable achievements in all spheres of intellectual activity, we find also a great deal of merely outward imitation of western forms, and a tendency to rest content with a veneer of western culture and a stock of western catchwords. Side by side with an unquenchable desire for scientific knowledge, which shuns no sacrifice and is constantly drawing new elements from the lower classes, there is only too often a total inability to put into practice and make an effectual use of what has been learned. Fancy and emotion are much more widely developed in the soul of the Russian than true energy and joy in creation. The upper classes are noted for their luxury and extravagance and for their reckless gambling, their better side showing itself in their unlimited hospitality. The lower classes live in unspeakable poverty and destitution. Beggars are very troublesome, especially in the vicinity of churches.'

Manufacturing industry was said to be much less important than agriculture, although 'the Government has done much to elevate it in recent times, but there is a lack both of native capital and of competent workmen. The entrepreneurs and managers of factories are largely foreigners.' Should our traveller coming up from Odessa call at Yuzovka he would find coal mines and iron-works established by Mr John Hughes in 1872, 'whose employees were many of them English, for which a church and chaplain were provided'.

Approaching Moscow, the train stops at Tula which, Murray tells us, is 'famed for its manufacture of fire-arms and generally for its hardware'. The gun factory, Baedeker says, was established in 1632 by a Dutchman, and is now 'under the superintendence of an Englishman named Trewheller'. Steveni, who also has something to say about this place, finds that: 'The Russian workman is generally very intelligent and works cheaply; but he is so extremely careless that he has to be carefully watched at his work.'

Tula is frequently called the 'Birmingham of Russia', Steveni says, but has 'no very high opinion of the quality of its small-arms, judging from the wretched specimen of a revolver I purchased when last passing through. It was cheaply and carelessly made, and did not possess that finish one finds in English and American weapons. If the Russian mechanic cannot make a first-class revolver, he is quite a genius as regards the manufacture of *samovars*.'

Steveni agrees with other writers that card-playing is a very important pastime in Russia. 'In a country where the pursuit of politics is not altogether advisable, many people who would other-wise dabble in public affairs throw all their attention into cards and gambling.'

It is not only the aristocracy who are dissolute, because peasants who become rich merchants gladly join in the high-life as well: 'One merchant used to come to the gardens with a pocket-book full of £10 bank-notes, and throw them broadcast among the singers and dancers. Sometimes the performances conclude with a drunken orgie, during which the merchants, in order to show their generosity and absolute contempt for money, finish off by smashing all the mirrors and wine-glasses, and then coolly calling for the bill! It must be remembered that the majority of the merchants spring from the peasant class, and have neither the birth, breeding, or social status of the merchants in England.'

Should the merchant go on holiday to the Baltic beach resort of Dubbeln he might need to exercise more restraint over his boisterousness, for Murray tells us that: 'The hours of bathing for ladies and gentlemen, respectively, are regulated by the ringing of a bell, and any infringement by the one sex on the hours allotted to the other is visited with a severe fine when detected', which penalty, however, the merchant may not have been averse to paying.

Travelling within Russian towns had its difficulties: 'The driver of the carriage often does not know how to read; he does not always know his way about, and sometimes raises difficulties about giving change', Baedeker informs us. 'The little one-horse *Sleighs* are wider and more comfortable than the cabs. When they are going fast, passengers must be on their guard against being thrown out.'

We are told that hotels in provincial towns, 'especially the older ones, satisfy as a rule only the most moderate demands, and they often leave much to be desired in point of cleanliness. In spite of these failings they frequently have high-sounding names, such as Grand Hotel, etc. The washing arrangements are generally unsatisfactory, usually consisting of a tiny wash-basin communicating with a small tank, from which the water trickles in a feeble stream.'

Murray comments in his earlier guide: 'Without wishing to detract from the merits of the best hotels mentioned in the Handbook, it is right to advise the traveller to be provided, when travelling in Russia, with remedies against insects of a vexatory disposition.'

The further one went from the main cities the worse was the accommodation, especially for those using Siberia as a route to Japan, or wanting to see something of Central Asia. On the Caucasian Black Sea coast, at Poti, there were many hotels but, says Murray of 1888: 'The climate is disagreeable, and fever prevails during the summer months. The marshy forests throw out most dangerous fogs which produce ague. The houses are infested by noxious vermin.'

On the Siberian route at Tiumen the hotels are said to be poor: 'It is well to come provided with sheets, towels, soap, and insect powder.' At Bokhara in Central Asia: 'Travellers are cautioned not to drink water that has not been boiled, and to be on their guard against boils, ulcers and contagious diseases.'

'In summer,' Baedeker writes, 'the heat is almost unbearable, while the dust irritates the respiratory organs in a highly unpleasant manner.' In the matter of social intercourse one is told: 'Immediately on arrival at Ashkhabad, Bokhara, or Tashkent, the traveller should call upon the Russian diplomatic officials (dress clothes *de rigeur*).'

Caution against drinking water is again heavily italicized. 'For washing, the traveller should be provided with an indiarubber bath or basin, and he should disinfect the water with lysoform. The so-called Sartian sickness or pendinka (identical with Aleppo or Baghdad boil) especially prevalent in Aug. and Sept., and the rishta (thread-worm) which burrows under the skin, seem both to be propagated by the water.'

Towards the end of the nineteenth century the overland journey to Peking via Siberia was attracting more and more travellers, including ladies, Murray says, and although the railway ended just beyond the Ural Mountains, 'with the assistance of the Russian Commissioner at the Chinese frontier, the journey has been performed in nine weeks from St. Petersburg'. After 1903, when the Trans-Siberian Railway was complete, the twice-weekly express took nine days to go from St Petersburg to Vladivostok on the Pacific, passengers being cared for by the International Sleeping Car Company.

On the way to Irkutsk the literary traveller might call at Omsk where, Baedeker reminds us: 'The building in which the author F. M. Dostoevski (d. 1881) was imprisoned from 1849 to 1853, and in which he wrote his "Recollections of a Dead House" stood in the N.E. corner of the fortress, but has been removed.'

Having reached Irkutsk, where carriages were changed, Murray says that the chief hotel is excellent, though the others are 'almost invariably dear and indifferent'. Baedeker informs us that one disadvantage is 'the inevitable concert or "sing-song" in the dining room, which usually last far into the night'.

If the traveller stays a while, and happens to have Bradshaw's *World Guide*, 1903 for his companion, he may be alarmed by the following: '... the sidewalks are merely boards on cross-pieces over the open sewers. In summer it is almost impassable owing to the mud, or unbearable owing to dust. The police are few, escaped convicts and ticket-of-leave criminals many ... In Irkutsk, and all towns east of it, the stranger should not walk after dark; if a carriage cannot be got, as is often the case, the only way is to tramp noisily along the planked walk; be careful in making crossings, and do not stop, or the immense mongrel mastiffs turned loose into the streets as guards will attack. To walk in the middle of the road is to court attack from the garrotters, with which Siberian towns abound.'

In 1901 Harry de Windt set out from Paris to northwestern Siberia, and reached Alaska by crossing the Bering Strait, his epic journey narrated in *From Paris to New York by Land*. At Irkutsk his party put up at the Hotel Metropole (mentioned in Baedeker, though not in Bradshaw, nor in the *Guide to the Great Siberian Railways*, 1901) which he found something of a shock to enter, 'such a noisesome den, suggestive of a Whitechapel slum, although its prices equalled those of the Carlton in Pall Mall. The house was new but jerry-built, reeks of drains, and swarmed with vermin. Having kept us shivering for half an hour in the cold, a sleepy, shock-headed lad with guttering candle appeared and led the way to a dark and ill-smelling sleeping-apartment. The latter contained an iron bedstead (an unknown luxury here a decade ago), but relays of guests had evidently used the crumpled sheets and grimy pillows.'

After some time in Irkutsk, de Windt continues his trek of thousands of miles across the Tundra armed with revolvers and two rifles, as well as a fowling piece.

It is now time to assume, however, that our traveller, with much heart-yearning, wishes to turn his tracks towards Home. Before he can do so he will have read in his Baedeker that on leaving Russia he must 'report his intentions to the *Police Authorities*, handing in his passport and a certificate from the police officials of the district in which he has been living to the effect that nothing stands in the way of his departure'. Having obtained this, he will go to the offices of the International Sleeping Car Company and buy a ticket to London for nine pounds in gold, which haven he will reach in sixty-five hours.

CHAPTER SEVENTEEN

ENGLAND, HOME AND BEAUTY

'How happy and green the country looked as the chaise whirled rapidly from milestone to milestone, through neat country towns where landlords came out to welcome him with smiles and bows; by pretty roadside inns, where the signs hung on the elms, and horses and waggoners were drinking under the chequered shadow of the trees; by old halls and parks, rustic hamlets clustered around ancient grey churches – and through the charming friendly English landscape. Is there any in the world like it?'

So Thackeray summed up the feelings of English travellers coming home from Abroad, but what would be the reaction of foreigners to the country who were seeing it for the first time or, for that matter, the ex-convict returning from the Antipodes after he had made good and become rich – and possibly changed his name? The difficulty here is that guidebooks for foreigners in their own language were somewhat scarce. The guidebook in the nineteenth century was, initially, a British and a German invention, people from those countries being the first to have the money and the intellectual curiosity to travel, at least in any numbers.

Most guidebooks to England were put out in English for the use of the English, and many excellent series soon provided total coverage of Great Britain and Ireland. A. & C. Black's of Edinburgh produced some forty-four volumes (the first one, to Scotland, appeared in 1826), and John Murray forty volumes of county and cathedral guides. Later in the century came Baddeley's *Thorough Guides* of nineteen volumes, with excellent maps and plans by Bartholomew. A little later nearly ninety volumes of Ward Lock's Red *Shilling Guides* went on the bookstalls, as well as fifty volumes of Methuen's *Little Guides* and twenty-four volumes of the excellent *Highways and Byways* series. This made the British Isles an extremely well guidebooked country, with something over two hundred titles, so that anyone going on holiday to Derbyshire, for example, had at least seven good manuals to choose from.

The question is, how critical were they, or how purblind, to the conditions of the country they so meticulously described? The first Baedeker to England (though in German) did not appear until 1862, a French edition following in 1866, while the *Guide Joanne: Londres Illustré* came out in 1865. The foreign traveller, each of them tells us, had no need of a passport for a visit to England, though it was wise to carry one as proof of identity, and so as to have no trouble when returning to their own country.

The only thing to worry about regarding the English Customs were '*liqueurs spiritueuses*' and cigars in excess of 250 grammes, though English books printed on the Continent could not be brought in. The *Guide Joanne* says that the crowds of people who besiege the traveller on his arrival at the London station offering to carry his baggage and take him to the best hotel should be ignored, since they are known in England by the name of sharks (*requins*) and are apt to prey on him.

The traveller should get himself into a cab as soon as possible. The foreigner who doesn't know English will be confused on getting to London for the first time, so it would be best if he could write to a friend beforehand, and also consult a plan of London. In any case he should get quickly to a hotel that has been recommended to him as economical, and only stay the absolute minimum of time necessary in which to find lodgings in a private house.

Baedeker says that if the traveller wants information all he has to do is ask a policeman. There are seven thousand of them in London, each, according to Murray, paid eighteen shillings a week, 'with clothing and 40lbs. of coal weekly to each married man all the year; 40lbs. weekly to each single man during six months, and 20lbs. weekly during the remainder of the year'.

The duty of the police is to control traffic and more or less guarantee the safety of people from – Baedeker tells us – the fifteen thousand pickpockets who infest the capital. 'The number of persons taken into custody between 1844 and 1848 inclusive,' Murray goes on, 'amounted to 374,710. Robberies during the same period were 71,000, and the value of property stolen was £271,000 of which £55,000 was recovered.'

One is advised by Baedeker to address a passer-by only in case of absolute necessity, and not to reply to any question addressed to him on the street, especially in French or German, for it is usually the preliminary to some thievery or trick. 'We recommend that in general the traveller should be on his guard, and above all to keep an eye constantly on his purse or watch, because London swarms with thieves, and even those who live in London do not escape their attentions.'

Murray tells us to beware of mock auctions at shops, and also not to drink the 'unwholesome water furnished to the tanks of houses from the Thames'. Should you become ill, beware of falling into the hands of a charlatan. It is better to get the address of a good doctor from someone who lives in the same neighbourhood.

In the hotel you should lock your door on going out and, even in the best hotels, lock it also before going to sleep. Valuables are best kept secured in your trunk, because the wardrobe locks are not sufficiently solid. Anything really valuable should be left with the proprietor of the hotel – but get a receipt. In private lodgings the traveller should take particular care in this respect.

Most hotels forbid smoking in the bedrooms and dining room, though special rooms are set aside for smokers. Cigars are an item of luxury in London, the expense being somewhat reduced since one is not allowed to smoke in crowded places, as on the Continent. One can't find cigars as cheap as in Germany or, if you can, they are usually bad, so it is better to buy them from the same place each day, where the shopkeeper will get to know you and give a good brand. Murray warns us never to listen to offers of 'smuggled' cigars on the streets.

As for restaurants, English cooking deserves neither the pompous praise often lavished on it, says Baedeker, nor the absolute condemnation of which it is sometimes the object. Murray's *Handbook to London*, 1864 tells us that the population is 2,803,634. 'The Metropolis is supposed to consume in one year 1,600,000 quarters of wheat, 240,000 bullocks, 1,700,000 sheep, 28,000 calves, and 35,000 pigs. One market alone (Leadenhall) supplies about 4,025,000 head of game. This, together with 3,000,000 salmon, irrespective of other fish and flesh, is washed down by 43,200,000 gallons of porter and ale, 2,000,000 gallons of spirits, and 65,000 pipes of wine. To fill its milk and cream jugs, 13,000 cows are kept. The thirsty souls of London need have no fear of becoming thirstier as long as there are upwards of 4000 public-houses and 1000 wine merchants to minister to their deathless thirst.'

In the restaurants one could have oxtail soup for eightpence, a chop for sixpence, a chicken for a shilling, or a rump steak for tenpence; for vegetables there were potatoes for a penny, cabbage for twopence, or spinach for threepence; as for dessert there was plum pudding or rice pudding for fourpence, and cheese at twopence, accompanied perhaps by a pint of stout for fourpence. 'The wine is generally expensive and bad in England. *Claret* is the name given to French red wine of an inferior quality. In many dining rooms it is the custom to serve every quarter of an hour a roast joint. At a given signal an enormous platter is wheeled in and you are free to cut the part which you desire. In these sorts of establishment the meat generally leaves little to be desired.'

Baedeker says that London is growing bigger by the day, and that its ten thousand streets contain nearly four hundred thousand houses, including '796 boarding houses, 330 restaurants, 883 cafés, and 398 hotels'. Furthermore, 'The census of 1861 listed 25,000 tailors, 45,000 dressmakers, and 180,000 domestic servants of both sexes.'

To light the city at night, '360,000 gas-lights fringe the streets, while to warm its people and to supply its factories, a fleet of a thousand sail is employed in bringing annually 3,000,000 tons of coal, exclusive of what is brought by rail. The smoke from this immense quantity of coal has often been traced as far as Reading, 32 miles distant.'

Murray tells us that the streets of the Metropolis would, if put together, 'extend 3000 miles in length. The main thoroughfares are traversed by 1200 omnibuses, and 3500 cabs (besides private carriages and carts), employing 40,000 horses.' The thought here occurs that if each horse deposited on the street five pounds of dung on average, the resulting hundred or so tons of overspread must have created an abominable stench, though not perhaps as piercing as that which comes from traffic today.

All books agree that the traveller could not fail to be astonished at the complicated enormity of London – the first city of the world in population and extent wherein, says Baedeker, 'everything seems rare and even unique. Nevertheless familiarity will exercise its influence, and the stranger will soon get so used to its peculiarities that they will cease to astonish.'

We are told to remember that: 'The English are attached with much tenacious partiality to their institutions that have been passed down to them by their ancestors; and it is true to say that Great Britain is indebted in some way to these institutions for a good part of its present grandeur.'

In the London Postal District there were eleven deliveries of letters daily, and those letters put into the box before six at night were delivered the same evening. Baedeker tells of the many marvels to be seen, but says also: 'The numerous churches in London, with the exception of the most important, are mentioned only in passing, the majority are not worth mentioning: a single glance which the foreigner casts on one or another of these temples will be enough to prove that they are absolutely devoid of interest from the artistic point of view, and that they merit only the attention of the theologian (of whom there are many from the numerous sects which exist in London).'

Special warning is given about the strict observation of the Sabbath. Hippolyte Taine's first Sunday in London was probably the unhappiest day in his life, since he tells us that he was prepared to 'commit suicide after an hour's walk past the closed shops. Everything is gloomy and sooty. Somerset House is a frightful thing, Nelson is hideous, like a rat impaled on the top of a pole', and so forth. He quotes a fellow-countryman's words to the effect that: 'Here religion spoils one day out of seven, and destroys the seventh part of possible happiness.'

All shops are closed but 'it is better to go out into the country on that day, where you may satisfy your appetite at any hour, and rest from the noise which you have had to put up with all week. You may also thus at the same time see how the middle and lower classes of English society, who make long excursions in the environs of London with all the family, including small children, lie on the grass, unwrap all sorts of toys, singing and enjoying themselves, and then going home late on the omnibus. Hampton Court is the only establishment open on Sunday: one must therefore take care to visit it in the week.'

The traveller is liable to be confused in the matter of money and coinage, for he will have to deal with such arcane rarities as guineas, pounds, sovereigns, half-sovereigns, crowns, half-crowns, florins, shillings, sixpences, fourpences, pennies, halfpennies and farthings. Possibilities for imposition must have been boundless.

Regarding public conveniences, there are: 'Closets for ladies in all the railway stations (the Ladies' waiting room) and at all the Pastry-cooks; then in the main stores. For men, at the stations, in the dining rooms and at public houses. If you are in doubt the best plan is to ask a policeman: *"Will you tell me, please, where is the nearest place of convenience?"* '

A list of the places to see followed by meticulous descriptions in the *Guide Joanne* include the *Prison de Newgate, Hospice de Chelsea, Musée Britannique, Galérie Nationale, Musée de South-Kensington, Galérie National des Portraits, Parc de Saint-James, Jardins de Kensington, Parc de Battersea, École de Westminster, Cathédrale de Saint-Paul, Abbaye de Westminster, Le Temple, Les docks, Banque d'Angleterre,* and the *Tour de Londres.* In the environs were such attractions as the *Palais de Cristal* and the *Jardins de Kew.* Baedeker suggests three weeks in which to see everything, but adds that much more time could profitably be spent.

The outer environs were not without interest: a steamboat from Charing Cross would take you to Woolwich, where English subjects could visit the arsenal and citadel, accompanied by an officer of the garrison, while foreigners had to obtain a letter of introduction from their ambassador. Later in the nineteenth century a service of steamers on the Thames ran as far as Oxford, daily in the summer – though not on Sundays.

The map in Baedeker showed England as already covered by a dense network of railways, so there was no difficulty in going to all the main towns, while those off the beaten track could be reached by coach. Brighton was an hour and twenty-five minutes away, though the *Guide Joanne* is somewhat contemptuous of *Le Pavillon*: '... *un édifice du style le plus ridicule et le plus étrange: une pagode indienne ou javanaise sous un ciel moins beau que celui de l'Inde ou de Java.*' Baedeker, who knocks five minutes off the journey time, says that the Pavilion complex is a '*grand et disgracieux édifice en style oriental*...'

County and regional guidebooks in English gave no information on how foreigners should behave, and the only translated book which did so will be examined later. A curious book entitled *Foreign Visitors to England*, 1889, deals mostly with travellers' impressions from a somewhat earlier age. According to Misson (1688): 'The inhabitants of this excellent country are tall, handsome, well made, fair, active, robust, courageous, thoughtful, devout, lovers of the liberal arts, and as capable of the sciences as any people in the world.'

On the other hand, a certain Dr Gemelli-Careri (1686), perhaps knowing something of the Englishman's opinion of *his* countrymen, says: 'The commonalty are rude, cruel, addicted to thieving and robbing, faithless, headstrong, inclined to strife and mutiny, gluttonous, and superstitiously addicted to the predictions of foolish astrologers; in short, of a very extravagant temper, delighting in the noise of guns, drums, and bells, as if it were some sweet harmony.'

Returning to the nineteenth century, an American, Professor Poppin (1867), in a study of English character, says: 'If I could chastise my own intemperate nationality, and not let it stick out offensively, I soon made friends with Englishmen who, in the end, would volunteer more in reference to their own failings than I should ever have thought of producing them to. Mutual pride prevents Englishmen and Americans from seeing each other's good traits and positive resemblances. And all Englishmen are not disagreeable, neither are all Americans insufferable.'

In 1835 Frederick von Raumer pontificated in a book about England, as if he would rather like its inhabitants to become Prussians, that: 'The spirit of resistance to power, which grows with rank luxuriance on the rough uncultured soil of the people, has a native life which, when trained and pruned, bears the noblest fruit, such, for instance, as heroic devotion to country.'

We will now lure our intrepid foreigner into *terra incognita*, to those parts of Great Britain beyond London with which many natives even today are so little familiar that it might be as well to quote Thomas Fuller on the matter: 'Know most of the rooms of thy native country before thou goest over the threshold thereof, especially seeing England presents thee with so many observables.'

Going by the Great Western Railway, with Murray's handbook for *Wiltshire, Dorset & Somerset*, 1859, and the current *ABC Railway Guide*, we soon reach Swindon, 'the great central establishment of the company, the engine depot capable of accommodating 100 engines. A number of mechanics are here employed, and of their skill a curious specimen was exhibited in Hyde Park, 1851; it was a working model of a pair of non-condensing steam-engines, which stood within the compass of a shilling, and weighed three drachms.' Murray also reminds us that the church gives character to the town, 'and shows that this great railway company is not wholly absorbed in the worship of Mammon'.

Should the traveller break his journey and visit Laycock, he will read how the Talbots established their inheritance of the abbey. 'The young daughter and heiress of Sir Henry Sherrington, being in love with John Talbot, contrary to her father's wishes, and discoursing one night with him from the battlements of the abbey church, said she, "I will leap down to you." Her sweetheart replied he would catch her then: but he did not believe she would have done it. She leapt down, and the wind, which was then high, came under her coates, and did something break the fall. Mr. Talbot caught her in his arms, but she struck him dead; she cried for help, and he was with great difficulty brought to life again. Her father thereon told her that since she had made such a leap she would e'en marrie him.'

Going down to the Dorset coast, an interest in penal establishments will take us to Portland: '*Convict prison*, erected in 1848 (but to which strangers are admitted only at the dinner-hour, 11 A.M.).

It is a model building of the kind consisting of 8 wings, besides a hospital, chapel, barracks, and cottages for the warders. It accommodates a governor, deputy-governor, chaplain, 2 schoolmasters, and other officers, and about 1500 convicts, of whom the greater number are employed in quarrying stone for the breakwater. The arrangements are very perfect; the building is lighted with gas from its own gasometer, and abundantly supplied with both fresh and salt water, which are pumped into it by a steam-engine from reservoirs on the shore.'

Baddeley's guidebook of 1914 gives the number of inmates as seven hundred. 'The charitable address, and always used by officials, is "The Grove, Portland".' If we take a steep path we reach the plateau, 'and are amidst the quarries. Away to the left is the *Prison*, which is best left alone; in fact, the sight of a horde of excursionists deeming it the correct thing to stand gazing and making remarks on the gangs of those who *have* been "found out" as they return from the Government quarries to dinner is unseemly and unkind.'

Murray, in his guide of 1887, says that Devonshire 'has something to present to the curiosity of the traveller besides mere beauty and grandeur of scenery. It contains the greatest Naval and Military Arsenal combined, in the British Empire, planted on the shores of a harbour not to be surpassed for spaciousness, security, and scenic beauty. The sight of its docks, fitting yards, Steam factories, workshops, its palatial Barracks, gigantic Forts and Lines, gun wharfs bristling with rows of cannon, and, above all, the floating Armaments of iron and wooden war ships floating peacefully on the bosom of Hamoaze, combine to display to the fullest the power of Great Britain, and present alone a spectacle worth coming far to see.'

This refers, of course, to Plymouth and Devonport, and some indication is given of the hours of work: 'The *Dockyard* (hours of admittance are the working hours of the yard: observing that the yard is closed from 12 to 1 in winter, and from 12 to ½ past 1 in summer, except on *Saturdays*, when the workmen remain at their work during the usual dinner-hour, and leave the yard at 3 P.M. It is then closed altogether).'

The traveller in search of tranquillity may visit Widecombe in the Moor, but 'the only resting place is a very poor village *Inn*.

The place is interesting, however, because: 'In Oct. 1638, during divine service, a terrible storm burst over the village, and, after some flashes of uncommon brilliancy, a ball of fire dashed through a window of the church into the midst of the congregation. At once the pews were overturned, 4 persons were killed and 62 wounded, many by a pinnacle of the tower which tumbled through the roof, while "the stones," says Prince, "were thrown down from the steeple as fast as if it had been by 100 men." The country people accounted for this awful destruction by a wild tale that "the devil, dressed in black, and mounted on a black horse, inquired his way to the church of a woman who kept a little public-house on the moor. He offered her money to become his guide, but she distrusted him on remarking that the liquor went hissing down his throat, and finally had her suspicions confirmed by the glimpse of a cloven foot which he could not conceal by his boot." '

Crossing Dartmoor, we are told that the annual cost of maintaining each inmate in the famous prison was nearly thirty-six pounds – something like two thousand pounds in today's money. A free man might try better accommodation at Clovelly, where the small inn will entertain him 'with great hospitality (Inquiry as to rooms may be made by telegraph from Bideford). If it happens to be the autumn, he may regale at breakfast upon herrings which have been captured over night; for Clovelly is famed for its fishery.' Another place at which the traveller might put up, especially if he is a writer, is Babbacombe: 'A few years ago this pretty village was one of those romantic seclusions which have rendered the coast of Devon such a favourite with the novelist.'

Proceeding still further west, and carrying in his pocket Baddeley's *Thorough Guide to Devon and Cornwall,* our traveller will no doubt take a look at the Scilly Isles, passing between the mainland and St Mary's (the legendary Land of Lyonnesse). When he gets there: 'The men who pester tourists on their arrival at the new quay with cards, are quite capable. But among them are some more qualified than others, and some are merely boatmen in the intervals of cobbling or gardening.'

Should fog or a storm keep the traveller in the inn he can read of how an English fleet was wrecked on the rocks of the main island in 1701. S. Baring-Gould gives a good account in his book on Cornwall but, for the sake of brevity, I will refer to Baddeley.

When Admiral Shovel was sailing across the main on his way back to England, there was on board his ship a common seaman who kept for himself a reckoning of the vessel's course. This in itself was an unusual proceeding, very few sailors in those days possessing the necessary knowledge. The man declared that the ship's course would take her upon the rocks of Scilly, and this conclusion was brought to the knowledge of the officers. The unfortunate man was court-martialled on a charge of inciting to mutiny, and then and there convicted and sentenced to be hanged at the yard-arm. Before execution he asked, and got leave, to read aloud a portion of the Holy Scripture. The portion he chose was the 109th Psalm. It spoke of him who 'remembered not to show mercy, but persecuted the poor and needy man, that he might even slay the broken in heart.' It invoked upon him, among many other woes, fewness of days, fatherless children, and a posterity cut off. In a few hours the reckoning of the unhappy man was proved to be correct: the vessel struck upon the Gilstone Rock, and was lost. The body of the admiral, still alive (it was whispered that he was murdered for the sake of a ring he wore by the tenant of Sallakey farm), was carried by the sea to Porthellick, and for a while rested on the spot of ground marked by that strip of sand, and ever since that time the grass has refused to grow there!

The conclusion by S. Baring-Gould is somewhat different: 'The body of Sir Cloudesley Shovel was picked up by a soldier and his wife, who gave it a decent burial in the sand. It was afterwards conveyed to Westminster Abbey and laid there.'

Going out of Cornwall by railway, and then in a northeasterly direction through delectably bucolic counties, the traveller reaches the Black Country, the centre of which is Birmingham, the seat of the hardware, glass, gun, steel-pen and silver plate industries. 'A visit to the principal manufacturing establishments, and excursions in the neighbourhood of the town, are the sole attractions for the tourist,' Murray says.

Taking the train towards Crewe we read: 'Gliding out of the magnificent central station and passing through the tunnel, the traveller emerges at once amongst the blackened chimneys and smutty atmosphere of manufacturing Birmingham. This is abundantly evident, not only from the physical signs of labour, but from the dense population accumulated on either side of the line, the frequent stations, and the general character of the passengers – the first class being occupied by business men, who leap in and out as though to save every moment of time, while the third are filled with grimy-faced artizans.'

After nine miles the town of Tipton, with a population of 30,000, is 'spread over a circular area about 2m. in diameter, with coal-pits, iron-works, and dwellings, all mixed up together. In fact every inch of available ground is covered with furnaces, Tipton being celebrated for its iron as adapted for heavy works. It possesses a specialty for chain, cables, and anchors; and steam-engine boilers are also largely manufactured.'

Should the traveller decide to explore Shropshire and Cheshire he will note Mr Murray's difficulties in compiling the handbook to those counties. 'A list of a few good Hotels and Inns above the average is subjoined by way of help to the traveller and stimulus to hostelries below par. It is better in Shropshire, though there is still room for improvement; but in both counties it would be a proof of courtesy in the owners of "show places" and "historic houses," which they are duly desirous to find mentioned in Country Handbooks such as "Murray's," if they would make known at the chief Hotels and leading bookseller's shops of their nearest town, whether, when, and after what preliminary steps, visitors, presenting their cards, can be admitted. In one or two instances the Editor has been subjected to discourtesy, though it was the exception, not the rule.'

Ironbridge in Shropshire will be found 'terribly spoilt by the forges and foundries, the banks of slag and refuse that run down to the water's edge. Tiers of dirty cottages rise on the hill-side, which is very steep. Very near the station the Severn is crossed by an *iron bridge* of one arch, of 120 ft. span, being the first iron bridge on record.'

If our traveller in Crewe has to wait while changing trains he might look in at the nearby works, where steel ingots 'are made here by Bessemer's process, and it is one of the most beautiful sights in the world to see the blast put on to the huge converter. After a blow of 18 minutes, the spiegeleisen is added, and the whole fiery mass is then decanted out of the converter into a mould, a magnificent exhibition of fireworks and white heat.'

Tired of this spectacular industrial might, the traveller could pass a week at Matlock, having read Byron's encomium in his Murray: 'I can assure you there are things in Derbyshire as noble as Greece or Switzerland.'

The hotels are said to be 'very comfortable', and 'agreeable walks have been carried up the steep heights on both sides of the valley; but, being for the most part private property and leased out, they are accessible only on paying toll. Indeed, the tourist will soon find with what ingenuity the people of Matlock manage to make him pay "backsheesh," enough to exhaust a good amount of small change, for the privilege of beholding their charming landscapes. Nevertheless, he should on no account omit to ascend the Heights of Abraham.'

'I have never seen anywhere else,' wrote Nathaniel Hawthorne, 'such exquisite scenery as surrounds the village of Matlock.' the author of *Highways and Byways in Derbyshire* (J. B. Firth), however, bewails its spoiled condition, because 'the railway companies let loose daily in the summer-time among its sylvan beauties a horde of callous rowdies, who envy Attila his destructive secret, whereby the grass never grew again where once his feet had been planted. The debasing influence of the day tripper is everywhere visible in Matlock. His trail is unmistakable. His litter is omnipresent. He has tastes which must be catered for. The shops deck themselves out with vulgarities and banalities to please their patron. His ear is so accustomed to the roar of machinery and the din of streets that there must be a bawling salesman on the pavement to shout crude invitations to buy. It is these shops, these refreshment bars, these permanent preparations for the coming of the tripper, which ruin the place, and, once begun, the descent to Avernus becomes a veritable glissade.'

Ruskin inveighs against the 'civilization' which 'enterprised a railroad through the valley – you blasted its rocks away, heaped thousands of tons of shale into its lovely stream. The valley is gone, and the Gods with it.'

Or perhaps instead of Matlock our traveller might call at Chester on his way to Wales. Murray says: 'Few, if any towns attract so many visitors of all classes and tastes as does this ancient city.' During the races 25,000 people a day pass through it. Dr Johnson had previously observed to Miss Barnston: 'I have come to Chester, Madam, I cannot tell how; and far less can I tell how to get away from it.'

Henry James, in *English Hours*, 1872, says: '. . . if the picturesque be measured by its hostility to our modern notions of convenience, Chester is probably the most romantic city in the world . . . it is so rare and complete a specimen of the antique town . . .' If he stayed at one of the two first-class hotels he would have learned from his Murray that both were expensive.

From Chester it is a mere twenty-four miles to Llangollen where, Murray says, the Hand Hotel is 'one of the best in Britain, a pleasant house, thoroughly comfortable, and very moderate, kind landlady, Mrs. Edwards.' He then leads us on a ten-minute walk above the church to a 'small cottage ornée, once the retreat of two maiden ladies, Lady Eleanor Butler, and the Hon. Miss Ponsonby. In 1799 they came hither together in the heyday of their youth and charms, influenced only by a romantic attachment to each other, which never was sundered, and a fancied desire to retire from the world. Here they set up their tent and lived together amidst their books and flowers. An assiduous correspondence carried on with their literary and fashionable friends kept them always *au courant* of the latest gossip and scandal of the outer world, and as their hermitage lay on the Holyhead mail road, it allowed many a passing friend to drop in upon them, such as young Arthur Wellesley on his way to embark for Spain, in 1808. The costume which they adopted, though it seemed singular to strangers, was only that of the Welsh peasant woman, – a man's hat, a blue cloth gown or riding habit, with short hair, uncurled and grey (undyed). After a happy friendship of 50 years Miss Butler died, 1829, aged 90, and Miss Ponsonby in 1830 at the age of 78. Their house is now converted into a sort of Museum. Visitors pay a fee of 6d., which goes to some local charity.'

The *Gossiping Guide to Wales*, 1905 gives more details of the association, calling them 'two queer old souls who, when they were young, vowed, as violently attached ladies do vow, for celibacy and a cottage, only with this difference – they fulfilled their vows. They were Irish, and they fled from matrimony as from a pestilence, and found in Llangollen a haven of rest, where, for more than half a century, they lived, and where their remains now repose under a tombstone in the churchyard near the church door. Mathews the Elder describes them as they first burst on his astonished vision in the Oswestry Theatre, which is now, by the way, a malthouse. "Oh, such curiosities! I was nearly convulsed. I could scarcely get on for the first ten minutes after my eye caught them. As they are seated, there is not one point to distinguish them from men: the dressing and powdering of the hair; their well starched neck-clothes; the upper part of their habits, which they always wear even at a dinner party, made precisely like men's coats; and regular beaver black hats. They looked exactly like two respectable superannuated old clergymen." '

Any distinguished visitor who passed that way a second time was expected to bring a present of carved oak. 'The Duke of Wellington was here in 1814; and Wordsworth, who called on his tour through North Wales in 1824, composed a poem in the grounds, in which he called the house a "low-roofed cot," greatly to the annoyance of the Ladies, who declared they could have written better poetry themselves! Amongst other visitors were Madame de Genlis, with the young Mademoiselle d'Orléans, in 1791, and Sir Walter Scott in 1825.'

Baddeley's *North Wales* adds this intriguing detail: 'In one of the bedrooms is a double secret cupboard containing authentic copies of the garments worn by the romantic pair.' A French guidebook of 1914 gave the two ladies some philanthropic credit by remarking that 'well before the beginning of the feminist movement they established in the district a refuge for young girls seeking to escape the deceits and wiles of men'.

For more upland scenery the traveller would go to Snowdon where, on its peak: 'The visitor will be much mistaken if he comes prepared for mountain solitude, for in the season it is one of the most crowded spots in Wales. The guides have erected 2 or 3 huts on the highest point, where refreshments, such as eggs, cheese, tea, and bottled beer, may be obtained at tolerably reasonable prices, considering the labour of getting them up. In foggy or wet weather it is no slight relief to find a dry room and blazing fire. A charge of 6s. is made for bed and breakfast, to those who wish to see the sun rise.' By 1914 the price had risen to ten shillings.

After a flying visit to Aberystwyth ('the Biarritz of Wales') we may track our way north again, to Liverpool. Hawthorne, the American consul for four years from 1853, said about the people, and the English in general: 'I had been struck on my arrival by the very rough aspect of these John Bulls in their morning garb, their coarse frock-coats, gray hats, checked trousers, and stout shoes. At dinner-table it was not at first easy to recognise the same individuals in their white waistcoats, muslin cravats, thin black coats, with silk facings perhaps. But after a while you see the same rough figure through all the finery, and become sensible that John Bull cannot make himself fine, whatever he may put on. He is a rough animal, and his female is well adapted to him.'

Liverpool's prosperity was founded, Black's guidebook relates, on slaves and cotton. In 1874, it had a population of 500,000, and was the second city in the kingdom. Large scale manufactures included 'sugar refineries, chemical works, foundries, wood and iron ship-building yards, steel works, anchor and chain cable foundries, and roperies'. Though the city's five public parks had cost an immense amount of money the site of Liverpool was, from some unaccountable cause, 'unhealthy. But between 1786 and 1868 upwards of three hundred million pounds have been expended in improving the town, in the formation of new streets, purchasing old obnoxious property, and in carrying out stringent sanitary improvements.'

W. H. Davies tells in his *Autobiography of a Super Tramp* how in the 1890s he lands at Liverpool after working his passage from the United States. The men who came with him intend to live by begging during their few days ashore: 'They are an idle lot, but, coming from a land of plenty, they never allow themselves to feel the pangs of hunger until they land on the shores of England, when courage for begging is cooled by the sight of a greater poverty. Having kind hearts, they are soon rendered penniless by the importunities of beggars.'

Murray's *Yorkshire* gives grim pictures of its industrial cities. 'Sheffield is beyond all question the blackest, dirtiest, and least agreeable of towns. It is indeed impossible to walk through the streets without suffering from the dense clouds of smoke constantly pouring from great open furnaces in and around the town.'

As for a particular industry, we are treated to an account of saw manufacturing, 'in which the grinder, holding the steel plate cut into the shape of a saw with both hands outstretched and nearly prostrate, leans his whole weight upon the grinding-stone, balancing himself on the points of his toes, and pressing the plate against the stone with his knees. There is a risk of being whirled over by the grindstone if he loses his balance.'

Guidebooks of thirty or forty years later give the same picture of pollution, which in any case lasted well into the present century. A tragedy which did not find an account in any guidebook comes from *The Professional Papers of the Corps of Royal Engineers*, 1883, telling of the collapse of a stone chimney at the Ripley Mills in Bradford on 28 December 1882. The structure, 255 feet high, was built over old coal workings. The only witness who saw the fall of the chimney reported that a few minutes after eight o'clock in the morning, 'during a heavy gust of wind it burst out suddenly, at a considerable height above the ground, then the upper portion just settled down vertically, and finally seemed to turn slightly on its heel and fall, cutting down the Newland Mill, a four-storeyed building occupied by three different firms of worsted spinners and wool-top makers'.

The greater part of the building was razed to the ground, and some fifty-four people killed, in addition to many injured. 'Had the chimney fallen but a few minutes sooner, the loss of life would have been far greater; fortunately it happened when most of the hands had left for breakfast. The failure of this chimney was undoubtedly due to the operation of straightening. The only wonder is that it survived that operation for twenty years.'

On our somewhat zig-zag way to the Lake District we will pass through Durham and Northumberland, with Murray's handbook for 1890. Scenic beauty both counties have, but some of the route from Newcastle to Berwick is 'blackened by the smoke of its innumerable coal-pits, and the unprotected plains in the upper part are blasted and parched by the fierce winds which sweep across them from the North Sea'. Now and then, however, as the traveller is hurried across the bridges, 'he will catch glimpses of lovely valleys, with rich green meadows or deep woods'. An interesting break in the scenery might come at Haws Peel where a murderer was hanged in chains in 1792, 'within sight of his victim's abode, where a gibbet, a modern erection, but on the site of the original, still exists, with a wooden head (painted to imitate a dead man's face) hanging from it'.

If the traveller wishes to stay at a hotel in the Tyneside area those in Gateshead are 'hardly to be recommended: sleep at Newcastle'. The same remark is made regarding Jarrow.

As for the industrial workers, they are 'now comparatively sober, and very peaceable, but very immoral, as is attested by the large proportion of illegitimate children. This is partly owing to the barbarous nature of their courtships, but more so to the infamous condition of their cottages, large families being crowded together into little cottages of a single room, by which overcrowding all natural sentiments of modesty are sapped. Among the great faults of the inhabitants are suspicion and an utter inability to forgive. They brood over an insult for years, and over wrongs that are quite imaginary. On the other hand, they are as firm friends as they are unforgiving enemies. Kind-hearted and charitable, their hospitality is simply patriarchal. In every house you are offered bread, cake, cheese, whisky, or milk, according to the means of the owner. From constant intermarrying there is a good deal of tendency to madness among the people.'

The lead miners are considered to be rather special, much influenced by the barren and secluded moorlands in which they live, 'but beneath a rough exterior they have great kindness of heart and much natural intelligence. There is little poverty among them, for the lead miner, who works only 8 hrs. a day, and works only 5 days in the week, obtains from 15s. to 20s., and as a rule they have small plots of ground to assist in their maintenance. There is little intemperance; but bastardy is still very rife, though generally followed by marriage. Excellent schools have been built, and a library for the use of miners has been opened at Newhouse. In the books chosen from the latter, the great popularity of mathematics is evident. The miners of Coal-cleugh have published a selection of poems, and four of them conjointly have written a pamphlet illustrating the benefit to be derived from well-conducted Friendly Societies.'

Nevertheless, regarding the County of Durham's ancient customs: 'There is a general belief that bread baked on Good Friday is a cure for most disorders. Waifs or waffs of dying persons are seen by their neighbours, and many persons even see their own waifs. Garlands are occasionally carried before the coffins of virgins. Salt is placed upon a corpse after death, and is supposed to prevent the body from swelling; and the looking-glass in the death-chamber is covered with white, from fear of the spirits which might be reflected in it. The straw used to be taken out of the bed in which a person had died, and burnt in front of the house; then search was made in the ashes for a footprint, which would be found to correspond with the foot of the person to whom the summons would come next.'

The most noticeable characteristic of the middle and eastern parts of the country is its dirt, 'for the smoke of the collieries, which envelops these parts, injures vegetation, scatters black ashes over the fields, and hangs in a thick cloud overhead'. We are told of a terrible accident at Heaton Main Colliery on 30 April 1815. 'There were 95 persons in the pit: 30 escaped on the first alarm, but 41 men and 34 boys perished. Of these 56 had gained a point which was not reached by the water, and perished from want of air. Their corpses were found within a space of 30 yards of each other; their positions and attitudes were various; several appeared to have fallen forwards from off an inequality, or rather step, in the coal on which they had been sitting; others, from their hands being clasped together, seemed to have expired while addressing themselves to the protection of the Deity; two, who were recognised as brothers, had died in the act of taking a last farewell by grasping each other's hand; and one poor little boy reposed in his father's arms.'

We will end our visit to the area on a less pathetic note, on reading that the villages belonging to the Duke of Northumberland had had almost all their cottages rebuilt within the last few years. 'The village of Denwick is perhaps one of the best examples of the improved condition of labourers' dwelling-houses. The inhabitants, however, still cling to their ancient customs of sleeping in box-beds, which occupy one wall of the common sitting-room, being generally placed opposite the fire, for the sake of warmth, and being closed all day by shutters, which are opened at night. It is still almost impossible to persuade a Northumbrian peasant to do anything so "uncanny" as sleeping upstairs. The dwellings have generally a great appearance of prosperity and plenty, which is obtained as much from abundance and cheapness of coals as from the high rate of wages. The chief peculiarity of dress among the peasantry is the high *buckled* shoe, which is almost universally worn by the women and children.'

The traveller to Westmorland and Cumberland could supplement his Murray with Wordsworth's *Guide Through the District of the Lakes in the North of England, with a Description of the Scenery, &c. For the Use of Tourists and Residents*, using the fifth edition of 1835: 'In human life there are moments worth ages. In a more subdued tone of sympathy we may affirm, that in the climate of England there are, for the lover of nature, days which are worth whole months, – I might say – even years.'

Such a guidebook emphasizes pedestrianism as the ideal (and expected) mode of locomotion, for then the traveller is able to see everything, and has time to reflect on what scenery he passes through. The often idiosyncratic style provides a calm and healing read while catching breath among the Fells, or after a hunger-slaking meal by the fireside of inn or hotel in the evening. It is not a guide in the Baedeker or even the Murray sense, for Wordsworth was too singular for that, and in any case he would have despised guidebooks which brought the undiscriminating horde to his favourite haunts. He sees the landscape with the eye of a poetic geographer, to whom the coming of the railway was little short of an assault on his soul. His guide awakens one to subtle combinations of sky and landscape, predating Ruskin's monograph *Storm Cloud of the*

Nineteenth Century – a classic of meteorological description.

The author of A. & C. Black's later guide, however, attempts to put Wordsworth in his place. 'Till about the middle of the eighteenth century, indeed, the rest of England took much the same Philistine view of Lakeland. Mountains in those days meant bad roads, poor inns or none, the fear of robbers, and the chance of losing one's way. But it is a mistake that, as commonly supposed, Wordsworth and Southey *made* the Lakes, from the tourist point of view. An older admirer, one of the first who taught our prosaic forefathers to look for less tame models of the picturesque, was the poet Gray. The journal of his tour may still be read with interest and amusement. One well-known guide-book was fifty years old when Wordsworth wrote his hand-book; and both he and Southey complain of the crowds of holiday "Lakers" who every summer invaded Grasmere and Keswick.'

Another Victorian guidebook to the Lakes was that of Harriet Martineau, who lived in the area after 1850. She is more down to earth and systematic, though writes for a somewhat simpler traveller than either Murray or Wordsworth: 'There is one thing more the stranger must do before he goes into Cumberland. He must spend a day on the Mountains: and if alone, so much the better. If he knows what it is to spend a day so far above the every-day world, (unless there is danger in the case); and, if he is a novice, let him try whether it be not so. Let him go forth early, with a stout stick in his hand, provision for the day in his knapsack or his pocket; and, if he chooses, a book: but we do not think he will read today. A map is essential, to explain to him what he sees: and it is very well to have a pocket compass, in case of sudden fog, or any awkward doubt about the way. In case of an ascent of a formidable mountain, like Scawfell or Helvellyn, it is rash to go without a guide: but our tourist shall undertake something more moderate, and reasonably safe, for a beginning.'

Her tone is rather like a nanny telling the infant what to do, but she is very sensible about the perils of boating on Lake Windermere. 'The stranger should be warned against two dangers which it is rash to encounter. Nothing should induce him to sail on Windermere, or on any lake surrounded by mountains. There is no calculating on, or accounting for, the gusts that come down between the hills; and no skill and practice obtained by boating on rivers or the waters of a flat country are any sure protection here. And nothing should induce him to go out in one of the little skiffs which are too easily obtainable here, and too tempting, from the ease of rowing them. The surface may become rough at any minute, and those skiffs are unsafe in all states of the water but the calmest. The long list of deaths occasioned in this way, – deaths both of residents and strangers, – should have put an end to the use of these light skiffs, long ago.'

There is no such warning in Black's *English Lakes*, 1905, so one can assume that the matter was put right. However, we are told by Black's that it was not always easy to find your way about. 'The lake roads, and even the mountain paths, are well off for guide-posts, sometimes better represented by stone tablets, since foolish tourists, in exuberance of spirits, have been known to set the arms of a post awry, so as to deceive those coming after them, a most mischievous trick that deserves a tour on the treadmill.'

ENVOI

Having brought our traveller safely back to his own by no means unendowed country from foreign parts I will now mention, as a means of conclusion, a guidebook to the homeland published in French, dealing mainly with spas, seaside resorts, and known beauty spots: *Through Great Britain* by Charles Sarolea, issued by the Fédération des Syndicats d'Initiative des Municipalités Britanniques. Published in the fateful year of 1914, it was unable to serve its intended purpose of drawing French holidaymakers to Britain.

The main feature of the book is not so much its contents as the long introduction by the author who, though he may not have known it, sounded the perfect lights-out on an age of travel which, on the familiar routes at least, had reached the apex of comfort and freedom. The *fédération* in whose honour the book was produced was to hold its first congress in Great Britain that summer. Dignitaries from England and France were to take part and, it was hoped, on their return home the French were to tell 'their compatriots of the friendship and hospitality they had received, and of the beauties of the English landscape. To frankly appreciate the importance of the task, account must be taken of the lamentable isolation of England, and of the extraordinary insularity of the English character. The European Continent is becoming more and more internationalised, and only Great Britain is not participating in this movement.'

Sarolea gives a picture of a more or less culturally united Mainland Europe, proved, he goes on, by the fact that many cities have large foreign colonies: 'Ostend, Biarritz, Wiesbaden, Carlsbad, and even the far-off small towns of Bohemia and the Carpathian Mountains; even Biskra on the edge of the desert in Algeria has become a cosmopolitan centre, while the English towns remain the preserve of the English.'

With uncanny echoes of the early English guidebooks to the Continent, only in reverse, because England was now in need of the revenues from tourism, Sarolea explains: '. . . the English hotels are not yet good enough to rival those of Switzerland, and English hotel keepers have not yet learned to cater to the desires of foreigners, though these inconveniences may be exaggerated, and English hotels in general do not deserve the bad reputation that they have among those who live on the Continent.'

The author's reasons as to why the French in particular should be attracted to the United Kingdom are curious. Ever since the Norman Conquest, he says, the two peoples have had very strong feelings for each other, either an invincible revulsion, or attractions not less irresistible, and yet the best qualities of the French and English have much to teach both nations.

> The Englishman is an individualist, the Frenchman is socially and civically inclined. The Englishman is practical, the Frenchman an idealist. In England the imagination dominates, in France intelligence. The Englishman believes in versatility, the Frenchman in unity. The Englishman triumphs in local administration, the Frenchman in centralisation. The Englishman glorifies the spirit of enterprise and adventure. The Frenchman prefers to cultivate the art of good living. It is because of that diversity of civilisation and difference in national temperament that France will always be for the English the country of intellect and art, and England for the French the teacher of initiative and energy. It is not too much to say that Great Britain can show the French traveller a new world. Even a short stay will be for the Frenchman the best school in moral and political science.

It is a long and intelligent essay on the necessity of French and English union, and of European friendship and cooperation, but it was too late, for in August of 1914 the Great War began. In the immortal words of Sir Edward Gray, the lights went out all over Europe, only to come on again, finally, in 1989, two hundred years after the Cannonade of Valmy had ensured the survival of the French Revolution.

The bibliographies of many guidebooks before the Great War refer the reader to articles on the various countries in the *Encyclopaedia Britannica*. Because of their authority and comprehensive range such entries were sometimes the length of short books, written by people of experience and scholarship. The *Britannica* of 1911–12 – the famous Eleventh Edition – could in fact be said to have been the guide of guides, a thirty-volume handbook to all that had been of note in Western Civilization. No more perfect encyclopaedia has been produced since.

A paragraph to a supplementary volume put out just after the Great War is worth quoting in full as a sad and fitting summing up to the end of a great era. The editor explains the difficulties of bringing out a new edition, similar to the Eleventh, after 1918:

Irrespectively, indeed, of the question whether as good a complete edition as the Eleventh could have been produced *de novo* now, it would cost in any case at least twice as much to make as it did in 1911, and it would have to be sold at a far higher price. But, from the editorial point of view, the important fact is that it could not be made to-day so as to have anything like the scholarly value of the work produced before the war by the contributors to the Eleventh Edition. Neither the minds nor the wills that are required for such an undertaking are any longer obtainable in any corresponding degree, nor probably can they be again for years to come. This is partly due to sheer 'war-weariness,' which has taken many forms. A shifting of interest has taken place among writers of the academic type, so that there is a disinclination to make the exertion needed for entering anew into their old subjects – a necessary condition for just that stimulating, vital presentation of old issues in the light of all the accumulated knowledge about them, which was so valuable a feature of the Eleventh Edition; the impulse has temporarily been stifled by the pressure of contemporary problems. Many of the pre-war authorities, moreover, have died without leaving any lineal successors, and others have aged disproportionately during the decade, while the younger generation has had its intellectual energies diverted by the war to work of a different order. Again (a most essential factor), it would have been impossible to attain the same full measure of international cooperation, among representatives of nations so recently in conflict, and in a world still divided in 1921 by the consequences of the war almost as seriously as while hostilities were actually raging.